# BORDERLANDS

After completing his graduation in chemistry and post-graduation in computer application, Pradeep Damodaran pursued a successful career in the software industry for nine years before quitting IT to take up journalism. He is the author of *The Mullaperiyar Water War* and was chief of bureau, *Deccan Chronicle*, Chennai.

## Praise for *Borderlands*

'Pradeep Damodaran's engaging travel book takes us to places we would never visit… [It] is an eye-opener, if you are willing to listen to the varied voices… Crucially, the book makes you ask questions about the identity you take so much for granted.' – *The Hindu Businessline*

'Pradeep Damodaran's *Borderlands* makes for an unusual read because it is not merely a travelogue. The 10 places the author has chosen to visit and write about evoke some unsettling questions about identity, privileges and nationalism… *Borderlands* brings out how identity changes as we move farther away from our cities and towns and leaves you wondering about the idea of identity itself. While it is difficult to finish this book in a single sitting, the author successfully plants in the reader a desire to follow his trail across the country.' – *Hindustan Times*

'This book, in a way, also tells you how simple it is to "go abroad" without a passport or visa. But then, this book is way beyond the payscale of a travel book, in as much as it also becomes a very readable sociological experiment on why land and sea border outposts in India are what they are… I found the book difficult to put down, and have a gut feeling that for a certain kind of traveller, this may become a cult reference manual.' – *Outlook*

'The author has delved into his decades of experience in reportage, personal histories and travelogues to bring us face-to-face with this reality. He tries to raise the questions of national identity, citizenship and loyalty, which most of us, living in the mainland, take for granted.' – *India Outbound*

# BORDERLANDS

## TRAVELS ACROSS INDIA'S BOUNDARIES

PRADEEP DAMODARAN

hachette
INDIA

First published in 2017 by Hachette India
(Registered name: Hachette Book Publishing India Pvt. Ltd)
An Hachette UK company
www.hachetteindia.com

This edition published in 2018

SRD



ISBN 978-93-5195-225-1

Hachette Book Publishing India Pvt. Ltd
4th & 5th Floors, Corporate Centre,
Plot No. 94, Sector 44, Gurugram 122003, India

Typeset in Adobe Devanagari by Surya, New Delhi

Printed and bound in India
by Manipal Technologies Limited, Manipal

# Contents

# Introduction

Dictionaries define borderlands as vague or intermediate stages between two concrete realities. Borderlands, as most of us understand them, are those territories that either lie near the borders of a country or are separated by a politically demarcated boundary. In a vast nation like India, however, borderlands are usually those ambiguous spaces whose inhabitants find themselves trapped between two distinct national entities.

I do not exactly remember when the idea of writing a book on borderlands struck me. Several images come to mind when I try to recall the precise moment. The most poignant among them is the memory of sitting, well past midnight, on the moist, surf-kissed sands of Marina Beach in Chennai. Beside me was a friend, trapped in a hopeless marriage and contemplating the idea of wading into the water and swimming off to another country, simply to escape the feeling of being shackled and start life afresh in a new land, free of the tags conventionally attached to a person to define identity – name, family, friends, employer, citizenship and everything in between. Even exploring the possibility of such a flight seemed to be an exhilarating experience.

Thus began my fascination with borderlands – namely, those towns and villages so remote and distanced from what represents the concept of national identity that an element of ambiguity persists when trying to match these spaces with a specific country. In my imagination, these borderlands were inhabited by people who preferred to lead free lives on the fringes, unhindered by the boundaries or societal obligations of a particular nation, with the choice of simply walking – or swimming – away to the other side, whenever the urge seized them.

Several years later, I was visiting a remote fishing hamlet on a desolate strip of land, flanked on both sides by the beach, in the Rameswaram district of Tamil Nadu – the site of the once-thriving border town of Dhanushkodi. Instead of bumping into the usual hippies and free-spirited seafarers I had expected, I came across the impoverished families of fisherfolk forgotten by the rest of the nation. They were not part of the vote bank; nor did they have savings accounts in any bank. Untold suffering was an integral part of their lives, merely because their homes were situated close to the shores of another country – Sri Lanka.

For those of us who live in big metros and towns, citizenship and national identity are privileges we take for granted. Our identities are unequivocal and our loyalty to our country is never questioned. We seldom realize that these are luxuries denied to many of our countrymen.

When we think of India's neighbours and the long border we share with them, the three countries that usually come to mind are Pakistan, China and Bangladesh. We have gone to war with two of these nations and have ongoing border disputes with all three in one form or another. But a closer look at India's contours reveals that it shares territorial or maritime borders with at least ten different countries that are diverse in culture and heritage. People living in the small towns that have sprung up along these borders are often uncertain about their nationality and do not always share that sense of belonging inherent in Indians living on the mainland.

The thousands of men and women living in these remote places – whether it is Minicoy, a small dot of an island in the Arabian Sea barely a few dozen nautical miles from the Maldives; Campbell Bay in Great Nicobar, just a boat ride away from the Indonesian town of Aceh; or Moreh in Manipur, which shares a land border with Myanmar – have more in common with the citizens of a neighbouring country, with whom they have historical and cultural ties, than with their fellow Indians. This book is about those people, their lives and their aspirations.

* * *

In December 2014, my first book, exploring the conflict and controversy surrounding a 120-year-old dam along the Tamil Nadu–Kerala border, was published. Even I, its author, did not come to know that it had been published until I discovered it listed under my name after a random Google search. Like most first books by unknown authors, it did not do well. I had worked on it for almost two years, mostly between 11 p.m. and 4 a.m., as I had a day job. In a matter of weeks, hours of painstaking research and writing were consigned to oblivion. The experience was terribly depressing, to put it mildly.

I was working at the time with an English daily in Chennai, trying hard to please my bosses on the one hand, and live up to the expectations of my team members on the other. My workday started at 10.30 a.m. and wound up at 11 p.m. This punishing work schedule, coupled with an hour-long commute each way, eventually took a toll on my physical and mental health. I felt trapped, stifled, and could not wait to set off on a long journey in quest of something meaningful to write about. So taking a few days off from work, I wrote out a proposal of sorts for a travel book in which I intended to explore unfamiliar, unheard-of border towns in search of an Indian identity.

Five months after I had sent off that proposal by email, I was at Chennai Central railway station with a backpack on a weekday afternoon, waiting to board the Kamakhya–Bengaluru Cantonment Premium Express to explore India's border towns. The train, running late by over ten hours, reached Chennai only around midnight. Since it was the last run for that special train (the service was being discontinued due to lack of demand), no

Travel Ticket Examiner (TTE) was present through the long journey that lasted for over two days. It seemed like a free ride offered by the Indian Railways, except that the passengers were to experience the worst that the railways could offer. The toilets were anything but clean, the water tanks were filled only once or twice through the entire journey and there was not a single mobile charging point in any of the sleeper coaches. In many ways, that train ride prepared me for the gruelling and chaotic journey ahead.

Exactly a week after alighting from that train at Howrah, I was sitting outside a thatched hut in Talpukur village in West Bengal on the India–Bangladesh border, listening to Moina Beevi, a middle-aged Bangladeshi woman, recall how many years ago she had boarded a fishing boat on a moonless night to illegally cross over to the Indian side of the Ichamati River in search of an Indian husband – a spouse from India meant stability and a better life. As I did not know any Bengali beyond '*Ami tomake bhalobashi*' (thanks, of all things, to a Hindi film song), a young CPM cadre and aspiring policeman from the same village served as my interpreter. Sitting inside a hut in that remote hamlet surrounded by jute fields and shallow ponds, listening to the love story of Moina and Mohammed Shamshu, I realized that it had all been worth it – quitting my job, leaving my comfortable home and enduring exhausting journeys in filthy locomotive coaches.

Over the next weeks and months, I travelled across the country by train, bus, shared taxi, cycle rickshaw, ship and even helicopter, recording the fascinating stories of dozens of men and women who live on the peripheries of this vast nation, admiring the breathtaking landscapes their homes are surrounded by and delving into the chequered histories of those lands. Almost everyone I met on this voyage – be it the embittered Bihari activist-businessman from Gangtok, who claimed that Indian settlers had been less discriminated against when Sikkim was a kingdom ruled by the Chogyal, the former soldier from the remote island of Minicoy who had abandoned a career in the Indian Armed Forces because of alleged religious discrimination, only to return to his island and train young students for a life in the same Indian Army, or the septuagenarian Malayali wife of a soldier in Shastri Nagar, the last settlement on the Great Nicobar Island, whose family had been relocated with the promise of a better future and later forgotten by subsequent Union governments – had one common plaint: they had been ignored, forgotten and conveniently pushed away from the mainstream. This book is about their lives, their dreams and their regrets.

* * *

One of the most endearing personalities I would meet during my travels in the North East was former Special Services Bureau (SSB) personnel Lama Khandu. He was drinking beer outside a shop in Sheru village near Tawang in Arunachal Pradesh when I spotted him on a weekday afternoon. As I could not find another man in the village to talk to, I resigned myself to a chat with the sozzled old man. It turned out, however, that the senior citizen, who was a radio broadcaster and a Bodhi language teacher, had a fascinating story to tell about his family's horrific experiences during the Chinese invasion of India. The old man's account of his family's ordeal did not just move me, but also his fellow villagers who had gathered around to listen.

Back home in Chennai, I replayed the recorded conversation again and again and have reproduced most of it verbatim. But I refrained from getting an official version of the events that unfolded during that turbulent period.

If I have resisted meeting government officials and army officers, unless absolutely necessary, while presenting the perspective of the common man, it is for a reason: I believe there is a world of difference between established facts and the reality that emerges from experience. While facts are supported by corroborative evidence and are usually unambiguous, there are various levels of truth, depending on one's situation and perspective, as in the case of Lama Khandu, whose family was forced to eat animal carcasses for survival while fleeing the Chinese Army. The record books might not mention it, the Indian and Chinese armies might not acknowledge it, but to Khandu, his experiences are as much a reality as the Himalayas he admires every morning from the portico of his home in the hills. My intention in writing this book has been to explore other dimensions to the truth as we know it by putting together these various personal histories, along with my own experience of travelling through the borderlands in which they are set.

# 1

# Dhanushkodi

My first visit to Dhanushkodi was on a balmy January afternoon in 2008. But this eerie ghost town, poised, as it was, on the southernmost tip of peninsular India and as close to Sri Lanka as you can get from the mainland, had stirred my imagination much earlier. Few places in the world can cast as hypnotic a spell on you, especially by sheer virtue of their geographical location and mythological antecedents, as this sparsely populated, cyclone-ravaged region.

Dhanushkodi is supposedly the point where Lord Rama, of the Hindu mythological epic Ramayana, commanded his army of apes to build a stone bridge across the Palk Strait, enabling him to reach the island of Lanka (later known as Ceylon and then, Sri Lanka). There, he would engage its ruler, the ten-headed Ravana, in a fierce battle and vanquish him, returning in triumph to the mainland after rescuing his wife Sita from the clutches of the demon king who had abducted her. Once he crossed, Lord Rama destroyed the bridge, using the tip of his bow. And that, apparently, is how Dhanushkodi – meaning, 'tip of the bow' – acquired its unusual name.

Thousands of Hindus, devotees of Lord Rama and believers of the Ramayana, visit Rameswaram, the nearest temple town, and Dhanushkodi to perform the last rites of their loved ones in the hope that the souls of the departed will find peace in the afterlife. I went to Rameswaram looking for peace not for departed kin, but to appease my own restless soul. The thought of travelling to the very end of a vast, densely populated land mass seemed to promise what I so fervently sought.

A bumpy twenty-minute ride in a four-wheel-drive van with fifteen other passengers brought me to land's end – a slender strip of sand battered by the sea and buffeted by gale-force winds that made even a short walk virtually impossible, but for the shelter afforded by the few huts that sold souvenirs and snacks. In that strange, harsh terrain, I met families of fishermen who lived a life pared down to the barest minimum; for them, electricity, healthcare, educational facilities and basic sanitation – necessities we took for granted – were alien concepts; they did not even possess an identity card to prove their nationality.

* * *

'*Summa jaallya irikalam*, sir,' Mari declared, as we stepped off the bus seven years after that first visit.

This was not the first time that my local guide was uttering those words since our introduction the day before. But I was still clueless as to what he meant; what was so jolly about going to a remote fishing hamlet that had no electricity, healthcare facilities or treated potable water, let alone shops, hotels and bars – in other words, nothing, apart from a 100-odd fishermen and their families living in squalid little tenements within touching distance of the sea? But I kept my thoughts to myself. I needed Mari's help to make it to the hamlet and, more importantly, to get out of there in one piece.

Bus Route Number 3, supposedly connecting Dhanushkodi with Rameswaram from where we had boarded, was never actually meant to go anywhere near what remained of its proposed final destination. It dropped off its last passengers at its chosen halt – five kilometres short of the cyclone-battered town at a place called Mukuntharayar Chatram or M.R. Chatram. No state transport was available beyond this point.

'No outsider is allowed to stay after dark,' Mari informed me, as we left the bus behind and headed towards the beach. 'But don't worry, sir. I have made all the arrangements for your stay. Let's go and have a jolly time there and come back.'

There it was, again.

M.R. Chatram was the last point up to which roads had been laid for motorized traffic. Tourists visiting Dhanushkodi had to park their private vehicles in the public parking lot here and rent a 13-seater van – if they were travelling in a group – or share a ride with other tourists to the ruins and back for a fare of ₹50 per head. The vans ferried visitors back and forth from sunrise to sunset. Six p.m. was the cut-off time.

When we arrived at M.R. Chatram, it was a little after five in the evening. Winds roared at us from either side of the narrow strip of land on which we stood. On the beach to my right, young couples held hands as they waded through the waves. Ahead of us, vans packed with tourists were driving back from Dhanushkodi.

'Should we board one of those vans?' Mari asked. 'It's a pleasant walk, though, especially at this hour. *Summa jollya nadakalam*, sir. Do you think you could manage it?'

I quipped that I wouldn't mind walking all the way to Sri Lanka in such good company and proceeded towards one of the vans that was about to leave for Dhanushkodi.

In response, Mari simply grasped the hem of his *kayili* (as the lungi is known in this part of the country), flipped it up till it was half its length and wrapped it tight around his slim waist.

'Let's walk to Kodi, then,' he announced, setting off.

Adjusting my backpack so that its weight was evenly distributed between my shoulders, I snatched up my water bottle and hurried to catch up with him. A few minutes into the trek, however, I began feeling a little uneasy about being alone on a desolate beach with a complete stranger. I would soon be out of range from mobile-phone towers and cut off from all means of communication with the rest of the world. I came to a halt, asking my guide if we could just travel by van, instead.

'No sir, it's better to walk,' he replied. 'If we take a ride in the van, the driver will know that one of the passengers has not returned from the trip [since you're planning to stay overnight in Dhanushkodi]. He could tip off the Coast Guard or the local police. But if we simply go there on foot, nobody will know you are here.'

Well, that was precisely my concern too. So I took out my voice recorder, pressed the 'record' button and said, 'Starting to walk with Mari, CPM leader from Dhanushkodi, from M.R. Chatram to the fishing hamlets. The time now is 5.10 p.m.'

I winked at my guide and we set off again.

Strong winds now swept in from either side of the narrow strip of land, barely a few hundred metres wide. Between the two shores stood little mounds of sand, where dried seaweed had piled up, letting off a mild stench. From the smooth, yellow-white sand that lay between these mounds sprouted weeds and blades of sparse coastal grass. The further we moved from the parking lot, the fewer in number were the vans on the other shore. Our side of the shore was now completely deserted, as if we were on some tropical island forgotten by time.

The route to Dhanushkodi had not always been so desolate. Until 1964, this place had been as big as Rameswaram, if not larger. An important port in south India, it had been well connected by road and rail network with Rameswaram and the rest of Tamil Nadu. Two ferry services had connected Kodi with northern Sri Lanka and passengers from Chennai and other parts of Tamil Nadu could take a train up to the Dhanushkodi railway station and then board the ferry heading for Sri Lanka on a single ticket.

Situated south-east of Pamban, this lost town lies just 18 nautical miles from Talaimannar in Sri Lanka. Apart from a post office, a number of schools, business outlets and even a Customs office, this former railway junction had once even boasted of a well-equipped railway hospital. In 1897, Swami Vivekananda had stopped in Dhanushkodi on his way back from Chicago, after attending the World Parliament of Religions. Several other celebrities and prominent Indian citizens are known to have taken the Boat Express – the train between Chennai Egmore and Dhanushkodi – to travel to the island nation, making the port at Dhanushkodi an important transit point.

But that was not Mari's topic of discussion as we walked, stopping occasionally to click photographs of the breathtaking cloud formations and the colonies of seagulls alighting briefly on the shore before taking off together to fish in the shallow waters. Being a cardholder of the Communist Party, my guide neither believed in any of the mythical stories associated with Kodi nor cared to dwell on its past glory.

'Today, we are more concerned about the 250-odd families of fishermen who live there and the future of their children,' he said.

A day before we set out on our journey, a local journalist had introduced us in the lobby of Hotel Tamilnadu in Rameswaram, explaining that Mari was the local leader of the fishermen living in Dhanushkodi. Dressed in an all-white full-sleeved shirt and matching dhoti, with large spectacles perched on his prominent nose, the diminutive man fit the image of a typical Marxist politician quite well. And the diary he held in his hand, with a few envelopes tucked into its pages, further enhanced that impression.

Until a few years ago, Mari had, in fact, been living in Palam village. But his need to ensure that his daughters continued their education had prompted his move to Rameswaram. He now lived in Natarajapuram with his wife and three children and travelled to Kodi every day.

'The only school in Dhanushkodi is a government-sponsored

middle school that offers education up to class VIII,' Mari went on, as we walked along an undulating shore against a setting sun. 'After that, the students must either move to Rameswaram or forego their education altogether and return to their forefather's ways of earning their livelihood – from the sea.'

According to him, the 250-odd families which lived in Dhanushkodi had been ignored by successive governments. They had no electricity or any basic amenities and not a single family had ever been issued a ration card.

After a cyclone devastated the area in 1964, the then state government had declared Kodi and its surrounding areas unsafe for permanent habitation. They had decided to rehabilitate and resettle all the fishermen who had been living there in newly developed areas closer to M.R. Chatram, like Natarajapuram and Ramakrishnapuram. But the arrangement had not worked for many. Apart from Dhanushkodi being their ancestral home, its location at the confluence of two ocean currents made fishing in the area a far more lucrative proposition than elsewhere along the coast. Inevitably, several resettled fishermen had returned, abandoning their new homes inland, while others chose to travel several kilometres every morning to work out of Kodi. Outcasts and fugitives from other parts of the district had also found a haven here, safe from scrutiny and intrusive questions.

Forty-five minutes later, we were approaching the town's first visible ruin – a tower tilting to one side. About ten to twelve feet tall, it had been built by using some kind of concrete mix to hold solid chunks of rock together. Strings of sacred yellow thread hung from this structure in large numbers and countless pieces of yellow and red fabric were tied to it.

A temple had stood here once, Mari explained.

'All that remains now is this tower. People still come here regularly to offer their prayers and tie these threads. The deity is deemed to be the protector of fishermen.'

I clicked a few pictures and sat for a moment on the slope of a sand mound near the structure. Against the backdrop of sundown, with an engulfing darkness spreading behind it, the tower, tilted at an angle, seemed like some phantom image from another world. Apart from the ceaseless roar of the waves and the tearing gusts of wind, there was nothing around us but utter stillness.

* * *

By the time we reached Palam, one of the two hamlets sitting amid the ruins of Dhanushkodi, the sun had set and the sky had turned dark. The white surf gleamed along the shoreline as breakers, hit the sand before dispersing into tiny frothy bubbles. The wind had gathered force; it howled through the huts and the damp timber from dismantled country boats lining the shore. As we neared the settlement, the remains of an inundated, weathered road surfaced, leading us to rows of huts that flanked it on either side. Not a ray of light was visible anywhere around us. While the men of the community were nowhere to be seen, the women sat outside their homes, combing their hair. Their sole company was a number of sturdily built stray dogs, resting their bellies on the warm, rough surface of what remained of the tar road. Little children scampered between the huts, involved in some game, shouting at one another.

Mari, who had been walking ahead of me, turned and announced, 'This is the place you had wanted to see.'

I was conscious of attracting curious glances from the women. The dogs, fortunately, did not create a ruckus at the sight of a stranger in their midst.

'You do believe me now, don't you?' my guide went on. 'A place like this actually exists in 21st-century Tamil Nadu. Even in the early 1980s, the path we're walking on used to be a proper tar road, with a full-fledged bus service. But it was when the civil war between the LTTE [Liberation Tigers of Tamil Eelam] and the Sri Lankan authorities intensified that the Indian government wound up the service. This road has since been abandoned and left to rot.'

A few metres ahead stood a hut that turned out to be the village tea shop. Inside, a middle-aged woman stood behind a giant kettle filled with boiling water. She was pouring the water into glass cups, to which she added two teaspoons each of Amul milk powder, before stirring the mixture vigorously. The tea shop, a space measuring hardly five by five feet, had a pair of rustic wooden benches arranged in two corners. The remaining space was taken up by the woman and her collection of utensils. A kerosene lamp provided the only illumination. Half a dozen men, all in their sunset years, sat on the two benches and stared at me as we appeared in the doorway.

'Why are you all staring at him like that?' Mari enquired, addressing the customers. 'He is a friend of mine from Chennai. He's here to observe and record your lives.'

The woman promptly poured some boiling water into a glass tumbler and asked if I would like some tea.

'There's no reason why he shouldn't,' Mari replied, then turned to me. 'We don't use milk here, as it spoils very quickly,' he explained. 'By the time it arrives from the mainland, the day is already very warm and there are no fridges here.'

I stepped into the tea shop and explained the purpose of my visit to the customers, all local fishermen. Before I had even finished drinking my tea, the men were ready with a list of people whom I should meet and the things I could do while I spent time with them. After jotting down the names, I took out my wallet, intending to pay for the tea, but the woman turned down my offer right away.

'We don't accept money from guests,' she said simply.

Leaving the tea shop, we continued down the road for a bit, until it ended abruptly in front of a Mariamman temple standing right on the seashore. Two young men who had followed us from the teashop now approached us hesitantly.

'Who is he?' one of them asked Mari.

'*Machan*,' said my guide in reply, 'he is a reporter from Chennai. He has come to observe our way of life.' Then turning to me, he said, 'This is my cousin Muniappan. He was born and raised here. You can ask him all the questions you want.'

How did he feel about living in such a desolate place, I asked the young man.

'Doesn't it get to you? Don't you ever want to live somewhere else, where there is power supply and a TV connection, cinema halls, shopping malls and so on? Aren't you bored here?'

He pondered my questions for a while, scratching his head thoughtfully as he did so, then spoke up.

'What to do, sir!' he said. 'We were born here. So we make the best of it. I do, occasionally, go to Rameswaram to buy clothes and other stuff. Mostly, I go there to get my hair-cut,' he added, running his fingers through his hair that was neatly parted on one side. 'Otherwise, we like living here. Who has the time, anyway, to do all the things you mentioned? Between going out to sea and cleaning and weaving our nets, there is hardly any spare time.'

Like most youth who had grown up in these parts, Muniappan was illiterate, for during his childhood, Dhanushkodi had had no school to speak of. By the time the state government set up one in 2006, the boy was too old for class I and his parents decided that it was better he took to the sea like others in the family.

Muniappan's family, like other Kodi residents, had been allocated land in Natarajapuram after the area was devastated by the 1964 cyclone. But having lived here for generations and discovered that the catch was good, they had decided to return.

Muniappan's parents felt it was simpler to resettle in their ancestral hamlet and devote themselves to their traditional country-craft fishing than to set out from Natarajapuram every day at 1 a.m. to make it to Kodi in time to set out to sea.

After a while, I ran out of questions and lapsed into silence. Mari suggested that we proceed to Sakarapandi's home, where we were supposed to spend the night.

'There are four boys in the family and you will enjoy talking to them,' he remarked. 'We can have fun talking to them, sir.'

Sakarapandi or Umayasundaram, as he was otherwise known, lived with his wife Umayammal and their three sons – Umayavel, Mariraj and Santhanam – and their cousin Nagarathinam in a modest hut perched on the very edge of the Bay of Bengal. Their home stood at the far end of the village, beyond which lay a vast coastline dotted with colourful country boats and strewn with fishing nets of different sizes and hues.

Sakarapandi had come to Dhanushkodi 17 years ago, when he was just a young man. Like most other resettled families here, he had found the daily commute from New Road Junction too tiresome and had built a modest hut where he could live with his family. His sons were born in quick succession and when the family needed a more spacious home, Sakarapandi and Umayammal had built a larger hut closer to the beach. However, not only did the man have no documents to establish his ownership of the land, his three sons had no birth certificates or any other proof of their existence. During every election, local MLAs and councillors would provide every adult living in the area with a fabricated address-proof document and ensure that all the fishermen's families had voter identity cards. When election day came around, these political leaders would arrive in vans to pick up the Kodi settlers and their wives and herd them to polling booths of their choice to ensure that their votes were cast. With that formality over, Sakarapandi and his neighbours officially ceased to exist, to be a part of the country's 1.2 billion-strong population, until the next election.

We reached Sakarapandi's home to find him in a relaxed mood, sitting outside his hut with his family, engaged in lazy conversation. Pandi leaned against a pile of nets, his drawn-up knees serving as a backrest for his wife. Their youngest son Santhanam, was watching a movie on YouTube on his mobile phone with his head resting on another pile of nets, while Umayammal's sister, who was visiting them from Kambipadu, sat near, picking lice from hair. Inside the hut, the other two sons were huddled in opposite corners, engrossed in their mobile phones, sleek headphones in place.

All three boys were watching different movies on YouTube, their father informed me.

'This is the story of this village, sir,' he elaborated. 'These boys have neither shirts nor pants to call their own, nor even decent *kayilis*, but everyone here – boys and girls – has at least two mobile phones, that too the latest models. Every evening, they just sit and watch a new movie. They no longer chat with us as they used to or hang out with friends. They don't even get a good night's sleep any more, so busy are they, watching movies on their mobiles all night. It gets on my nerves, the different kinds of music and dialogue blaring out of each phone. With so much noise around, I just cannot sleep.'

Watching the Tamil horror flick *Darling* on his phone, Pandi's youngest son argued that mobile phones were their only means of keeping up with the rest of the world.

'We don't have TV or cinema halls here. Not even newspapers. It's only through this phone that we get to know what's going on.'

Listening to their exchange, I remembered how Kodi used to be during my visit in 2008. None of the mobile network providers had a tower anywhere in the vicinity and telecommunication was simply not an option for those living in the area. It was during the final phase of the civil war in Sri Lanka that the Indian government erected a giant communications tower beyond Kambipadu and Palam for the purpose of intercepting signals from the Sri Lankan Army as well as the LTTE. The tower had turned out to be a boon for Kodi's fishermen.

The huge solar panels put up on the premises of the government-run school by the local body and some NGOs had ensured enough power for each hut to light a single eight-watt bulb and use a plug point.

'All the youngsters here use electricity only for charging their mobile phones. They don't even allow us to switch on the one light that we have,' Sakarapandi grumbled.

Mari laughed and the women too joined the debate on whether mobile phones were a boon or a bane for the local youth.

A little later, loud devotional music blared out in the distance. I looked wonderingly at my guide. It turned out that the celebrations surrounding the Thai Poosam festival were on at the Santhanamari Amman temple that stood between the two hamlets Palam and Kambipadu. Mari and I set out for the place right away.

Unlike the fishermen's homes, the temple was a solid brick-and-concrete structure with a cement floor, its sanctum sanctorum a tiny room at the end of a long corridor, where we joined the queue of devotees, mostly chattering women and children awaiting their turn to receive the *sakkara pongal* (a dish made of rice and jaggery) being distributed by the lone priest. The sole source of illumination here was a solar-powered eight-watt bulb. Outside, on a wooden table stood a DVD player and a television set with a 20-inch screen. Music blared out from a loudspeaker connected to the DVD player. A diesel-fuelled generator provided the electricity.

While we were eating the *sakkara pongal*, my attention was drawn to the teenage boys who had appeared on the scene a while ago. I had noticed how small they were for their age and the way they hovered around the priest, trying to draw his attention. Having eventually managed to do so, they leaned over to whisper something in his ear. The priest glanced across, looking first at Mari and then at me.

'It's nothing important, really,' he said, addressing me. 'The boys just wanted to know if it wasn't time to switch on the TV and the DVD player. This is our only entertainment, sir. During every festival and holiday, we put a TV and a DVD player out under the banyan tree and show new films. Those who are interested gather here to watch them.'

Despite my promise to feign ignorance of the implied video piracy, the priest insisted on playing devotional songs that evening. To put the waiting audience at ease, I suggested to Mari that we leave them to enjoy their show and head back to Sakarapandi's home.

Although it was barely 8 p.m. when we returned, the doors to most of the huts were closed; their occupants having turned in for the night. At Pandi's home, dinner was being served. We sat cross-legged on the hut's floor, made a mound out of the sand and flattened it at the top to use as a table. Then we placed our plates on it and waited for helpings of boiled rice and fish curry. As among fisherfolk elsewhere, rice and a variety of fish, left over after the daily catch had been sold, constituted the main meal. Every other item of food was considered a delicacy and reserved for special occasions.

After dinner, Mari and I went for a stroll along the shore, while the men of the house set out to get their country boats ready for their pre-dawn fishing trip. Barring Friday, which was a day of rest for the fishermen here, fishing rights were evenly distributed through the week between those who used country boats and those who owned the larger fibre vessels; each group was allocated three alternate days in a week for setting out to sea.

Returning from our walk half-an-hour later, we found the men had retired to the hut. Now huddled together, they lay wrapped from the chest downwards in their all-purpose *kayilis*. The women, meanwhile, had gone to spend the night in a relative's hut.

Mari and I were provided with a huge tarpaulin to sleep on. We spread it on the ground outside the hut, using folded fishing nets for pillows. While I took out a thick blanket that I had brought along to cover myself with, Mari simply wrapped his *kayili* around his chest.

Lying on my back under the open, cloudless sky, I heard the faint strains of Tamil film music from the 80s floating out from one of the boys' mobile phones. Between songs, a radio jockey would speak in a weird Tamil slang. The music was being broadcast from a radio station in Jaffna.

'Oh, so you can catch programmes from Sri Lankan radio stations, can you?' I asked.

Mari laughed. 'Until a few years ago, they were the *only* radio and TV stations we could get,' he said. 'We don't get clear signals from stations based in Chennai or Madurai. Jaffna is less than 20 nautical miles away.'

'If you have a double-engine boat, you can reach Talaimannar in half-an-hour,' Pandi said, speaking from inside the hut. 'Before anyone knows it, you can cross over to the other shore, spend some time there and come right back – all in the space of a single night.'

Would he take me to Talaimannar that night, I asked, if I paid for the diesel? I was hoping he would take up the offer, but Pandi remained silent.

Excited at the idea of lying under the open sky almost within touching distance of the sea on a beach that was barely half-an-hour away by boat from another country, I couldn't sleep a wink. Finally, I turned on my mobile phone to check the time.

It was just 9.45 p.m. Had I been at my workplace, I would still be busy clearing news stories, after which, if I were lucky, I would head home. A good night's sleep lay at least three hours away, if not more.

Lying on this beach now, I would open my eyes every now and then at the thought of something crawling across my body. Could it be a crab emerging from the fishing nets on which I rested my head? Or perhaps a scorpion or even a sea snake? But I saw little point in getting up to investigate; even if I were bitten by something venomous, medical assistance was several kilometres and at least a few hours away.

* * *

Muniasamy who lived in a modest hut behind his spacious tea shop located at the far end of Kambipadu village was used to rising at three every morning. After washing his face, he would walk straight to his shop and light a kerosene stove. He then poured water into the giant kettle which was sitting neatly on top of the burner. Within 15 minutes, the water would be boiling. Samy added 250 gm of Red Label tea power to it and lowered the flame just enough to keep the kettle hot and the water boiling.

He lit another stove, placed a deep-frying pan filled with palm oil on the burner and set to frying *bonda*s, balls made of rice and white flour. By 3.30 a.m., his customers started trickling in and within minutes, Samy's modest tea shop, fondly named Santhanamari Chaya Kadai, was humming with conversation.

Swathed in lungis that hung from shoulder to ankle, men strolled in and squatted on the floor, waiting for a hot cup of tea and a quick bite. There were no daily dealings in cash. Each customer had a running account that was settled once or twice a month. Over tea and snacks, the men discussed the weather, the condition of the sea and the catch of the day, in addition to news and politics. Soon, they would be proceeding to their boats and heading out to sea, while Samy prepared to serve the next batch of customers.

During a lull, he would light up a beedi and move close to the fire for warmth. These days, his eyesight was no longer what it used to be and he liked to hover around the kerosene wicker lamp that sat next to the stove.

When Mari and I walked in that morning around 4.30 a.m., there were already three customers present, drinking tea and smoking beedis. Standing by the stove, Samy too was enjoying a beedi. The moment he saw us enter, he got to work and, in less than a couple of minutes, had two glasses of tea ready for us.

'This is how it works here,' he explained. 'You don't even have to ask me for tea; anybody who visits my shop gets a glass. If you can pay for it now, well and good; if you can't, pay whenever you can.'

Like most male adults in Dhanushkodi, Samy did not remember the exact year of his birth. Nor did he have a certificate to prove it. He claimed that he had just turned 59, but immediately added a rider that it could be two years this way or that. He had been around nine when the killer cyclone struck.

'I was staying in my grandparents' home at Munthazh when the disaster happened and we came back here only a month or so later,' he recalled. 'I've been living here since.'

When he was a young man, Samy would set out before dawn to go deep-sea fishing for a living. Those were the days, he recalled, when the experience of being out on the open sea and bringing back fish worth thousands of rupees was an adventure.

He had married young and fathered, within a few years, five

daughters and a son. As the family expanded, Samy found it impossible to meet their needs solely from the income he earned from fishing. It was at that point in his life that he switched over to shore-based activities like selling fishing nets, taking on the role of a middleman or broker to mediate between the fishermen and the wholesale buyers who came from various parts of Tamil Nadu and even Kerala. He would drive a hard bargain with the market vendors to negotiate a better deal for the fishermen and take his cut. Business was good and eventually, Samy was able to get all his five daughters married.

The stress of managing his business and bearing the expenses of his daughters' weddings had, however, taken a toll on his health. Eventually, Samy realized that his eyesight had deteriorated to such an extent that he could no longer carry on even with his second profession.

'Having little choice, I set up this tea shop,' he confided over glasses of black tea. 'For the past 18 years, this has been my life and my source of livelihood. I start my day at 3 a.m. and wind up at around 11 p.m., after spending time with my grandchildren.'

The shop, however, always downed its shutters around 6 p.m.

Despite making good money during his youth and in his middle years, Samy, like most other Kodi residents, had seldom travelled anywhere beyond Rameswaram. Cities like Chennai and Mumbai were just as remote and irrelevant to him as, say, Chicago or Istanbul. Samy had no inkling whether these places existed. Nor did he care.

'I once accompanied my family to the Meenakshi Amman Temple in Madurai,' he recollected. 'The city was too crowded and I did not like it there. I prefer it here.'

These days, however, he liked to venture out to nearby towns and villages, mainly as a pilgrim, but poor health and the demands of his business often prevented him from making such trips.

'Running a tea shop is like being in jail,' he quipped. 'You just cannot escape from it. You have to throw the doors open every day at 3 a.m., as people are waiting for you to serve them tea. If I don't wake up in time one fine morning, I'll end up ruining the day for many of my customers.'

Mari and I asked if he would like to join us on our planned walk to Arichal Munai or Erosion Point.

'It would be just lovely to walk all the way there and watch the sunrise. But how can I possibly tag along? I have to be at the shop for my customers,' he said.

Muniasamy's life wasn't so very different from that of his customers. For them, life began and ended in Dhanushkodi and it kept them so busy, they had little time to spare for other matters.

* * *

At 5.30 a.m., Mari and I set out for Arichal Munai, the extreme point of Indian soil closest to Sri Lanka and, thus, technically, the 'borderland' between the two countries. As is the case with most things in Dhanushkodi, Arichal Munai is unusual. Its location shifts every day, depending on the tide. At high tide, a large portion of land is submerged, bringing Arichal Munai much closer to Kodi; when the tide is low, one can walk at least a couple of kilometres closer to the Sri Lankan town of Talaimannar on Mannar Island, beyond which a chain of shoals, commonly known as Adam's Bridge, separates the two countries.

While geological evidence suggests that a land border which actually existed between India and Sri Lanka in the past had, possibly, been submerged during the cyclone of 1480 or even earlier, it is still widely believed that there is a land border just 45 metres long on a land shoal along Adam's Bridge. Given the unstable nature of these shoals and the pattern of sea tides, the governments of the two neighbouring countries had decided on an Imaginary Boundary Line located about 12 nautical miles from Rameswaram. Though this would later be deemed the international boundary line, it does not fulfil international norms. International Maritime Law decrees that for a boundary line to be feasible, the countries in question must be separated by a distance of at least 36 nautical miles. The distance between India and Sri Lanka, however, is just 18 nautical miles.

The sky was still grey, the sea dark, the huts and shrubs of karuvelan (*prosoposis juliflora*) eerie silhouettes against an endless horizon, when Mari and I set out from Pandi's home. Except for the few fishermen gathered in Muniasamy's tea shop and some stray dogs loitering nearby, no one was awake at that hour. Even the seagulls were nowhere to be seen.

Wrapping our *kayilis* tight around our waists, the two of us headed south towards Arichal Munai, armed with nothing but a bottle of water each. The wailing winds of the previous night had died, but a mild breeze still remained and there was a bite in the air.

When we reached a spot far enough to afford the privacy we needed to attend to our morning business out in the open, Mari pointed me to a nice little mound, while he himself headed, water bottle swinging from his hand, for a spot closer to the sea on our right. 'Just sit there and get on with your job, sir,' he said, before walking away. 'Nobody is around to watch you.'

Needless to say, for a man used to the convenience and privacy of a toilet for 40 years, the nippy air, the view of the sea flanking me on either side and the vast open spaces were major impediments in getting the job done quickly. Squatting there, I could not help but wonder how Samy or Pandi might feel if they were taken to Chennai and forced to get the job done within the confines of a four-by-four enclosure.

When Mari and I were done, we continued on our way. As

we progressed towards the erosion point, the trek became an increasingly pleasant experience. With thick clouds overhead, stretching away into the distance as far as the eye could see, the prospect of enjoying the sunrise was dim, but the arrival of dawn was spectacular. We could now see isolated country boats and catamarans closer to the coast, with lone fishermen busy casting their fishing nets and laying out other equipment. A little further on our way stood the giant communications tower, a sight that seemed totally out of place in that no man's land.

'Usually, one doesn't have to walk this far to reach the Munai,' Mari said. 'During winter, this stretch of land is mostly under water.'

With the strip of land having narrowed in width to barely a few feet now, he cautioned me to keep to the centre for my own safety. Soon it would end in a curve, where sea currents moving in opposite directions converged.

'Here we are, at India's very edge,' Mari announced somewhat dramatically.

I promptly looked at my watch. It was exactly 7.30 a.m.

'It took us two hours to get here,' I observed.

After soaking my feet and torso in the water at the confluence of two different seas, I returned to the shore and flopped down on the sand. From here, I speculated, any good swimmer could simply hop from one shoal to another and reach Sri Lanka in a matter of hours. Child swimming prodigy Kutraleeswaran had already covered the distance several years ago.

'Can we swim across the sea to Talaimannar?' I asked Mari.

It would be impossible for me to do so, he said confidently, but added, 'But we can, if we need to. Fishermen who are familiar with the shoals can swim across on days when the sea is calm. But you never know.' He was silent for a moment. 'During the late eighties and early nineties, when the civil war in Sri Lanka was at its height, refugee boats would land here every day and men, women and children, destitute and starving, would trudge up to our villages. We always offered them food and water, before the police and Coast Guard took them away. But these days, no one comes to India along this route. Besides, the government has enough spies here to alert them.'

I asked him if the local fishermen had ever been hostile towards these strangers.

'No sir,' Mari replied, 'they were just like us – poor people caught between two big governments. We helped them in every way we could, until the police warned us not to. Now we don't.'

He suggested that we return to Palam in time to interview the schoolchildren.

We had barely covered 500 metres on our return journey when the clouds completely obscured the sun. The wind had begun to rise and Mari feared that we might get caught in a shower, with nowhere to run for shelter. Removing his *kayili*, he packed his diary and both our mobile phones and wallets neatly within its folds and wrapped it tight around his waist.

'This way, they won't get wet. But we don't stand a chance of keeping ourselves dry,' he said.

I couldn't think of an appropriate response as I watched the dark clouds and the turbulent sea and listened to the moaning wind. Any moment now, it seemed to me, the little strip of land on which we stood could be swallowed by giant waves. Then it began to drizzle. We broke into a sprint, racing towards Dhanushkodi. Within minutes, the drizzle had turned into pelting rain. The wind had gathered velocity and was blasting our faces, the sand it carried so abrasive against our skin that I feared it would peel off.

'*Sooraoli*! *Sooraoli*!' Mari yelled into the wind, clutching my hand tight.

I tried going as fast as I could, but the nearest shelter or any kind of cover, for that matter, was the giant cell-phone tower more than a kilometre away.

For a fleeting moment, I wondered if I had done a stupid thing by not informing the Coast Guard office before coming down here. Had I got in touch with them earlier and saved their contact numbers, I could, at least, have called them now and sought help. I looked back once at Arichal Munai and noticed funnel-like clouds shrouding the point where we had been sitting not minutes ago.

'Did I not warn you, sir, that this place could be dangerous and you shouldn't have been visiting it?' Mari said. 'By the way, do you know how to swim? The sea here can submerge this strip of land any time and we would have to swim to the nearest sand mound.'

Fortunately, the rain subsided noticeably over the next ten minutes. Drenched to the skin, we watched the sky clear and soon, it was bright and sunny again, as if this were springtime in California. Those few minutes of rain and gale, however, had not only given me an idea of nature's overwhelming force in this climatically fragile part of the world, but also an insight into what had likely happened on that fateful night in 1964.

On the night of 22 December, more than half a century ago, a cyclonic storm that had formed in the South Andaman Sea five days earlier intensified and crossed Vavuniya in Sri Lanka with a wind velocity of 280 kilometres per hour, taking a heavy toll on human lives and property. The storm subsequently moved into the Palk Strait and made landfall in Dhanushkodi, virtually swallowing the bustling township.

One thousand and eight hundred people were reported to have perished in the storm. Among the casualties were 110 passengers and five members of the railway staff of the Pamban–Dhanushkodi passenger train. At 11.55 p.m. night, the train arriving from Pamban railway station was just a few metres from Dhanushkodi, when the signal failed. The loco pilot then took a decision to blow a long whistle and move ahead towards the Dhanushkodi railway station. At that moment, a giant tidal wave – well over five metres high, according to media reports – submerged all the coaches in deep water, washing away the six-bogey train. The devastation caused to Dhanushkodi was so extensive that the then government had made the decision to declare the township unsafe for habitation and permanently relocated its residents to other areas.

* * *

By the time Mari and I returned to Palam, the sleepy hamlet had come alive and was bustling with activity. A large number of women were out in the open, busy cleaning fish, washing clothes and vessels and attending to other domestic chores. The shops that sold snacks and souvenirs to tourists had thrown open their doors and were doing brisk business, while neatly dressed children in state-supplied school uniforms trudged along dirt pathways to the Mandapam Panchayat Union Middle School located beyond the settlement, the only concrete structure in Dhanushkodi, other than the temple, with a proper roof and a compound wall.

Until 2006, there were no schools in this area and children living here did not even have the option of getting an education. Following an intensive campaign by local activists such as Mari, who roped in the support of various NGOs over a period of time, the state administration conceded to public demand and sanctioned the setting up of a government-run primary school. As the number of students increased over time and those who wished to progress beyond the primary level were left with no choice but to discontinue their studies, the government granted permission to set up a middle school and released funds for the construction of three classrooms, a kitchen and dining area and toilet facilities for the students.

When we visited the campus, the school had a total strength of 69 students, divided into groups, with each group occupying one of the three classrooms. The classes were conducted by six government-appointed secondary-grade teachers, with a headmistress in charge of administration.

Headmistress Geetha lived with her family in the small town of Ramnad (also known as Ramanathapuram). She had to leave for work every day at 7.15 a.m. to ensure that she reached the school punctually by 9.30 a.m.

'I have to change two buses to get to M.R. Chatram. From there, the only way of reaching the school is to use those tourist vans plying to Kodi,' Geetha informed us. 'Sometimes, the van drivers offer us a free ride out of sheer goodwill, but during the tourist season, most visitors object to us riding in the vans along with them.'

On an average, Geetha and the other staff at the school spent a daily sum of approximately ₹150 to commute to work; the state did not pay them any extra allowances over and above their salaries.

'We look upon teaching in this school as a service to these poor children who would, otherwise, have no chance at all of getting an education. They would then be reduced to living the way their parents do,' volunteered Vijayalakshmi, who taught Classes II to V.

All members of the teaching staff are versatile enough to handle different subjects and deft at multi-tasking. Yet, things could be a little frustrating at times. While most parents on the mainland these days spoon-fed their children by helping out with their homework and school projects to ensure their wards obtain the best grades, the only grouse of the teachers at the Kodi school, according to Vijayalakshmi, was that despite repeated reminders, the parents of their wards weren't bothered about their offspring's basic hygiene. They made no effort to ensure that the children brushed their teeth and had a bath before going to school.

Mari, the president of the school's Parents Teachers Association (PTA), intervened, explaining that these poor folk knew no better.

'They go out to sea at 1 a.m. and return late in the morning,' he went on. 'Between selling fish, preparing food and getting their boats and equipment ready, there is no time to attend to their children. The children here fend for themselves and grow up on their own, the way I did. And when they are old enough, they either take up their father's occupation or get married. We are trying to bring about a change in this pattern. Last year, for the first time in decades, three youngsters from here completed their higher secondary education and went on to college. Many parents are still reluctant to allow their children to continue their education beyond class VIII, but that mindset is beginning to change. More and more children are now going to school.'

Later, Headmistress Geetha encouraged me to have an informal chat with seven of her class VIII students. I was introduced to 13-year-old Pandeeswari, considered one of the school's brightest students and among the few who attended school regularly and completed homework and assignments on time.

After she had answered some basic questions about her parents and her life, I asked the teenager what she aspired to be when she grew up. The meek young girl stared back at me with an uncertain smile. She thought hard, looked at her teacher and said, 'I want to be like her.'

Why not a doctor, an engineer, an astronaut or any of the other more lucrative professions, I enquired. The teenager responded that she did not know 'such people'.

'I know my teachers and like what they do,' was her candid reply.

This girl, at least, knew that she wanted to be a teacher some day. Most of the other students I spoke to hadn't a clue about what they wanted to be when they grew up. The only reason they came to school was because people like Mari had been regularly spreading the word about the importance of attending school and getting an education. No less important was the fact that a nutritious meal was served to the students every day during lunch break. Despite the incentive, less than half the children under fourteen had been enrolled in the school. The rest simply roamed around Palam and Kambipadu aimlessly, until they were old enough to go out to sea.

'It's a long, hard struggle, sir, but slowly, things will change,' Mari said hopefully. 'Boys and girls from Palam and Kambipadu will become successful in life and return to our village. Then all our people will be inspired to send their children to school.'

* * *

We left the school campus well past noon and not before Mari, who considered the school his pride, had pointed out in great detail every little development that had taken place over the last nine years. By now, I had covered the list of places I planned to visit and the people I wanted to interview in Dhanushkodi. Yet, I felt as though I had missed out on something.

So we walked back to the Santhanamari tea shop which was now deserted, devoid of even the flies that were such a nuisance earlier in the day. Muniasamy was playing with his five-year-old grandson Muthu, who refused to attend school, claiming that it was so much more boring than his grandfather's tea shop.

Outside, all the bustle of the morning had died down. The women who had surrounded the fresh-water hole, busy with their washing and cleaning, were nowhere to be seen, while the men, aged between eighteen and eighty, either dozed or huddled together in little shacks and played cards.

'This is what the men here do,' Samy informed me. 'They work hard all morning and earn their money; later in the day, they gamble and drink it all away, until their pocket's are empty.'

Until a few years ago, the most popular man in Dhanushkodi was Kali, an octogenarian well-known to the media who claimed to have survived the 1964 cyclone through his sheer strength and grit. He would describe his ordeal to tourists with great zeal, while providing them with pure drinking water from a coastal aquifier pit. His gigantic physique and intimidating beard had made him a darling of the media which projected him as Dhanushkodi's symbol of resilience. But that famed storyteller was now dead.

While discussing Kali and his allegedly dubious legacy – locals suspected the stories were fabricated and the man had been nowhere near the scene when the cyclone struck– Samy brought up the name of another old-timer from these parts.

'You could try talking to the blind man Muthandi,' he suggested. 'He has been around longer than most Kodi residents and knows a great deal about what happened here in the past.'

Muthandi's hut stood at the far end of the settlement, close to the ruins of the old town. He was inside when we arrived, seated on a coir mat in a dark corner, staring at the blank wall in front of him. His broad shoulders and agile legs seemed weathered by the years, but his face was sharp and youthful.

'He is completely blind and can't see even in broad daylight,' Mari explained.

'My father was such a healthy man,' Muthandi's second son told us, as he helped the blind man out of his hut. 'But all these years, he has whiled away his time smoking beedis and playing cards. It was mainly because of his addiction to cards that his eyesight failed and his health deteriorated. He has lived here all his life and is now 64. He was around fifteen when the cyclone wiped out everything.'

Mari, Muthandi and I settled ourselves on a mattress under a karuvelan tree. After exchanging pleasantries, I asked the blind man to share the details of his life with us and turned on my voice recorder.

'I was born in Munthazh and came to Dhanushkodi with my parents when I was just seven years old,' he began. 'We never went to school in those days. Within a year of arriving here, I got a job on the shore that involved pulling boats out of the water when they returned from fishing trips. I was paid ₹7 for a day's work. This was a magnificent town back then. Here, on the very spot where we are now seated, were two huge mounds of coal for the steam engine. One contained fresh fuel, while the other was made up of used coal. Behind those mounds was the main pier, where passenger ships docked. Hundreds of passengers would arrive every day and take the train to the mainland. Two ships sailed between Talaimannar and Dhanushkodi twice a day, morning and evening. All of it was destroyed in a night.

'I still remember that day so well. There was nothing ominous about the sea until 4.30 p.m. A mild drizzle started in the evening and it gradually intensified. The wind continued to gather momentum and by nightfall, it had acquired terrifying force. The tidal waves were so high, they simply swept Kodi away. An entire area of the town, covering at least three-and-a-half square kilometres, was submerged.

'Fishermen like us were not as badly affected as the other residents, for we were protected by the huge sand mounds on the shore,' Muthandi went on. 'Crawling behind our boats for shelter, we waited out the storm. By early dawn, the western winds had begun to blow, offering us a much-needed reprieve. The weather calmed and we were safe. Had it not been for those winds, the sea would have devoured the entire area.

'It was not until the next morning that we found out about the tidal waves toppling a train from its tracks and learnt that a large chunk of the island had been submerged. We were told that thousands of people had died. But there were far fewer casualties in the fishing community. I have not seen the sea in such fury since.'

Describing the horror of those moments, Muthandi stared at the sky, as if he could visualize every single, traumatic detail.

'The next day, we were all taken to camps in Mandapam and provided food and shelter for a few weeks. Then they allotted us new homes in the Pudu Road Junction area. But I could not bear to stay away from our hometown, away from this sea which is our source of livelihood. I returned to Kodi just two months after the cyclone had struck and have been living here since. Life was peaceful for a few years after my return, as we quietly went about our fishing activities. Technological advances were taking place and more and more mechanized boats were being introduced by fishermen from Pamban, Rameswaram and Kodiyakarai areas. The fishermen in Kodi had switched over to blast fishing by using explosives obtained from the mining companies in this region. But everything went haywire after the war broke out. '

'Tell him how you lost your eyesight,' Mari urged.

'During one such fishing trip,' Muthandi continued, 'I mishandled the explosive and its dust penetrated my left eye. Later, I consulted a local healer who would pour some herbal juices into the injured eye. But when I finally went to the town hospital, I was told that all the nerves in the eye had died and that I would never be able to see again. It was mainly because of the local healer's poor judgement and chosen mode of treatment that I lost my eyesight. In those days, we were ignorant about the white man's medicine. But what I have suffered is nothing compared to the torture we endured at the hands of Sri Lankan Navy officers. My eyesight is long gone, but this eye doesn't hurt any more. Yet, the stinging pain in my back keeps recurring.' Muthandi turned on his side and pointed to a spot on his body. 'They kicked me all night in the same spot – all thirteen of them – till my back broke.

'As the war between the LTTE and the Sri Lankan Army escalated, our life became hell. During those years, officers of the Sri Lankan Navy would pick us up at random and beat us brutally. Even the memory of those days makes me shudder.' Muthandi's face worked with inexplicable emotions and his voice trembled. 'I have been caught many times by the Sri Lankan Navy and forcibly taken to their ships. They would never take us to their country, as is the case now, but would thrash us on their ships, until we were bruised and bleeding, and then send us right back. While torturing us in this way, they would hurl abuses at us, blaming us for helping the LTTE.'

Muthandi remembered, in particular, a one-legged Sri Lankan Navy captain who was the most brutal of them all.

'He was the most notorious, *nondi* captain. I owe this to him,' he observed, pointing to his ribs.

Even as Muthandi described his ordeal, Mari, who had been patiently listening to him until then, suddenly sprang to his feet and hurled abuses at the Sri Lankan Navy officers.

'Those bastards should be stripped naked and shot!' he seethed. 'Those officers are riddled with communal hatred, especially the young ones. They despise Tamilians and think we all belong to the LTTE. I have been nabbed several times by their navy, sometimes even in Indian waters, and brutally thrashed. My private parts have been mutilated and I have been forced to do things that nobody should ever be made to do. You people don't know about it, but every fisherman here has been exposed to sights they can never forget in their lifetime.'

As Muthandi and I remained silent, he went on, 'In 1992, five steamers with Indian fishermen were intercepted near Katchatheevu by the Sri Lankan Navy. At the time, I was just a teenager like him.' Mari indicated Muthandi's second son, who had joined us under the tree where we sat. 'We were taken to their navy vessel at around 8 p.m. and subjected to rounds of beating by one officer after another, until we could barely move.

'Then another group of naval officers seized two fishing boats bringing in refugees, one carrying the men, the other, women and children. After forcing the women and children to board the navy ship, the officers opened fire on the other fishing vessel. All the men who were on it – some of them mere teenagers – were killed and their boat was sunk with a grenade. Their mothers, wives and daughters watched the horror from the Sri Lankan ship they had been forced to board. This happened before our very eyes.

'The officers would later molest the women. If they resisted, the officers grabbed one of us and tried to force us on the women. They stripped the women and brushed their private parts against our bodies. If we turned away, we were beaten up. I even saw one of those officers tear open a pregnant woman's stomach.' Mari's voice had grown louder.

'The Sri Lankans – one should never forgive them! They are all butchers and only we, who have been through the horror of facing them, know how much they hate us,' he continued. 'For an entire month after that incident, I could neither eat properly nor enjoy a night's sound sleep. When we returned to Dhanushkodi after our traumatic experience, we found severed hands, dismembered torsos and other body parts washed up on our shore. It was such a ghastly sight that I have never been able to go fishing since.'

I asked Mari if they had reported the incident to the Coast Guard.

'We always do,' he replied, 'but they merely blame us for straying into Sri Lanka's waters. And like those navy officers, the Coast Guard too beat us for the same reason. Our troubles ended only after the LTTE came to know about the incident. Exactly a fortnight later, the Tigers bombed that Sri Lankan Navy ship.'

'It was after that ship was sunk that LTTE songs and slogans became popular here,' Muthandi volunteered, cutting into Mari's account. 'People realized that even if the Indian Navy failed them in a crisis, the Tigers would come to their rescue. So many similar incidents have taken place since then and, as usual, we have always been blamed by both the Indian and Sri Lankan navies. It is only now that our officers have become more sympathetic towards us. Earlier, they would never stand by us in an emergency, because they suspected all fishermen were involved in smuggling medicines, diesel and other essential items to the LTTE.'

Mari, who had managed to compose himself by now, conceded, however, that the officers could not be blamed entirely, as smuggling of drugs, fuel, medicines and other essential items had been rampant between Rameswaram and the northern and eastern parts of Sri Lanka for generations. With just 18 nautical miles separating the two countries, fishermen in boats equipped with a twin-engine motor could reach the other shore in mere minutes without a passport, visa or any form of documentation whatsoever.

Anyone with a little daring and driven by the spirit of enterprise could make a quick buck, every once in a while, smuggling clothes, medicines and other goods that were in demand in the other country.

'It is an open secret that the navies of both countries are well aware of these rackets,' Mari remarked. 'Locals in Rameswaram know for a fact that most of the town's wealthier residents actually started out as smugglers and later diversified into other businesses. With the war in Sri Lanka escalating, the demand for a different set of contraband items, such as prosthetic limbs, painkillers and even aluminium bars, soared and most fishermen set sail with these goods, instead of fishing nets, returning home with gold bars or cash in Indian currency.

'The number of atrocities committed by the Sri Lankan Navy peaked during this period, as they were well aware of how deeply entrenched were the contacts made by the Tigers in the Rameswaram area. Initially, Tamil fishermen, who were largely seen as LTTE sympathizers, were tortured and killed by the Sri Lankan Navy. Later, however, owing to the intervention of the Indian government, the torture stopped; when found trespassing in Sri Lankan waters, the fishermen were simply shot to death.'

After the war ended, the Sri Lankan Navy had apparently stopped shooting Indian fishermen, arresting them, instead, and remanding them to judicial custody in Sri Lankan prisons. The practice continues to this day. Fortunately, Dhanushkodi's fishermen, who still use traditional country boats, have been spared this ordeal; the Sri Lankan Navy now targets only mechanized fishing vessels.

* * *

Later that afternoon, Mari and I returned to Sakarapandi's hut and sat down for a meal of rice and fish curry, prepared and kept ready for us by his wife. Pandi, I was told, was about to set out for Rameswaram to purchase some household items. It was also his night for unwinding with a drink or two. Tonight, he would be able to sleep longer, as the following day was allocated exclusively to those who went fishing in mechanized boats. Small country boats could venture no more than a couple of kilometres from the coast without disturbing the bigger players.

I asked Pandi about the day's work.

'It wasn't so bad today,' he replied. 'We caught 40 kilos of fish and sold them for ₹2,000, which means that after deducting diesel costs, each member of our team made ₹200 for the day. Yesterday was better, though. We had made ₹500 each.'

Pandi would be a different person tonight, Mari quipped, 'with all that money flowing out in alcohol!'

Pandi smiled in response to the other man's teasing laughter and walked towards the parking lot.

When we were alone, Mari asked me if it wasn't time for us to return to Rameswaram.

'But I've hardly been here for a day!' I protested. 'We planned for a couple of days, at least, didn't we?'

'Sir, you've already stayed a day too long,' he countered, his expression grave. 'Let's go back to Rameswaram. If you're really keen, I'll bring you back here again.'

I saw no point in arguing further. By the time we packed our bags and were heading for the parking lot, the souvenir shops were shutting down for the day.

The long conversation at Muthandi's had darkened Mari's mood. He had lapsed into silence and I could barely recognize him as the jolly fellow I had met earlier. When I said as much, he replied that there was so much more to a fisherman's life than met the eye.

'There's so much sorrow buried deep in my core,' he said. 'I try to be cheerful and forget all that has happened, but the moment I come here, the memories come flooding back and leave me seething with hatred. That's the reason I've given up fishing and have turned to social work and some other small businesses I take care of. For the six years I spent out on the sea, I was a witness to such unspeakable horrors that I can never go back to fishing again.'

# 2

# Minicoy

The SMS announcing the delay in boarding *MV Lakshadweep Sea*, the passenger ship to Minicoy, arrived at around 2.30 a.m. I was wide awake, tossing and turning on the lower side berth of the sleeper-class coach of Trivandrum Express, when a beep from my mobile alerted me to the delay. The train was expected to reach Ernakulam Junction at around 4 a.m. and I did not want to be dozing when it did, for I could not imagine a more nightmarish scenario than missing the ship to Minicoy, the tiny island located on India's southwestern tip.

When I began planning this trip about a month ago, I was intrigued at the thought of how distant and isolated Minicoy was. The closest land mass is Thurukanu, the Maldivian island that lies approximately 70 nautical miles away. The nearest Indian island is Kalpeni, situated at a distance of 114 nautical miles, while the closest mainland port is Kochi, separated from Minicoy by around 215 nautical miles. Historically and culturally both, Minicoy or Maliku, as it is locally known, is more connected with the Maldives than any island in the Lakshadweep archipelago.

Internet search engines proved to be of no help as I tried to find a hotel or resort online. So I called up some travel agents, contacted a number of Lakshadweep government officials and even put out queries on travel-forum message boards. But my efforts were in vain. I simply could not get in touch with anyone who had visited Minicoy, could help me with accommodation there or simply provide some inputs from their first-hand experience of the island. Finding myself at a dead end, I sent off an email to the office of the Administrator of Lakshadweep.

A couple of days later, I received a response from his office, providing me with the phone numbers of government officials posted at Minicoy. When I eventually called them, however, I was told in no uncertain terms that outsiders were denied access to the island, unless they could get their permit documents processed through either a family member or a close acquaintance living there. And if you didn't have that advantage, the only way to travel to Minicoy was to sign up for the package tour organized by the Lakshadweep Tourism Department. The Society for Promotion of Nature Tourism and Sports (SPORTS), Lakshadweep, offered special package tours to the island at least once a month at a cost that was way beyond my budget. With no other option to fall back on and the tourist season about to begin there in a month's time (package tours were booked well in advance during peak season), I paid the amount in full a week in advance – and have been suffering since then from nightmares of the ship sailing without me.

Putting an end to that tormenting dream, the train reached Ernakulam on time and I was waiting at the Lakshadweep Wharf in Wellington Island, Kochi, at 10.25 a.m., five minutes ahead of the scheduled time for boarding the *MV Lakshadweep Sea*. The security-clearance area was crowded with native islanders waiting to check in. Hundreds of men, women and children stood about in little groups, chatting noisily in an unfamiliar language that I later came to know was Mahl, Minicoy's lingua franca.

Since I was travelling through SPORTS, I was given precedence and allowed to move ahead of the waiting crowd. In mere minutes, I was on the dock, preparing to board the huge white ship. A SPORTS official led me on board and guided me to a first-class cabin on the third deck. The cabin was compact, clean and air-conditioned. A pair of neatly made double beds, complete with crisp white sheets, took up most of the space. A centre table separated them. A narrow passage running behind the beds led to the bathroom which was equipped with a shower, a washbasin and a commode. Soft music played from speakers in the room. I asked the SPORTS personnel if the other tourists were yet to arrive.

'So far, we don't have information about any other tourist on this ship,' he replied.

'Am I the only tourist to Minicoy?'

'Very likely, but some may check in later.'

Before leaving, he handed me a bottle of drinking water and informed me that my lunch would be served on board. I was also told that the ship would only leave the port around 4 p.m., after all the cargo had been loaded.

Once I had settled in, I stepped out of the cabin to explore. *MV Lakshadweep Sea*, I discovered, was a medium-sized vessel, with bunk cabins on the lower decks and first and second-class cabins above them. Two VIP cabins were also available for special guests. Reserved for the owner and his guests on the topmost deck was a special cabin, on par with that of the captain's own, with the best view of the ocean. The ship had two cafeterias – one for the cabin class and another for the rest of the passengers – a first-aid unit and enough lifeboats to accommodate all the passengers in the eventuality of an emergency evacuation.

By noon, most of the locals had boarded the vessel and were either strolling around or squatting on the decks and chatting in little groups. Mothers balancing their babies on their hips paced back and forth in the sun, trying to calm them, while the smokers stood apart and took quick puffs from their cigarettes. Ignoring the cacophony around them, the sailors went about their business all afternoon, preparing the vessel for the voyage.

I returned to the cabin to find a stout, bearded man, probably in his mid-thirties, lying on the bed next to mine. He wore a white collarless t-shirt, faded denim jeans and a black cap. Two younger men were busy pushing huge cardboard boxes under the reading table and the beds and even into the bureau. My backpack had been moved to one corner. The bearded man smiled and said that he would be sharing the cabin with me. I asked him if he was a tourist.

'No,' he replied, 'I'm from Minicoy. What about you? Are you a tourist?'

I answered that I was, indeed, one and probably the only one on the ship.

The man introduced himself as Ismail, shook hands with me and said that the boxes in the cabin contained nothing but fruits and other goods that he was taking home for his family.

'We don't get these items on the island,' he explained, 'and even when we do, they are so expensive.'

I reassured him that I had no problem with that, as long as there was no contraband stuff.

After a while, I went out on the deck again and found more Minicoyans gathered there; they seemed restless and eager to go home. The only other person on the ship who was neither and islander nor government official, was a tall lean man from Pune. He was visiting the island as a guest. I met him on deck and since he looked as lost as I probably did myself, I assumed he was a tourist like me. But I soon learnt that he was on his way to Minicoy to conduct a four-day training programme for teachers of the first private school on Minicoy.

Discovering that I was a journalist, he said anxiously, 'I've heard the island's entire population is Muslim. Is there likely to be trouble because of that, do you think? My wife was really concerned when she came to know about it.'

I said that I was just as clueless about the matter.

At 3.30 p.m., an announcement came through the speaker system that the ship was ready to set sail. I returned to my cabin and found Ismail back on his bed, leaning against the headrest. He looked fresh and relaxed. After a moment of awkward silence, he asked me about the purpose of my visit to Minicoy. I told him how eager I had been until a week back to meet a real, flesh-and-blood resident of the island and how surreal the idea of the place had seemed to me, until I actually boarded the ship.

'Well, now you have a shipload of Minicoyans to talk to and you can ask us anything you like!' he said with a laugh.

Soon, we were chatting like old friends.

Ismail was a sailor, currently employed as a petty officer on an international cargo ship. Following an uninterrupted stint of nine months on the sea, he had returned to Minicoy in June for a short break. He was now on his way back home after spending nine days in Kochi, where he had gone to have his mother treated for an ailment. He had also spent time with his wife and daughter there.

'I had to wait in a queue for three whole days to get tickets to board this ship. And yet, all I managed was one cabin-class ticket,' Ismail confided. 'My wife, daughter and mother are down in the bunk. I can afford cabin class for all of us, but the ship always sails with a full load of passengers and tickets are hard to come by; getting even a bunk ticket is so difficult. It's a mystery as to how all the places on board get taken so quickly that only twenty to thirty people are fortunate enough to obtain tickets at one shot.'

Like tourists visiting the island, its natives too need a permit, issued by the Lakshadweep administration, to leave Minicoy and are required to specify the purpose of their visit to other destinations. A waiting period of several days at the Lakshadweep administration office in Kochi follows, before applicants are issued their permits and tickets, with each applicant being issued a maximum of five tickets.

'The officials in Kochi treat us like dirt,' Ismail complained. 'They doubt our intentions and are highly suspicious. We are

Indian citizens too, are we not? If the [Indian] government won't allow us easy access to the mainland and provide us with adequate facilities, why doesn't it simply give the island away to some other country? Why hold on to Minicoy if they can't provide us with a good life?'

Much of our conversation centred on the transportation problems that Minicoyans face while travelling back and forth from the mainland. This island, which they consider home, is among the few areas of the country that are completely disconnected from the mainland. The direct ship service between Kochi and Minicoy is available only four times a month, the alternative being the fortnightly island-hopping ferries – the only options a Minicoy resident can avail of, which explains the perpetual, frenzied rush for tickets among outbound islanders. Failure to procure tickets on a ship means that the prospective passenger must wait an entire week until the next vessel sails. The only airport in the Lakshadweep archipelago, located in Agatti, is quite far from Minicoy and not that well connected through the inter-island ferry service.

All through our conversation, Ismail did not utter a word of Malayalam, the official language of Lakshadweep. When I tried speaking to him in the language, he responded in kind, but his accent sounded quaint to my ears. His Hindi, though, was fluent and thereafter, we conversed almost entirely in that language and occasionally in English. When he chatted with his friends, though, Ismail lapsed into Mahl, which not only sounded like Urdu, but was written from right to left, just like the Urdu script.

At 4.30 p.m. on the dot, the *MV Lakshadweep Sea* set sail from Kochi port on its west-bound journey. I ended my conversation with Ismail and rushed to the deck to click a few selfies, with the fading Kochi skyline as the backdrop. I remained there all evening, admiring the gleaming, endless sea, the crimson glow of the sun setting on the distant horizon, the flying fish that seemed to skim over the surface of the water like sparkling silver coins flipped in the air, until darkness descended and all I could see was the movement of the frothing, choppy waves.

When I returned to my cabin, Ismail was nowhere to be seen. I tried catching up with some reading, but could not focus as the ship's constant rolling motion made me feel uneasy and nauseated. The more I tried concentrating on my book, the more the urge to puke gripped me. Eventually, I lay down on the bed and rested until dinner was announced.

It was around half past seven that I went to the cabin-class mess to try and see if I could get some food down without throwing up. I found a bespectacled young man in denim shorts and a dark red t-shirt sitting at one of the tables. He definitely did not look like an islander to me. I approached the table, introduced myself, pulled out the chair facing him and sat down. To my surprise, the young man turned out to be the highest ranking official on Minicoy – Deputy Collector Jatin Goyal, an IAS officer on his first posting.

Jatin belonged to rural Punjab. He was now on his way to join work after the 22-day leave he had applied for to sit for the Civil Services exams. His previous attempt had secured him a Group B service and he had opted for Union Territory service, which had landed him in Lakshadweep.

'I like it there,' he admitted over a dinner of rice, chapattis, chicken curry and dal. 'It's very nice, challenging and all. But my heart is not really in it. I was aiming for either the IAS or the IFS service. That's why I'm giving it one more try.'

Before joining the civil services, Jatin had been working with the NGO Pratham, also known as Aid India, in certain areas of the country and had focussed mainly on improving the quality of education in rural schools. When offered his first posting in Kavaratti, Jatin moved with his wife to the capital, where he worked for two months before being posted on Minicoy as Deputy Collector.

'Nobody had opted for this posting,' he confided. 'Over the past four months, I have been trying to get a grip on the various problems the islanders face and making every effort to solve them. My most pressing responsibility is to handle the port traffic. Almost half the budget allocated for Minicoy goes into ensuring that ships sail back and forth regularly from the mainland and supplies reach the people in time. Even a minor glitch risks setting off street protests. The island is highly politicized.'

As recently as the previous week, a shortage of kerosene created by infrequent supply, had triggered protests on the island. Unlike most other parts of the country where kerosene was hardly used as cooking fuel, it was still a much-valued commodity on Minicoy. Without kerosene, kitchens in most island homes would be virtually impossible to run.

After dinner, Jatin and I moved to the deck and continued our conversation. Being the island's administrative head, the IAS officer had more information at his disposal about Minicoy and its woes than any other official I could meet. It was from him that I would come to know that the island was among the very few areas in the country whose entire power supply was managed through diesel generators.

'If there is a shortage of diesel, the island will remain plunged in darkness, as there are no alternative sources of power generation,' he explained. 'Thermal, hydroelectric and even solar power are still decades away. Even hospitals and other emergency services are provided electricity through diesel-powered generators. Barge services to the island primarily transport diesel, kerosene, LPG, fruits, rice and other essentials on a regular basis. Only if there is any free space left, can it be reserved by residents to transport their vehicles, building materials and other goods.'

When I pointed out how irked the locals were about hardly ever being able to get tickets on an outbound ship, Jatin informed me that the government was doing all it could and going out of its way to please Minicoyans. Apparently, the Government of India had ensured that the price of tickets for ships sailing to the island was heavily subsidized. And this was not merely the case with passenger ships. Even cargo vessels had a significantly subsidized rate for transporting goods, as every other product had to be shipped from the mainland.

'But we do have to draw the line somewhere, don't we?' Jatin said. 'Most islanders will even feign illness to get a permit and visit the mainland, simply to roam around and take in the sights. We try to prioritize and only issue permits when they are genuinely needed. After all, the number of berths on a vessel is limited and we have to be judicious in granting permits.'

Jatin also had several bizarre facts to share about the island. For instance, the biggest threat to an islander's safety, while outdoors, was, of all things, falling coconuts. The IAS officer dished out statistics to prove his claim, declaring that this hard-shelled fruit posed the most serious hazard to pedestrians and motorists on Minicoy. Last year, for example, four people had sustained head injuries from falling coconuts; that exceeded the number of people who had been injured in road accidents.

We talked for a long time, gazing at the dark sea until I was so drowsy that I could barely stand. Jatin too felt it was bedtime and we parted company and headed for our cabins a little before ten. I entered my cabin to find the lights switched off and Ismail fast asleep.

* * *

I was awakened the next morning by the clatter of suitcases and boxes being carried out of my cabin. In the corridor, groups of men moved with frantic urgency, carrying duffel bags, cardboard boxes and other luggage, shouting and yelling at one another. Ismail was not in the cabin and two boys, whom I had never set eyes on before, were moving his luggage out.

I asked them if we had reached Minicoy.

'Yes, we have,' one of the boys replied. 'We are just three hundred feet from the shore.'

'Don't worry,' said the other, 'it will take at least another hour before you can step out on shore.'

I left the cabin and walked out to the deck on my right. Before me, about a hundred metres away, lay a narrow sliver of land on which coconut trees grew in abundance. The sea was a deep blue, the shoreline steep and ragged and dotted with fishing boats. A large number of men and women had gathered on the shore to watch passengers alight from the ship and make their way safely to land. As they cheered, about a dozen young men pushed one of the fishing boats into the water and climbed aboard, rowing it frantically towards our ship. When it had moved a few feet away from the shore, the motor was turned on and the boat raced towards us. As soon as it had closed in on the exit gate below my deck, the boys climbed on the hull and fastened the boat to the ship with nylon ropes.

At the exit, a large crowd of passengers waited to be guided on to the boat with their luggage. Four of them hopped on to the fishing vessel with a few suitcases and other odds and ends. Once the boat had been filled to capacity, it returned to the shore, dropped off the passengers and made its way back to the ship for the next lot. By then, three more fishing vessels had set out from the shore and were on their way to pick up more passengers.

'This is the first of your surprises,' said Jatin, who had come to stand by me with a coffee mug in hand. 'After the recent accident, the captain and crew of every ship arriving here have been advised not to dock at the jetty until the season for rough weather is over. As a result, all passengers are expected to wade through the water to reach the shore. Remember to keep your wallet and valuables in your luggage, as you are likely to get fully drenched by the time you step on shore.'

The previous week, another ship – the *MV Arabian Sea* – had had a minor mishap when the crew was trying to dock the vessel. Due to inclement weather, the ship had rammed against the jetty. Though the accident was not a serious one, it had cost the island administration ₹1 crore to repair the vessel, Jatin informed me.

Although sea-transportation options to and from the mainland are limited, it is virtually impossible for private players to enter the fray and fill the gap, because there is no way they can compete against government-operated ships which offer heavily subsidized tickets. While a single trip to Minicoy costs the Lakshadweep government at least ₹50 lakhs, they charge passengers only ₹200 per head for air-conditioned bunker tickets.

'This is the story of Lakshadweep,' Jatin observed. 'We spend fifty per cent of our funds on managing the ports and vessels. The residents protest whenever a transportation problem crops up and their concerns are genuine, but the fact remains that the government spends vast amounts just to keep these people happy.'

I asked him if he too had to wade through water to reach the shore. The official nodded and went back to his cabin.

Half an hour later, three young men approached me and announced that they were from SPORTS; they had come to escort me to the resort where I was being put up. They carried my luggage to one of the two exit gates and placed it in a waiting fishing boat. One of the oarsmen extended his hand and helped me down into the boat.

I glanced at my fellow passengers. Sitting next to me was a young woman in an all-enveloping burqa. Ahead of me was an elderly woman who had been carried out of the ship in a wheelchair and placed on the boat. The engine roared back to life and in minutes, we had reached the shore.

I was asked to leap from the boat and into the water, which was at least three or four feet deep. I complied and waded towards the shore. My luggage was taken off the boat by two youngsters and carried out. The men who had been operating the boat hoisted the wheelchair-bound woman on their shoulders and set her down on the shore. The other woman had to follow my example, leaping off the boat into the water and wading through to the shore.

At the beach, a staff member from the resort was waiting for me with a bright red Willys jeep and an even brighter smile. He shook my hand and introduced himself as Nizam. I dumped my backpack in the rear and climbed into the passenger seat in front.

As the jeep moved through the island towards the resort, Minicoy seemed, at first glance, like any other village in Kerala, dotted with tall coconut, breadfruit and other tropical trees whose foliage was so dense that sunlight hardly filtered through. But here, the ground was flat, no more than a couple of feet or so above sea level, and wherever you went, the roar of the waves seemed to follow you.

There was just one main road on the entire island. It was barely seven feet across and had been built with concrete. There were no traffic signals. Barring a few bicycles and bikes, we saw no other vehicle on our way to the southern part of the island where the resort run by the Tourism Department was located.

* * *

At first, I could not believe what I had heard: apparently, apart from me, there were no other guests in this sprawling, world-class twenty-cottage lodging facility overlooking a turquoise lagoon. It was as if a childhood dream had come true, except for the fact that I had no companion to share it with. Being the only tourist in the entire resort, I was given a cottage closest to the restaurant, with not only a beautiful view of the lagoon, but a bathroom larger than the living room and a roof that was open to the sky.

Since the tourist season was still a month away, a skeleton staff was on duty at the resort. Besides Nizam, two young men managed the restaurant, while an elderly woman took care of the kitchen. The SPORTS Assistant General Manager (AGM) arrived a little later and apprised me of all the water sports and other entertainment facilities available at the resort. When I confided that I had actually come to the island to write about the place and needed to visit the villages, he suggested that I remain at the resort during the day and go out nearer sundown.

'It is so hot during the day, na, that nobody comes out of their homes,' he explained. 'Go out to the villages after 4 p.m. and you'll be able to meet the locals.'

The AGM was right. On the island, the month of August was, indeed, disagreeable. The days were hot and humid and the nights only slightly more bearable. Rainfall was sporadic and heavy, making life difficult. The only way to reach the islands was by crossing the sea, which was the biggest attraction here. It could be rough and unpredictable between June and September, making it difficult to anticipate when a ship might arrive or depart. Given the circumstances, it was no surprise that I was the only tourist staying at the largest resort in the Lakshadweep archipelago. The management of this swank property had earlier played host to several national political leaders and to VIPs like the president of the Indian National Congress party Ms. Sonia Gandhi, who was here in 2014, just before the Lok Sabha elections. The islands and Minicoy, in particular, have been a bastion of the Congress Party from the time elections began taking place in India. The only credible opposition to the Congress here is the National

Congress Party (NCP), headed by Sharad Pawar. In fact, other than Maharashtra, Lakshadweep is the only state/Union Territory where the NCP has a stronghold, though nobody, not even politically aware Minicoyans, has a clue as to how that came about.

* * *

Being the sole tourist in the only resort on a remote island with a population of just over 10,000, I was accorded the kind of special treatment which, I suspect, is usually reserved for important guests. The meals, including a delectable selection of south Indian, north Indian and continental delicacies, were served on time; snacks and beverages were available on demand and the service was exceptional by any standards. If I informed Nizam, for instance, that we would be starting out for the villages at 4 p.m., as the AGM had suggested, he would not only arrive at my cottage promptly by 3.50 p.m. and wait outside with the red Willys jeep, but would ensure that we set out exactly at four – unless the delay was from my side.

Apart from the resort and a lighthouse built in the year 1885, there is nothing in the southern part of the island but forests. The island itself, shaped like a pea pod with a bloated middle portion, covers just 4.8 square kilometres and stretches 10 kilometres from north to south. The entire population of Minicoy lives in the northern part of the island, crammed together in tiny, close-knit villages spread over an area of about 500 square metres. After a brief halt at the lighthouse, Nizam and I drove north along the island's single main road to Falassery, Minicoy's oldest village, dating back to 1701.

Every village on the island had a village house – the first having come up at around the same time as Falassery itself – which was a community hall owned collectively by all the residents, who had also contributed towards its construction. This house, where a hall was reserved exclusively for the womenfolk who gathered there to hold their own meetings, was meant to serve as a venue for all communal activities, including weddings and other family functions. While a Bodukaka or Moopan headed the men's village house, a Boduthatha or Moopathi was in charge of the women's house and was deferred to by the women in the village. All villagers sought the advice of their Bodukaka or Boduthatha before taking any major decisions – a community set-up that prevails to this day.

A fifteen-minute ride through several narrow roads and alleys led us to the present Falassery village house, a solid concrete structure last refurbished in 1985. Nizam parked the jeep outside it, but on alighting, we discovered that the building was locked, as the village officials had gone for their evening prayers. A colourful traditional race boat, known locally as a *jahadhoni*, was on display outside the village house to give tourists a glimpse of the island's unique culture. Nizam and I went and seated ourselves on a parapet near the boat and I listened to him with interest as he explained what made this unique vessel so important for the islanders.

*Jahadhoni*s are the traditional snake boats of Minicoy. Unique to the island, they are not found anywhere else in India or even in the Maldives. These boats are symbolic of the Minicoyans' age-old maritime culture and serve as a link to their past. Treasured for these reasons, the *jahadhoni*s are rowed by a crew of 43 oarsmen (with 21 on each side) and have a coxswain sitting at the mast. Long and narrow in shape, these boats were traditionally used to tow the larger fishing vessels, known as *odi*, to the shore, as the *odi*s that went out on long voyages could not navigate the shallow waters and variable tides closer to the shore. Whenever an *odi* returned from a voyage, a *jahadhoni* rowed by these oarsmen would peg it to their own boat and tow it back home.

Over the years, however, the *odis* have been replaced by more modern vessels and the *jahadhoni* is now predominantly used for a fiercely competitive festival-related race, one of the island's more prestigious events involving participants from rival villages. This annual boat race, held every December, has been helping the island's youth to hone their seafaring skills and prepare them for a career out on the ocean. The islanders believe themselves to be the best sailors in the world after the ancient Greeks and sailing continues to be the most popular profession among Minicoyan men to this day. Among the competing local villages, Falassery enjoys the reputation of being home to champions who have continued to hold the trophy for several years running; in fact, the snake boat on display here was the very vessel that had fetched the much-coveted honour.

While the village house in Falassery stands testimony to the island's 300-year-old civilization, local legend, which historical evidence bears out, claims that Minicoy was inhabited much before the 1700s. According to the Anthropological Survey of India, there is evidence of human habitation on Minicoy after Boduthakrufan, the Muslim ruler of the Maldives, set foot on the island in Hijra 981 (1573 CE) and recorded his visit by inscribing the fact on a stone.

King Boduthakrufan was arguably the most revered national hero of the Maldives, celebrated above all others for his courage and patriotism. During the Portugese invasion of the Maldives, he is said to have come to Minicoy in a special boat called a *kaluafummi*, accompanied by his brothers Ali and Hassan and a small band of loyal soldiers. Minicoy was then ruled by the Ali Rajas of Cannanore, who extended full support to Boduthakrufan and even constructed a small house and mosque for him in Sedivel village. From his base on Minicoy, Boduthakrufan made several surprise attacks under the cover of darkness on the Portuguese stationed on various islands and eventually defeated them. His mission accomplished, Boduthakrufan and his team left Minicoy, only to return later with his two daughters Kamborani and Koharathukamana and other members of the family.

Another theory holds that the inhabitants of Minicoy, along with those of the Maldives, had embraced Islam as early as 1153 CE (Hijra 548) and that Kamborani and Koharathukamana were not, in fact, King Boduthakrufan's daughters, but prominent women belonging to the era that witnessed the conversion to the new faith. Recently, in December 1995, archaeological excavations carried out on a small hillock on the island led to the discovery of an ancient structure resembling a Buddhist *palli*, suggesting that Buddhism had arrived in Minicoy much before the advent of Islam and probably as early as the later period of Emperor Ashoka's reign (265–238 BCE).

Despite these contradictory claims on Minicoy's history, it is clear that this remote island has been hosting a civilization for many centuries now and, despite its precarious geographical position – standing roughly two feet above sea level, it is at the mercy of tidal waves and a gradual rise in sea levels – has sustained life since time immemorial.

As Nizam and I continued to sit outside the village house in Falassery, the breezy evening gave way to a balmy starlit night. The beach stretched before us. Groups of elderly women in *libus*, the traditional local attire which consists of an ankle-length printed dress gathered at the waist with broad pleats, worn with white headscarves, could be seen walking down the clean, narrow streets, running errands for their families, while the men returned to their workshops or yards to resume their professional duties. Unlike in other parts of the country, Minicoyans were accustomed to working late into the evening and winding up only around nine p.m. Typically, there were fewer men on the streets of Falassery than women who, I soon came to know, played an active role in all aspects of island life. According to Nizam, while the village panchayats held elections and elected their chairmen and ward council members, it was the Moopan and the Moopathi who held sway over the people and commanded their respect.

'The elected officials here merely act as nominal heads,' Nizam clarified.

After giving me a basic round-up of life on Minicoy, he suggested that we visit the home of one of the village's oldest residents. To help tourists understand the unique village system that prevails on the island, the Tourism Department regularly organizes a guided tour that includes a lecture by a senior citizen on Minicoy and its culture. As the village head was unavailable that evening to offer us more detailed insights into the island's life and culture, Nizam took me along to meet Hassan, secretary of Falassery village.

Hassan's home was a modest concrete house adjoining a grocery shop in a narrow lane. When we knocked on his door, the 67-year-old was painting, with his daughter Nazeema's help, a piece of carved wood in the traditional style to decorate his living room. Hassan was stout and dark-skinned, with the typical look of a man from south India. Like most islanders, he had strong hands. Neither of his two sons, Nadir and Basheer, one of whom worked at the resort where I was staying, while the other was pursuing his seaman course in Chennai, were home.

After Nizam had introduced me to the family, Hassan led us into his living room and offered us chairs to sit on, while he himself sat cross-legged on the raised platform where he had been painting.

Like most men living on Minicoy, Hassan too had spent a good part of his active life out at sea. After 21 years of sailing around the world, he had resigned from his job and come home for good to spend the remaining years of his life with his family. The senior citizen now worked as the secretary of the Falassery village, taking care of accounts and other paperwork. His father Hussain, also a former sailor, had spent his adult life on various ships across the world. His son-in-law, Nazeema's husband, was a sailor as well. He worked for a British sea-cargo firm and was, at present, out at sea.

'It is quite common in Minicoy,' Hassan said in broken Malayalam. 'You will find at least a couple of sailors in every home here. For as long as I can remember, sailing has been the oldest and most popular profession for men living on this island. Minicoy seamen and captains are much sought after in the shipping world and over the years, we have built our reputation as honest, hard-working and trustworthy employees. Besides, even a ten-year-old boy from Minicoy will be a good swimmer. Throw him into the sea and he will find his way home.'

As the men spent a lot of time at sea, the island's women had learnt to manage their domestic affairs on their own. Such self-sufficiency in the realm of household matters had led to the island's culture evolving in a unique way; Minicoyan women were not required to leave their parents' home after marriage. In the lectures they held for tourists, Hassan and other senior citizens not only liked to highlight this aspect of their culture, but celebrate it as well. He contended, in fact, that unlike the rest of the country, where the girl child was considered a burden and dowry-related crimes were still a distressing reality, the women of Minicoy enjoyed great respect and authority.

'When a man from here gets married,' Hassan explained, 'he inherits his wife's home as well. In short, he has to take care of two homes; he spends the night at his wife's ancestral home and returns to his parents' place for the afternoon meal. Unlike in other parts of the country, a man has to take care of all marriage expenses and only those men who can afford to get married, do so.'

Nazeema was a living example of the system. Her husband had approached Hassan with a proposal for his daughter and taken care of all the wedding expenses. After marriage, Nazeema had continued to live with her parents, while her husband returned to his job, sailing the seas. When on shore leave, he spent most of his time at his in-laws' home, returning to his parents' place once a day to see to their needs. Nazeema too paid her in-laws a daily visit and washed and cleaned for them while she was there, but returned to her parents' home for the night. Hassan confided that when his sons began earning enough money to afford a wife, he planned to look for suitable girls for them, preferably from the same village.

'After they marry, my sons too will have two homes and families to take care of,' Hassan went on. 'Due to this unique custom of ours, most Minicoyans prefer to choose their spouses from among the island's residents. In recent times, however, there have been instances of men from other islands in Lakshadweep marrying our women and settling here.'

Much of the island's culture had evolved in tune with Minicoy's geographical isolation, not just from the mainland, but also from other islands within the archipelago. The idea of a village house had also evolved for much the same reason. Since most of the island's men were out to sea for a greater part of the year, their families were sometimes left to fend for themselves in an emergency, with not a single male member available to fall back on. The close-knit village system, where every family event, be it a celebration or a contingency, was jointly handled by the entire village community, reassured seafaring islanders that their loved ones would be taken care of during their long periods of absence.

'On Minicoy, we are all one family,' Hassan said proudly. 'Even if I am out on the ocean, I don't really need to worry about what's happening back home. If there's a marriage or any other function in my family or if someone falls ill, I know that our neighbours, as well as other members of the village, will join hands to help us. Nobody on this island is ever alone or helpless; that is why you won't come across beggars or homeless people. If anyone on the island is in trouble, the entire village will reach out to that person and help him resolve his problems.'

In recent years, however, the traditional values and community support that had sustained the islanders for generations have been eroded to some extent by the very technological advances – mobile phones and social-media networks – which enable them to keep in touch with their loved ones, wherever they may be. In fact, until a few decades ago, any form of communication between the islands and the mainland was so unreliable, Hassan recalled, that most natives of Minicoy were unaware of India's independence from British rule until 1951, four years after the momentous event! Until the early 1960s, when Hassan was about ten years old, the island did not even have a formal school and children of his generation went to local madrassas, where the only subjects taught were Islam and Mahl. It was only after the Lakshadweep Administration had established the first school on Minicoy, with lessons offered up to the level of class VII, that Hassan was able to avail of a proper education at a government school. On completing class VII there, he was sent to Calcutta by his father for a seaman training course.

'At that time, there were seamen training institutes only in Bombay and Calcutta. When I failed to get admission to the institute, I attended a regular school there and studied up to class X,' Hassan recalled.

Later, he would enrol himself for a seaman course and join the merchant navy in 1974. In those days, Hassan and his fellow sailors would be out at sea for a year and return to Kochi for a six-month vacation. But ferry service between Kochi and Minicoy was so infrequent that seamen from the island had to wait for up to three months on the mainland to get a berth on the ship. As a result, a greater part of Hassan's shore leave was spent waiting in Kochi. By the time he was able to set foot on the island, there were barely a couple of months left of his vacation. Soon, he would be preparing to return to the mainland for another year of sailing. During those long years of separation from his family, Hassan remembered that it was his neighbours and fellow villagers who had provided his loved ones with the help and support they needed.

With the introduction of passenger ships, the ordeal of waiting for months for a ticket back home no longer haunted the Minicoyan sailor, but Hassan claimed that life was still difficult enough, as travel to and from the island could not be undertaken at will.

'Even now, we feel so isolated from the rest of the world,' he lamented. 'One of the most crucial problems we face is lack of medical-evacuation facilities. While there is a helicopter service to airlift critically ill patients to the mainland, it is seldom available when we need it. The concerned officials always explain away its unavailability by claiming that the helicopter is in use on another island or in Kochi. Seriously ill patients are often made to wait indefinitely for the helicopter to transport them to the mainland. Our demand for a second standby helicopter has yet to be met.'

Hassan considered these problems minor inconveniences, however, when the subject of relocating to the mainland or sending his children away to other areas of the country came up for discussion.

'We don't ever consider leaving our island, because here, we are one close family,' Hassan declared, reiterating their unity, while

Nizam nodded in agreement. 'It is our great asset. Elsewhere, I would have had to struggle for a living all alone, with no support whatsoever from the community.'

Nizam was among the few men on the island who did not opt to go sailing across the world and was happy enough living within the 4.8 square kilometres of land that Minicoy covered. When I asked him if he wasn't curious about the rest of the world, he answered that there was no reason for him to be, with the world coming to his doorstep every year. There was no dearth of visitors to his island.

'Why would I need to go out?' was his rejoinder.

It was already half past nine when we left Hassan's home, but the roads were brightly lit and groups of young women and even children were out and about, engaged in animated conversation with each other. I could not help remarking to Nizam how different the scene was from elsewhere in the country, where women and children were expected to be indoors so late in the evening, primarily in the interests of their own safety.

'It is how we live, sir,' he said simply. 'There is nothing to fear on the island. People stay outdoors as late as 11 p.m. and leave their doors unlocked when they go to bed. We live life as we please and are not dictated to by time. Our day begins at around eleven or half past eleven in the morning and ends only around midnight.'

And what he claimed was, indeed, true. Clothing outlets, grocery shops and even internet cafés were open as we drove back to the resort. On the way back, I asked Nizam if the islanders ever came to know through newspapers and TV channels of what was happening in the rest of the country. Were they familiar with the robberies, rapes, scams and murders that rocked the nation from time to time?

'We don't get newspapers here,' he replied, 'and though we do have access to a few TV channels, not many of us are really bothered about news from the mainland. Just as you mainlanders are not all that interested in Minicoy, we islanders are not particularly interested either in what goes on in the rest of the country.'

I asked him why he felt this way.

'There are neither newspapers nor journalists on Minicoy,' Nizam explained. 'No outsider really keeps track of what goes on down here, despite so many of the islanders travelling across the world.'

Until social media came alive in this place in the form of Facebook and WhatsApp, whatever happened on Minicoy was likely to remain confined to this remote island, I mused.

As if reading my thoughts, Nizam went on, 'Now everyone either has a Facebook account or is on WhatsApp. So we islanders share with others news of important events and incidents that take place here. That is our only way of communicating with the rest of the world.'

A delectable dinner awaited me when we returned to the resort. After doing it full justice, I went for a walk on the beach to digest all the delicious food I had consumed. Returning to my cottage about half an hour later to quench my thirst, I found Nizam and his associates waiting to hand me two bottles of drinking water before calling it a day and going home, leaving me alone in the huge resort.

Once the boys had left, I went back to the beach and continued my stroll, although the eerie feeling of being all alone persisted. As the island followed a curve, I could see occasional lights in its northern part from my vantage point. Besides those pinpoints of light and the dark silhouettes of coconut trees, there was nothing but the vastness of the ocean around me.

I stretched out on one of the beach chairs and just sat facing the lagoon for a long time that night. But for the gentle murmur of the waves, not a sound could be heard. Neither of my two mobile phones had a signal and internet was not even an option. I pondered my situation. On this vast planet spread over roughly 150 million square kilometres and inhabited by over 7 billion people, I had chosen to be isolated on a tiny island with a surface area of just 4.8 square kilometres and populated by a few thousand human beings. If a tsunami were to sweep Minicoy off the face of the earth that night, I mused, few would even remember that such an island, along with its people and their unique culture, had ever existed; it would be too minuscule a loss to register on the world's consciousness. For the Minicoyans, however, these few square kilometres of land were their world and being present in it right now, I could appreciate how remote and unreal Chennai, Kochi or even New Delhi might seem to these seafaring islanders.

* * *

Having come to know of the islanders' habit of waking up late and seldom venturing out before 10 a.m., I made no specific plans for the mornings and preferred to go for long, leisurely walks along the shore skirting the lagoon, looking for pretty pieces of dead coral the waves had washed ashore overnight. I felt they would be attractive souvenirs to carry home from Minicoy.

The resort was built right at the mouth of the turquoise-blue lagoon. It was about two kilometres wide and its depth ranged from two feet to around five or six feet, as you moved further away from the shore. At the point where the lagoon curved towards Viringili Island, thousands of pieces of dead coral, washed in by the waves, had piled up all along the shore, looking uncannily like human bones from a distance. From the spaces between the debris emerged colourful little snails and periwinkles, scurrying around busily in the wet sand, until they sensed my footsteps and retreated beneath their attractively patterned shells.

About half a kilometre from the resort, smooth, slippery rocks replaced the dead coral, forcing me off my chosen path and on to the beachside road that stretched far beyond and into the wilderness. To the north of the lagoon, the shore was clean, level and more conducive to walking. The mouth of the lagoon opened out into a backwater which was home to countless snails and other marine creatures. Occasionally, I would even spot a school of lagoon fish darting its way past me towards the backwater and then making a U-turn to return to the lagoon, as if they were on a patrol mission.

On alternate days, my morning walks ended in a snorkelling session offered by the resort staff. With Mujeeb and Raum, part-time snorkelling instructors, accompanying me on bicycles loaded with snorkelling equipment, I would ride down to the part of the lagoon closest to the coral reefs. There, we would park our bicycles and wade into the water. Once we were in waist-deep water, the two would ask me to don my snorkelling mask and bite down hard on the tip of the dry snorkel to practise breathing through the mouth.

While the instructors wore swim fins to help them navigate their way with greater ease through the coral, I was barefoot. When I signalled my readiness, Raum and Mujeeb would take me by the hand and guide me through the coral, while I bit down on the edge of the snorkel and allowed myself to float, breathing hard through my mouth and admiring the wonders of the reef.

I felt impelled to return to the splendours of the reef every other day, mesmerized by the sight of the brightly coloured fish, the giant sea clams, whose mouths opened and closed like gargantuan breathing vaginas in blue and purple, the coral that seemed to dance to the rhythm of the water, its pores apparently blinking at the ripples set up by our movements. During the long hours I spent in the lagoon, I came to know from my instructors that brown-black patches in the sea indicated a seabed rich in coral. If the water was turquoise or emerald green, it meant that we were in shallow waters. And dark blue water meant the sea was deep at that point and unsafe for swimming.

It was while spending time with Mujeeb and Raum that I also came to know about the island's youth and their aspirations. Like most young men living on Minicoy, my instructors too dreamt of a career out on the sea. Mujeeb's family was relatively poor, as none of the male members were sailors. While his father made a living as a barber, Mujeeb's older brothers did not hold stable jobs, as they had failed to complete their schooling, which might have improved their career prospects. And it was only with great difficulty that the family had arranged for funds so that Mujeeb, their third son, could complete his CDC (seaman training) certification course, return to the island and take up the snorkelling instructor's job at the resort, guiding tourists through coral-rich areas, leading them by the hand as a parent would his child when weaving their way through traffic. Some day in the near future, Mujeeb hoped to get a call from a sailing vessel and turn around the family's fortunes. Until that moment arrived, swimming among the coral reefs would be his occupation.

Raum was in a similar situation, except that his family was quite well off and under no great pressure to send him away soon so that he could prepare himself to earn a living. Most other youngsters who worked at the resort were also there to earn some money while waiting to get a call from a sailing vessel. No other occupation, except a government job, was considered worth pursuing.

It was during my pleasurable moments in the water that I chanced upon one of Minicoy's cultural taboos. Much as I loved the snorkelling sessions, kayak rides and simple freestyle swimming in the lagoon, I would learn to my exasperation that if I took off my t-shirt to enjoy the sensation of the warm waters on my bare torso, I would be offending local sensibilities.

'The locals would disapprove if you took off your t-shirt,' Nizam cautioned me before I set off on my first snorkelling trip. 'Please keep it on. No problem.'

A little later, when I did take off my t-shirt and waded into the lagoon, I was asked to put it back on before I went swimming.

On Friday and Sunday mornings – public holidays for Minicoyans – groups of young men and women thronged the southern part of the island to picnic with family and friends. They parked their vehicles close to the beach, set up giant speaker sets and played loud Bollywood music from the 1990s all through the day. These families brought food, sodas and enough games and toys to keep themselves engaged. The men and children in the groups wore trendy Western outfits; the women were mostly clad in black burqas. After a hearty meal and some dancing, these partying youngsters would leap into the waters of the lagoon, just like their cousins in the rest of the world. The only difference was that the men and women here remained fully clothed. Subsequently, whenever I thought of Minicoy, the image that would come to mind was of black burqas floating in the salty waters of an emerald lagoon on a sunny afternoon. For some reason, it saddened me.

* * *

Other than sailors, few Indians know about Minicoy and its people. Hardly any literature is available about the island and its unique culture. What little there is, deals with Lakshadweep in general, with minimal focus on Minicoy. Most local heroes live and die on the island, unknown to the rest of the country and the world. Not many islanders have managed to step out into the big bad world beyond Minicoy to leave their indelible mark. One of the rare few who have is Ali Manikfan from Funhilol village, known among fellow Minicoyans as 'the scientist'.

Ali is probably the only islander to have a Wikipedia page dedicated to him and even a fish named after him. A marine researcher, agriculturist and automobile mechanic, he is also credited with attempting to set up a new Hijra calendar for Muslims. The septuagenarian speaks and understands at least a dozen languages and has a keen interest in astronomy. A documentary filmmaker from the mainland has even made a 50-minute film on Manikfan and his achievements. But I wasn't aware of all that when I met Mr Manikfan on a dark, windy night at his home by the sea in a remote corner of the island.

Ali Manikfan lived in his friend's guest house, a dilapidated two-room building on the southern tip of the island beyond the resort where I was staying. Cycling down to his home late on a weekday night, I found the lean, frail man with a flowing goatee in the midst of his evening prayers. He was clad in a lungi and a worn-out cotton vest. I parked my bicycle next to a grey wheelchair scooter at the entrance and looked around. Tall almond, breadfruit and other tropical trees surrounded Ali's home. Flowering plants and shrubs, which I failed to identify in the dark, were planted at the entrance, with a thin, twisted bark from a tree blocking it. But for the gentle murmur of the waves, the silence was palpable.

Standing in his garden, I was savouring the darkness and silence all around, when I heard the front door open. Ali stepped out to invite me in. The living room was bare of furniture; a couple of crumpled coir mats lay in one corner, while a jumble of electrical wires surrounded a table fan, whose motor compartment had been opened up. The room was crowded with bicycle spare parts, electrical wires, plugs and various other contraptions that the self-taught scientist had built over time to keep himself occupied and useful. Ali led me to the centre of the room, where we both sat down on flattened cardboard boxes and chatted for over an hour about his life, Minicoy and everything under the sun.

Barely five minutes into our conversation, the scientist began expressing his concern over the issues that most troubled him, venting his frustration at the direction in which the younger generation of islanders seemed to be headed and lamenting the manner in which precious skills, acquired in various fields by their forefathers over several centuries, were being driven to extinction by the growing indolence of the younger generation and its lack of interest in keeping ancestral traditions alive. Manikfan deplored the islanders' increasing dependence on the mainland for even their day-to-day needs and felt that it was a dangerous trend.

'Youngsters today board ships sailing out from the island and return, a year later, loaded with money. Once back home, they are loath to do any work themselves. Instead, they prefer to hire labourers from the mainland who will do all their work for them, while they themselves go off to Kochi or some other Indian city on the pretext of getting medical treatment, roam around these places and return home empty-handed after losing all their money to shady touts,' he rued.

'Minicoy never used to be this way. Not so long ago, our people were skilled masons, carpenters and plumbers and could take care of all their needs on their own. In the old days, an islander who wanted to build a house never needed to hire labourers. The prospective house owner would purchase all the required materials and transport them to the site. Then all the able-bodied men in his village would pitch in and help construct the house. It was such a beautiful concept that is lost now, possibly forever.'

Owing to the influence of consumerist culture invading the island, industry could never thrive here. Even the local small-scale industries that had been the island's mainstay were now gone. As coconuts were in abundance, several coir rope-making units used to operate in Minicoy, providing a livelihood to many families for generations. But they had all been closed down due to lack of interest among the locals in continuing with the business. The only operational factory unit in Minicoy was a tuna-canning factory owned and run by the government.

'Today, we have to buy even choir ropes from the mainland,' Manikfan observed, blaming this state of affairs on the indifference of successive governments towards promoting local industry.

All through our conversation that night, Ali continued with his litany of complaints against the present state of affairs on Minicoy. At first, I could not quite grasp what had fuelled such intense anger and frustration. But my understanding and empathy grew as the night wore on and I gained more insight into the 'scientist' and his life.

Ali Muraiduganduar Manikfan was born in the year 1938 in Funhilol village to Moosa and Fatima Manikfan, members of the Manikfan community that enjoyed the highest social status among islanders. Its members were either owners of sailing vessels or engaged in other island-based enterprises. The next rung of Minicoy's social hierarchy was occupied by members of the Thakrufan community, who were usually employed as captains of ships. The Thakruks, ranking third, worked as sailors and engineers on ships, while the humblest position was occupied by the Raveris, who were, traditionally, tree climbers.

Ali's father Moosa, a member of the island's elite, served as the Amin (or administrative head) of Minicoy until 1954, when the traditional system was abolished and tahsildars and other government representatives took over the island's administration. As the scion of a well-to-do family in the Manikfan community, Ali's early life was one of refinement and grandeur.

Growing up in one of the island's largest homes, Ali attended a madrassa for religious education at a time when most local children rarely went to school. Like most Manikfans, his father owned shipping vessels that transported cargo and passengers to and from the mainland and even to other countries as far away as Sri Lanka, Malaysia and Singapore and brought back goods to Minicoy. Belonging to a privileged island family, Ali's parents had decided that he was destined for a better life than that of a sailor and sent him away, while he was still very young, to Kannur in Kerala for his education. But the budding naturalist could not bear the constraints that formal schooling imposed on him and returned to the island after three years.

During those pre-Independence days, the British government usually sent Sinhalese men to work in the lighthouse on Minicoy as headlight keepers, as the local language Mahl was very similar to Sinhalese. Ali, who was as fascinated by the lighthouse as he was by the sea it overlooked and the sky above it, frequented the place and learnt a lot about the ocean and the intricacies of sailing from those headlight keepers who, moved by his enthusiasm, taught him the basics of science and astronomy. With an avid interest in all that surrounded him and the urge to pick up information through observation and practical experience, rather than from what was offered at school, the teenager learnt more about the world around him than he would have from textbooks. Ali would take up odd jobs, including that of a clerk, and even worked as a teacher in a local madrassa for a year. One of the few islanders gifted with a scientific bent of mind, he assisted visiting scholars and researchers during his leisure hours.

In 1965, a miscommunication between the islanders and the authorities triggered a minor revolt against the Indian administration. As a result, criminal cases were registered against 300 young local men who had taken part in the riots. Several of them were even advised by their families to leave the village to avoid prosecution. One of those men, Ali Manikfan, who had been working with the Central Marine Fisheries Research Institute (CMFRI) at the time, was transferred to the Mandapam office in Tamil Nadu, where he would remain for the next two decades.

On the mainland, Ali purchased a 14-acre plot in Valliyur in Tirunelveli district, where he set up a farm, using a variety of native plant species that would thrive in the region's relatively dry climate. Confident that it could sustain itself without any human intervention whatsoever, he named his creation the 'Do Nothing Farm'. This unique farm and Ali's unconventional lifestyle and choices – instead of applying to the government for electricity or any other utility, he built a windmill and fixed solar panels to generate power – soon came to the public's notice and won him recognition and accolades from various quarters.

During his 20-year stint with the CMFRI, Ali helped the institution's research heads to identify and study various marine species. He was even credited with discovering a new fish species – *Abudefduf manikfani* – that would be named after him. Despite his growing success on the mainland, Ali kept himself updated on Minicoy-related affairs and continued to visit his family whenever he got the opportunity. He was also among the few islanders who would succeed in tracing their relatives in the Maldives, thus proving that they shared the same lineage as the Maldivians. It is, therefore, rather unfortunate that his four children, who preferred to settle down with their families on the mainland, have failed to maintain close ties with the island. Ali's son, an engineer, is now working on a ship based out of Mumbai.

After serving the CMFRI for two decades, Ali opted for voluntary retirement and took up odd jobs in Tamil Nadu and elsewhere in India, before returning to the island. For the past several years, he was busy working on a new Hijra calendar that he claimed would serve as a uniform calendar for Muslims across the world. He regarded it as his most significant contribution to the Islamic world and had even travelled to the Middle East on several occasions to propose to the religious heads of the various countries in that region that his calendar be adopted for use. He was now awaiting a response from them.

Six months ago, Ali returned to Minicoy for good and has been living as far away from the villages as possible. Every evening, he rides down to the village on the other side of the island on his bicycle, has his meals there and returns to his home-cum-laboratory to continue with his research.

Despite his age, Ali works at least sixteen hours a day, trying to solve his problems and those faced by his friends by using simple, unique techniques. The grey scooter I had seen parked outside his house is one such original contraption that he had built for a friend who recently lost the use of his legs. All the wires and plugs in his home are similar inventions, 'works in progress', as it were. Ali apparently does not believe in finding instant solutions to his problems by importing goods from the mainland. Rather, he tries to resolve them by using indigenous material.

'It is the way my forefathers lived on this island for centuries,' he said, explaining the reason behind his choices.

By the time my conversation with Ali drew to a close, I had sensed why the ways of the present generation dismayed him so greatly. This island, where he had been born and bred, had developed through the efforts of Minicoyans like him – independent, free-spirited, enterprising people, who were unafraid of going out into the world alone in their attempt to explore new frontiers and start a new life. Ali's forefathers had arrived from somewhere in the Maldives and established a settlement in this village known for its plentiful coconuts and tuna. They had tried out new recipes with whatever ingredients were at hand and built homes using indigenous material and skills that were locally available. In a place so far removed from the rest of the world, the only way to survive and be happy was to embrace the isolation and solitude the island offered and be content with what one had. And Ali's ancestors had sought to do so.

Minicoy does not have much in the material sense of the term, but it has enough to sustain life and that is all humans ultimately need. Ali Manikfan, the scientist, is one of those rare islanders to have grasped this profound truth.

* * *

One of the topics that kept coming up during my conversation with various islanders was their essentially peace-loving nature. Locals believed that it was owing to their tranquil disposition and industriousness that they were such assets to the shipping industry. I also came to know that Minicoyans were seldom involved in disputes which each other and on the rare occasions they were, the clash never escalated to the level of physical violence. A government official posted on Minicoy even suggested that I visit the local police station to find out for myself how little the police on the island had to do by way of maintaining law and order.

So impelled by my interest in checking out Minicoy's crime scene, I rented a burgundy Ladybird bicycle – curiously, all that the resort had to offer were ladies' bicycles – from Nizam late on a sultry weekday morning and pedalled my way to the island's police station that stood, along with other government buildings, near a public park. With the main police-station building undergoing renovation, the local policemen had been temporarily shifted to the office of the coastal police in the building next door.

I arrived at the police station to find the head constable, a middle-aged Malayali from Alleppey, standing outside the building, deep in discussion with a young man. Upon seeing me, he broke off for a moment, asked me to wait outside as the Inspector was in a meeting and took up his conversation where he had left off. I waited until the head constable was free and asked him if the island was, indeed, devoid of crime, as the government official had claimed.

The senior policeman laughed at my comment. 'No crime here, is it? If I had my way, every man here would be behind bars!'

With that repartee, he went into the building. At almost the same moment, two men walked out of Inspector Nazeer's room and I was summoned inside.

The inspector had been transferred to Minicoy only two months ago. A native of Androth Island, the stout, cheerful man with a thick, black moustache, typical of police officials in this part of the country, had worked on different islands under the Lakshadweep government administration. This, however, was his first posting on Minicoy.

In immediate response to my queries about the island's crime graph, the Inspector sent off his subordinates to fetch the registers. When they were handed to him, he started going through them and offered me some statistics on the situation. Between January and August 2015, Minicoy Police had apparently registered just three cases: a trespass-and-assault case and two cases against individuals for possession of marijuana, a contraband item. The previous year, the police had registered only four cases, including one of 'death under mysterious circumstances', which basically meant suicide, and cases against people in possession of marijuana and liquor, another banned item. No murder had allegedly been reported on the island since the time a police station and legal machinery were set up and not a single resident of Minicoy had apparently been convicted of a crime since Independence.

Taking note of my surprised look, Nazeer tried to explain why this was so.

'It is mainly due to the existence of the Moopan system that there have been few convictions on the island,' he began. 'The islanders usually resolve their disputes through the intervention of the village head or Moopan, whose word on all matters is final. If the rare case comes to us, we try our best to settle the concerned dispute amicably.'

It was during my interaction with the Inspector that I discovered yet another reason for Minicoy's relatively crime-free status: its geographical isolation. Theft on the island is virtually impossible to get away with, as the culprit would have nowhere to take refuge, with the nearest island or land mass lying around 100 nautical miles away. Besides, since the islanders know each other well, the moment one of them is seen in possession of valuables that don't belong to him, word spreads fast and the culprit is apprehended in no time at all.

This is the case as far as theft is concerned. Other issues like assault, family squabbles or property-related disputes do arise, but are usually resolved at the police station, as this is the most convenient way of doing so. However, while Minicoy has a police station and a jail, the nearest magistrate court is on Androth Island – about 90-odd nautical miles away at the end of an eight-hour voyage by ship. Even if the police were to register a case, they would have to file the charge sheet in court after waiting indefinitely for a ship to arrive, boarding it when it did and sailing for eight hours, before remanding the prisoner to custody, that too after producing him or her before a magistrate on Androth. Assuming that the police are willing to go that far to follow up a petty case, there are few lawyers – and not a single one on Minicoy – in the Lakshadweep archipelago to take up the case against the prosecution in court. As a result, lawyers have to be engaged from Kerala, brought in by ship, provided food and lodging and paid a huge sum to run the case. All the police do is explain to the aggrieved party the logistical and financial issues involved in filing an FIR. The concerned man or woman immediately agrees to a compromise.

'Here, on the island, we act as a kind of welfare police and serve mainly as a liaison between disputing parties,' Inspector Nazeer contended. 'Unlike in other parts of India, Lakshadweep Police do not mediate cases to make money, but to make life easier for both the victims and the accused.'

While this was the official explanation for the island's nearly crime-free state, locals offered an alternative theory that seemed just as credible. With over 80 per cent of all men on the island either working as sailors or aspiring to be seamen, a police case against one could end his career for good. Prospective seamen had to produce a police-clearance certificate before they could join international shipping firms. Therefore, a criminal case against a candidate could destroy his career prospects, thereby denying him his livelihood. According to the locals, this in itself was the biggest deterrent to crime and the main reason why Minicoyans were careful to avoid disputes with fellow islanders.

With not a single conviction handed out in the last several decades, the jail on Minicoy is among the island's many enduring mysteries. Strange though it sounds, nobody really knows where the jail is located, though it exists on paper. Even Inspector Nazeer had to discuss the matter with some of his senior colleagues before confirming the presence of such a building.

'Ah yes, it is there all right,' he finally conceded, 'but it is not actually a jail. It is a building like any other, which we have been directed to use as a jail.' Then turning to his constables, he asked, 'So where is this jail building?'

* * *

Curious strangers approaching you with queries about who you are and what you are up to in their neighbourhood are a common enough feature of obscure little places like Minicoy. When they are a little too familiar, however, it's usually a sign of impending trouble. My initial impression of Aslam was, therefore, not a favourable one.

I was having lunch at the resort, when the young man with a lean, hunched frame approached my table and introduced himself as a former soldier of the Indian Army. My first thoughts as I took in his appearance – gelled hair, thick beard and cheap, dark sunshades – were speculative: was he a conman, a junkie or a guy looking for a same-sex partner? It was a spontaneous reaction, originating, partly, from encountering strangers from every one of the categories I had just mentioned while travelling to gather material for this book. When Aslam volunteered to take me around the island, without any prompting on my part, I acknowledged his offer with a polite nod and suggested that he meet me later that evening, knowing quite well that I had other appointments lined up and would not be back until late at night. Driven by sheer curiosity, I could not resist enquiring about his rank and the name of the unit he had served while in the army.

'Oh, I could not stick it out in the army for more than six months,' he replied. 'You know how it is on the island, so free and laid-back. In comparison, every moment of my life in the army seemed regimented. It was just too much for me!' He laughed and started walking away, then turned to say, 'It's only now that I'm beginning to think I made a mistake. I've started feeling trapped on this little island and would probably have been better off in the army.'

With that, he vanished into the kitchen.

For most youngsters on Minicoy, life begins only on the day they leave the island. Every youth eagerly awaits that call from a merchant-navy ship, government institution or university that will provide the stepping stone for his departure from home. All the boys I had met so far, with the exception of Nizam, were on their way out to make a better life for themselves. So I was taken aback to find in the midst of such a crowd a young man like Aslam. He had virtually thrown away a career in the Indian Armed Forces that could have taken him across the length and breadth of the country, simply for the sake of returning to the freedom he had enjoyed on this tiny morsel of land in the middle of the Indian Ocean. Keen on delving deeper into the reasons that had led to this unusual decision, I decided to stay at the resort that evening for a chat with him.

Aslam Samanagutha arrived much before the appointed hour and was waiting at the restaurant when I came out to look for him. He was neatly dressed in denim jeans and a dark blue full-sleeved shirt. His hair had an unnatural gleam to it and looked so greasy that I wondered for a second if he had emptied an entire tube of gel over it. We greeted each other and shook hands.

'Have you been to the other end of the island?' he asked, pointing to its northernmost tip. 'Why don't we drive up to that point? It's nice out there and you'll enjoy it.'

It seemed like a good idea to go for a spin and we set off on his bike. Soon, we had passed the narrow concrete roads that ran through the villages and travelled beyond them to a desolate part of the island. Sitting behind Aslam, I pondered over the various possibilities for the evening. I could either wind up stoned, after smoking weed on a virgin beach with a complete stranger, or return to the resort alone, having categorically stated my sexual preference in a manner that was not likely to be construed as friendly. I could not think of any other end to the evening.

All along the way, Aslam talked non-stop about the village system, the islanders, their lifestyle and pretty much every other topic I had obtained insights on from various people over the past few days. By the time we reached the end of the road where the

Coast Guard was building a new compound, daylight had waned and dusk was almost upon us. Due to the dense vegetation all around, visibility had been greatly reduced.

Aslam now announced that in order to reach the island's northernmost tip, we would have to walk half a kilometre through the woods. My wariness must have been quite apparent, for he suggested an option: if I wasn't keen on venturing through the forest to the tip of the island, I could visit his home, which was close by, and meet his family, instead.

Since no islander had invited me to his home as a guest so far, I jumped at the offer. After I finished smoking a cigarette outside the Coast Guard compound, we turned around and left for Bada village, where Aslam lived in his family's large ancestral home with his mother, his three younger sisters and their children. Thankfully, the evening was not turning out the way I had feared.

As is typical of most homes on Minicoy, the living room of the house where Aslam and his extended family lived was long, rather than broad, and ended in a podium to the right, on which colourful carpets had been laid out for the family elders to sit on. The LCD TV mounted on the wall behind it was tuned to a religious channel. At the other end of the room was the kitchen, where Aslam's mother and sisters were preparing dinner for the family.

Having introduced me to the women, Aslam offered me black tea and a variety of unusual snacks, which included salty coconut-flavoured biscuits, samosas stuffed with minced tuna and spices and sweetened flakes made from white flour.

As we munched on the samosas and flakes, Aslam began describing his life on the island and followed it up with an account of his stint in the army, explaining why he had had to leave the armed forces.

Like other young boys growing up on Minicoy during the

1990s and in the beginning of the new millennium, Aslam had enjoyed a happy childhood, playing cricket and football with friends, spending weekends at the beach or simply wandering around the island without a care. Doing well in studies was the least of his concerns and the government-run higher secondary school where he studied had neither the infrastructure nor the qualified teachers essential for its pupils to achieve the kind of academic excellence that would put them at par with students from reputed mainland schools.

But as he grew older, Aslam developed a fascination for the armed forces, with a particular interest in the Indian Navy. While men on Minicoy have been known the world over as expert seamen and sailors, the island had rarely produced a navy man. Young Aslam dreamt of a career in the Indian Navy, even as his friends and family advised him to take up the CDC after completing class XII and work for an international cargo liner.

With his schooling over, Aslam left Minicoy to attend coaching classes at the teachers' training college in Kavaratti. There, he aimed to prepare himself for the selection tests he would have to pass if he wanted a career in the armed forces. He sat for the exams the same year and cleared both the written and the physical tests on his first attempt. But it was the Indian Army and not the Navy which recruited him. He was asked to report for training at the Army Recruitment Office in Kozhikode.

Setting aside his disappointment, Aslam joined and was sent off to Hyderabad, where he underwent artillery training. Joining him was another youngster from Androth Island, who had also made it through the written and physical tests. They would be the only two cadets from the Union Territory of Lakshadweep to join that particular batch of recruits in the Indian Army.

Until then, the two teenagers had merely heard of or read about India's diversity. But in training, they were plunged into the realities of living in a multicultural society. Most of their unit mates came from different parts of the country and practised a variety of faiths. Hardly any were fellow Muslims. As cadets from the same state usually hung out together, Aslam and his friend felt isolated in the crowded battery.

'I had heard about the training period being the toughest part of a career in the army,' Aslam recollected, as we sat in his island home that evening. 'In a short span of time, the recruits had to go through all the ordeals that might be in store for them in anticipated combat situations in the future. Some of our officers and seniors treated us with understanding and respect, but there were others who could be obnoxious and abusive. As if it wasn't difficult enough for cadets from different religions and cultures to live and work in enforced togetherness in the same unit! Problems invariably cropped up. But when it came down to certain officers abusing us simply because we were Muslims, we were not prepared for it.'

Having grown up on an island where every resident was a Muslim, Aslam had never faced discrimination on the basis of his religion, appearance or native language. His experience of humiliation in the army, therefore, came as a shock.

'But I managed to get over it and moved on with my work,' he recalled.

After basic training was over, the cadets were given regular work within the unit for the next several months. It was during this period that Aslam's troubles began in earnest.

'My friend from Androth, who was acutely sensitive, would complain incessantly about how badly his seniors were treating him,' he confided. 'He insisted that we had made a big mistake by joining the army. He would come to see me at four in the morning, soon after I had woken up, and shed tears of regret over his decision. He bemoaned the fact that we were being forced to put up with abuse from our superiors, all for the sake of making a little money – which we could well have earned through other means. Over a period of time, his words began to influence my views as well and soon, I too was longing for a life outside the army.'

When his friend was caught slacking at work, Aslam's superiors, who had discovered that the two of them spent a lot of time together, started tracking his activities too.

'My friend had taken to calling his mother every week and telling her that he could not stand it any longer and was desperate to be discharged from the army,' Aslam went on. 'Finally, fed up with his cribbing, his family sent a letter to the Commanding Officer, asking that he be discharged from service. It was at this point that we came to know that leaving the armed forces was not going to be easy. My friend's plea was rejected. When his brother sent a letter to the CO again, seeking discharge for his sibling, the CO summoned me as well and asked if I too wanted to leave. Too young and impressionable to know better, I replied on the spur of the moment that I did. It was a big mistake.'

The discharge petition was turned down again, however. Soon after, the youth from Androth deserted his unit and absconded. As was to be expected, Aslam, known to all as the missing man's best friend, was picked up for questioning. From then on, things turned from bad to worse. Aslam was sent to a punishment unit, where all soldiers facing punitive action were brought together, and made to work in the kitchen.

'I had hoped to become a soldier and fight for my country, but found myself assigned to the kitchen, instead, where I was put to work making rotis,' he said. 'To make matters worse, all those undergoing punishment like me were also in the bad books of their army superiors and cribbed and complained non-stop about their current situation. When I could take it no longer, I announced to my CO that I wanted to be discharged so that I could pursue further studies and become a graduate. I told him that was where my heart lay.'

Convinced about the seriousness of his intent, Aslam's CO arranged for his formal discharge and a few months later, the young man who had turned twenty by then was sent back to Minicoy, having served for a few months in the army.

Once back home, Aslam repented his decision of throwing away a career whose worth he had only begun to appreciate in retrospect. Deciding to complete his graduation, he enrolled himself for a degree in English Literature at a reputed college in Ernakulam.

'I wanted to finish my graduation and try for the Navy at the officer level,' he explained.

But even in college, there was no respite from his problems. Aslam felt that his background and upbringing were working against him yet again, making him something of an outsider among his peers. He was not fluent enough in Malayalam to converse freely with his classmates and found it difficult to keep pace with the trendy youth of Kerala's fashion capital. As for his classmates, they could neither understand his language nor make sense of his sartorial style, which was clearly dated. Yet again, the islander took refuge in what he knew best: he joined the college's NCC unit.

Due to his army background, fitness, commitment and general passion for a life in defence, Aslam soon grew to be a popular cadet and was sent to an increasing number of camps, including the Republic Day camps. He claimed, however, that even in the NCC, his religion and background were frowned upon by some of the officers who needlessly made life difficult for him.

'But despite all the trouble and humiliation I went through,' he said, 'I did not want to quit midway, like I had earlier. I stuck it out this time and in 2015, completed the three-year course. But I am yet to receive my mark sheets, as the university and college are now refusing to give me credits for the time I spent at the NCC and for the camps I have attended so far.'

More than an hour had passed since he started telling me about his life. I listened to him, dazed, without uttering a word. Outdoors, the weather had changed drastically. Giant raindrops pelted us from the skies when we stepped out. While we waited outside his house for the rain to subside, Aslam continued with his account, telling me how often he had been travelling to Kochi just to enquire about his yet-to-be-released mark sheets.

'It's all so difficult,' he said wearily. 'To get a berth on the ship is hard enough and even if I manage it and reach the mainland, the university authorities will ask me to return in a week's time. Since I cannot return to the island, I will have to stay on the mainland for a week. By then, the ship I was expecting to sail by would have left for Minicoy and I would have no option but to wait for another week in Kochi.'

Aslam's main regret these days was that he had precious little to show for the 25 years he had already spent on this planet. 'The years are going by so fast,' he sighed. 'I have no record of army service and even my formal graduation is getting delayed, because I have yet to receive my mark sheets. My father retires from service this year and I still don't know where my life is heading.'

Half an hour later, it was still raining. We decided to ride back to the resort, as it was getting late. Back in my room, Aslam took out his smartphone and showed me a few photographs of the Republic Day Parade he had organized at the island's public park a few weeks before my visit. Following his discharge from the army, he had decided to organize NCC units in his school and obtained permission from the principal to conduct a parade. A few days before 15 August, he had handpicked some students and trained them to participate in a modest parade celebrating Independence Day. He now planned to remain on the island and motivate youngsters to join the armed forces.

'Now that I have been there and know what it is like out in the army, I feel I have the necessary experience to prepare young boys for a career in defence,' he declared.

Just as he was leaving, I asked him if he had ever felt that his religious affiliation could have some bearing on all the problems he had faced in his life on the mainland.

'I have often brooded over it,' he replied, 'and, to some extent, believe it's true. Others had it much easier than I did.'

I pointed out that there were many Muslims in the armed forces as well as in other paramilitary units.

'They must have been used to the discrimination,' he countered. 'On this island, nobody has ever treated us differently.'

* * *

The night before I was scheduled to leave Minicoy, I came to know that the ship that was supposed to take me back to Kochi had developed a technical snag, extending my stay on the island by a day. By then, I was so used to the place that I could have reached any destination on the island blindfolded if I had a bicycle to ride. All I had to do, as I had done so many times before, was turn left from the resort and follow the winding road beyond the helipad, cross a narrow bridge over a backwater past woods flanking the road on either side for about five kilometres until the point where the road turned left at the Jawahar Navodaya School, then carry on past the tuna-canning factory, the public park to my left and the local police station, the Deputy Collector's office and other government buildings to my right. A couple of bends later, I would hit the villages where the roads became really narrow and cramped and continue all the way to the sea, where the Coast

Guard buildings were coming up. I would thus have covered the island from one end to the other.

During these rides, I often stopped at the only internet café on the island and drank a glass of chilled pista milkshake at the juice shop in the same shopping complex near the jetty. Behind this complex was a series of shops, including a grocery and a stationery retail unit. The nucleus of the island, according to locals, was the tea shop near the jetty, where most of the menfolk gathered during the day to exchange local gossip. I often stopped by on the pretext of drinking tea to eavesdrop on the conversations of the locals. Apart from the juice shop, a few tea shops and a handful of fast-food outlets that opened only in the evenings, there were no real hangouts on the island. The only decent restaurant on Minicoy – the one in the resort run by the Tourism Department – was closed to the public except on Friday, Saturday and Sunday evenings. On those particular evenings, the restaurant would be crowded with locals, mostly married couples, who made an occasion of their outing by arriving with their children and listened to loud Bollywood music of a bygone era while eating masala dosas by the sea.

It was on those evenings that I usually avoided the restaurant, preferring to visit the villages and meet the locals. By the end of the fourth day, I was so familiar with the island that I had started venturing down little dirt tracks in the woods, just to see if I could get lost, which was virtually impossible. Most of the locals here had begun to recognize me and would wave out in a friendly manner when they spotted me pedalling down from one end of the island to the other. So with the extra day in hand, I could think of no better place to spend it, but at the public library near the Navodaya School, hoping to stumble on some interesting literature on the island.

What I did stumble on at the Minicoy Public Library was an

interesting woman. Dressed in a brown printed salwar kameez, with her head covered in a black hijab, librarian Anisa Asif was about to lock the door to the library building and go home for lunch when I rushed in a little after noon. Like most business establishments and government offices on the island, the public library too closed in the afternoon and reopened in the evening for a few hours. When I pleaded my case, the dusky young woman with big eyes and a bright smile agreed to keep the library open for a little while longer and even helped me with some reference material.

Anisa, I learnt, had started working at the Minicoy Public Library only nine months ago. Earlier, she had worked at the public library in Kavaratti for three years. An islander from Seduvel village, the 30-year-old had completed her schooling at the Navodaya School here and gone on to NSS College in Ottapalam, Kerala, to pursue a Bachelor's degree in English Literature. Completing her post-graduation in Library Science at Calicut University, she had cleared the UGC NET examinations, qualifying for a lecturer's post. After completing her studies, Anisa had returned to Minicoy and married Asif from Falassery village. The couple had a four-year-old daughter, Aira.

Meeting Anisa was a stroke of luck. For during the past week, I had been trying in vain to initiate a conversation with Minicoyan women for insights on island life, viewed from their perspective. Most of the women I had attempted to talk to either understood no language other than Mahl or were too shy to respond. So when I chanced upon a young woman from Minicoy, who was educated and suave to boot, I was keen to know as much about her life as I could and, most importantly, find out why an educated young woman would leave the freedom and opportunities offered by the mainland and return to her home on a tiny atoll, where even the men were discouraged from taking off their shirts while swimming in the sea off the beach.

'Women enjoy more freedom on this island than on others in the Lakshadweep archipelago or even on the mainland,' Anisa declared, surprising me. 'Parents living on Minicoy send their daughters to college on the mainland after they have completed their schooling here and encourage them to have a career. Most of my friends who studied at the Navodaya School are now working in different places.'

Anisa was also proud of the fact that Minicoyan women were in charge of their lives.

'As a majority of the men leave the island to work either on the mainland or elsewhere, women here are accustomed to running their homes, holding community events and even managing family businesses,' she explained. 'On Minicoy, men are seen as money-making machines. It is the women who hold the island and its culture together.'

'But don't you miss going out for a meal, watching a movie in a theatre or even wandering through a mall?' I asked her. 'You've lived in big cities; don't you miss the life there?'

'We do go out for meals and movies when we visit the mainland,' Anisa replied. 'But back on the island, we do not need any of that. We rent DVDs of films and watch them at home with friends. My classmates from school organize a picnic on weekends every once in a while. We pack food and drinks and go out in large groups to the beaches at the other end of the island, play games, dance to music and swim in the lagoon late into the evening. Even when we don't, we are always in touch with our friends through Whatsapp, Facebook and so on.'

Anisa claimed that she had never felt vulnerable on the island and that unlike mainland men, their Minicoyan counterparts did not harass or pass lewd comments on local women.

'Generally speaking, there is nothing to be afraid of on the island and that is what I love about life here,' Anisa declared.

'You may have noticed it yourself. Young girls go out for special tuition or to the madrassa late in the evening and return home, unescorted, yet safe. Here, we are absolutely free of fear, even from snakes and other animals.'

I had to agree with her. There were no poisonous serpents on Minicoy to imperil lives or frighten its human inhabitants. As for the danger from predatory men who might dare to sexually harass the island's women, it was remote, with most men out at sea and the rest waiting to follow their example.

* * *

The next morning, I checked out of the resort by ten. Nizam, Raum and the other boys sent me off with warm hugs and sad faces. The red Willys jeep was unavailable and I travelled to the harbour in a white Maruti Omni that Nizam had arranged for me.

Even on the ship, the ambience was one of quiet melancholy. The cacophony and excitement I had witnessed during my onward journey was missing. I spent most of my time in my air-conditioned cabin, pondering over the past week, overcome by a sadness that I used to experience as a child every summer while returning from my father's hometown in Kerala after a week's vacation. It was the gloom that took over on leaving a beautiful place.

My thoughts turned, once again, to the women I had seen wading in the lagoon in black burqas. The image had disheartened me then, making me wonder what kind of a place this was that would not allow a woman to swim in the sea without covering herself from head to toe. How could any woman be happy in such a restrictive society, I had wondered.

And then I remembered Anisa. Despite living on the mainland for several years and tasting its many freedoms, knowing quite well that with her level of qualifications, she could get a job anywhere in the country, this young woman had chosen to return to Minicoy. For her, it was home, a place where tradition demanded that she wear a burqa, like the women I had seen swimming in the lagoon. It was also a place where like other Minicoyan women, she felt happy and secure in the belief that she could live without fear. And in these troubled times, I asked myself, wasn't that the greatest freedom of all?

# 3

# Hussainiwala

There was something about the opulence of Punjab's verdant countryside that gave me goosebumps. It was early spring and the scene was picture-perfect. Lush green wheat fields, interspersed with strikingly yellow mustard fields, stretched into the distance. Beyond them stood rows of tall trees, their branches bare of foliage, shrouded in day-long mist.

Like the trees, the men were also tall, broad-shouldered, with flowing beards and the women were mostly curvy and loquacious, both in a pleasant way. Even the cows and buffaloes looked well-nourished here, reflecting the land's natural bounty.

Like most visitors to the state, I was glad to be in Punjab on a sunny February afternoon, right from the moment I reached the Ferozepur Cantonment railway station after a three-hour journey on board the Ludhiana–Ferozepur Passenger train.

The popular Wagah Border sits right on the Grand Trunk Road between Lahore and Amritsar and is famed for the Samjhauta Express, also known as the Friend Express, plying between Attari and Lahore with a halt at Wagah railway station. Unlike the showy retreat ceremony at Wagah that attracts tourists in droves, the Hussainiwala border, my next destination, is nondescript in appearance, revealing little, initially, of what it has endured – two major wars and umpteen natural calamities. Before I arrived in Ferozepur, a major railway junction situated about 12 kilometres from India's international border with Pakistan, I expected it to be yet another impoverished shanty town like most other border towns I had visited so far. But the train ride from Ludhiana had changed my perception. The icing on my cake was the hotel where

I had booked a room; it had a full bar on the ground floor and at its entrance, printed in bold letters, were the words: 'Chilled Beer, Hard Bar.'

Having landed up in such a fecund region, I did nothing on my first night in town but visit the bar downstairs. The next morning, I woke up at seven, managing to struggle out of bed and brave the numbing cold only an hour later, merely to find the entire town engulfed in dense fog. The hotel's owner promised to arrange for an autorickshaw to take me to Gulam Hussainiwala, the Zero Point border village, at around eleven, as I was not likely to get a vehicle to head out to the border until later in the morning. So a little before noon, when the fog had cleared and the sun seemed tolerably warmer, I left for the international border in a diesel-run autorickshaw after a sumptuous meal of three aloo parathas and thick, homemade curd.

Unlike in other border areas, where roads either did not exist or were in an appalling condition, the one to Hussainiwala was a surprisingly well-maintained, neatly paved, two-lane expressway, flanked on both sides by lush farmland. A railway track ran parallel to it, adding to its appeal. Every two kilometres or so, a village would appear – an untidy cluster of dilapidated brick homes whose walls had been slapped with fresh cow-dung cakes left out to dry in the sun. Sitting in easy chairs outside these houses, indolently massaging their large paunches as they kept an eye on the family's toddlers playing in the dirt at their feet, were old men with flowing grey beards. Despite being so close to Ferozepur, these villages seemed far removed from twenty-first century luxuries. More surprising still was the presence of a handful of international residential schools with sprawling campuses that had come up in the past few years in the midst of these sporadic ramshackle dwellings along the expressway.

The first indicator of the perils the route presented made its appearance when Hussainiwala was about five kilometres away: Sandbags – piles and piles of them – accumulated on vacant land on both sides of the road. I asked my lean, mean auto-rickshaw driver Baljit Singh (the only lean guy I had met in Ferozepur so far) about them and received the prompt reply that the Indian Army always stored the bags along this route to counter possible surprise attacks from the enemy. Geographically, the Hussainiwala border offered an advantage for hostile foreign troops aiming to infiltrate Indian territory and the army was obviously taking no chances in the aftermath of two India–Pakistan wars.

Around ten minutes into the ride, the railway track that had been running parallel to the road came to an abrupt end and a board, planted at the spot, announced the end of the Northern Railway line. By then, the road we were travelling on was almost deserted, but for Border Security Force (BSF) trucks and Maruti Gypsy SUVs criss-crossing the stretch with armed guards. A few kilometres ahead of the place where the Northern Railway line had officially ended lay the border town of Hussainiwala.

Gulam Hussainiwala village was named after a Muslim pir, in whose memory a shrine had been built nearly a century and half ago. The tiny durgah now sits a few hundred feet from the international border's Zero Point on the Indian side and is reportedly visited by Pakistani pilgrims with special permission from the BSF. The shrine is apparently popular among childless couples who believe that their offering of prayers here will bear fruit. Baljit shared the local legend about the white-robed Hussaini Baba still being sighted roaming the neighbourhood at night. On the afternoon of my visit, I found the shrine locked from outside and could see very little through the peephole window at the entrance.

About half a kilometre before Zero Point, at the last BSF check post, a rifle-wielding jawan stopped our auto-rickshaw. He suggested that we return by 3.30 p.m. so that we could visit Zero Point and also watch the colourful retreat ceremony. While the ceremony at Hussainiwala is not as popular or talked about as the one at the Wagah border, at least a few dozen people from either side of the border turn up every day to watch. Visitors need an entry pass to do so and are allowed past the check post only an hour before the ceremony is due to begin.

Heeding the jawan's advice, we decided to check out the National Martyrs Memorial that stood right next to the border check post-cum-gallery. The memorial is a sprawling park spanning several acres, where three of India's most revered and well-known freedom fighters Bhagat Singh, Sukhdev and Rajguru had been cremated in March 1931. They were hanged to death in Lahore following their conviction in the sensational murder of British police officer John Saunders, which was later referred to as the Lahore Conspiracy Case. The bodies of the three patriots were discreetly brought to Hussainiwala and cremated on the banks of the Sutlej River. Although the cremation site became a part of Pakistani territory during Partition, the area would be returned to India in January 1961, when the two countries exchanged enclaves. The memorial, erected in 1968, is located barely a kilometre from Zero Point and was badly damaged by retreating Pakistani troops during the battle of Hussainiwala in 1971.

A picturesque open area with neatly laid out benches in lush green gardens, the National Martyrs Memorial park, unlike most such places in the rest of the country, was surprisingly free of young lovers canoodling behind bushes or in isolated corners. It is likely that the proximity of soldiers peering through their binoculars had chased the lovebirds away from this peaceful haven. When I strolled around the park, there were hardly any visitors in sight, except for a few old Sikh men who were taking photographs near the memorial stones dedicated to the martyrs.

However, the freedom fighters' memorial is not the only one in the park. There is also a memorial to the martyrs of the 1971 war with Pakistan, during which Hussainiwala served as one of India's most important battlefronts. Several soldiers from the 15 Punjab (First Patiala) unit laid down their lives for the country here. The park also houses the dilapidated Hussainiwala railway station, built in colonial times, in memory of a railway line that had gone past the station and all the way to Lahore during the British Raj. Shelling during the 1971 war severely damaged the building's structure, but a small portion of the old railway track remains, neatly preserved in the building for interested visitors.

After exploring the memorial park for more than an hour and taking in the region's war-ravaged history, Baljit and I left for the villages that lay closest to the international border. A gravel pathway, barely one-sixth the width of the expressway, branched out to the right, just before the National Martyrs' Memorial, and led to the border villages of Gatti Rajoke, Chandiwala and Tendiwala. We had barely covered half a kilometre of the stretch when the autorickshaw was forced to come to a halt; a large amount of gravel had been dumped on the road which, I learnt, was being laid for the first time since Independence. Since the three-wheeler risked overturning while navigating its way through the mounds of gravel, we had no option but to park the vehicle by the roadside. If I wanted to continue my journey to the villages, I would have to make it on foot.

Unwilling to turn back without visiting at least one village, I requested Baljit to accompany me and act as my interpreter for some extra cash. The sardar reluctantly accepted my offer and we were about to set out on foot, when help arrived in the form of a crowded minibus that was going all the way to Chandiwala village, the last hamlet on this side of the Sutlej. Baljit ran towards the bus, flagged it down and soon, we were on our way, along with about fifty other passengers. The vehicle creaked and croaked as it bumped and bounced its way over tons of gravel.

Most of our co-passengers were students from the villages of Gatti Rajoke, Tendiwala and Chandiwala, returning home from their school in Ferozepur, while the rest were poor peasants who noisily chatted with one another, while enjoying Punjabi film songs screened on the LCD TV mounted above the driver's seat. Most of the passengers seemed to have a nodding acquaintance with Baljit and were quick to make enquiries about me. I also noticed a large, plump man with a sunburned complexion and a thick grey moustache staring intently at me. He wore a long white kurta and a muffler was wrapped around his head. Wary of inviting unwarranted attention, I turned to the window and feigned keen interest in the scenery outside as the bus passed many dilapidated brick homes like the kind I had seen earlier and heaps of cow dung.

At Chandiwala, the last destination on the route, perched on the banks of the Sutlej River, Baljit and I got off, along with some of the local villagers, who led us directly to a street corner lined with shops. Here, right outside a barber shop, they set out a couple of chairs for us. The fat man with sunburned skin whose hard stare had made me uneasy in the bus now approached and introduced himself as Makhan Singh, the pradhan of Chandiwala village.

Sixty-five-year-old Makhan had been living in Chandiwala since birth and claimed to be a landowning farmer. He, along with his family, lived in one of the few conventional homes (built using bricks and cement) in the village. As he spoke no language other than Punjabi, I had to use Baljit as interpreter. Living as Makhan did, so close to an international border with a hostile country, our conversation inevitably veered towards the two wars that had taken place between India and Pakistan. Between Partition in 1947 and now, nothing else of great import had happened in these areas.

Makhan recalled how his family had fled to Ferozepur, escaping in the nick of time as Pakistani tanks rolled past their village, bombing everything in sight and leaving a trail of destruction in their wake. While homes and most household goods were heavily damaged and cattle killed, there were no human casualties, as all the villagers had fled the place by then. It was only two years later that they would return home. But the war and its impact on their lives were not what Makhan Singh wanted to talk about. These were not his immediate concerns and certainly not of any interest to any of the dozen-odd youngsters from Chandiwala who had gathered around us.

'Living so close to Pakistan is not as great a source of anxiety for us as the frequent flooding of the Sutlej that destroys our crops,' Makhan said frankly.

He was more worried about the fact that children from his village had to travel over 15 kilometres to attend school and return in the evening on foot or in private vehicles that were rarely available. And it irked him that despite 65 years of independence, it was only recently that the government had decided to lay proper access roads to these villages. The youth gathered around Makhan also urged him to highlight and elaborate on their civic woes, instead of dwelling on some battle from the past that had forced the villagers to flee from the invading Pakistani Army.

The pradhan, who disapproved of this rude intrusion by the younger generation, berated them loudly in Punjabi. Soon, a heated exchange of words followed. Before things could get out of hand, I decided to leave Chandiwala, assuring the crowd that I would return the next day and spend more time with them.

By then, the bus that had dropped us off at the village had left on its return trip to Ferozepur. Baljit turned to warn me that luck might not favour us this time and we would probably have to walk the entire distance to Hussainiwala, if we were to be in time for the flag-retreat ceremony. So we left Chandiwala in a hurry and set out on foot along a narrow dirt road, flanked by homes that had been built using red bricks and clay and wore the eerie look of a 1970s Bollywood movie set representing the dust pans of central India. The walls of some of the homes were plastered with cow-dung paste and in most of the houses we passed by, cattle and their human masters lived under the same roof, sharing the same space, separated, however, by a low wall.

Baljit even claimed that since these impoverished villages were caught in a kind of time warp and little had changed here since the 1940s and 1950s, scouting for locations that would be appropriate for shooting period films set in that era sometimes brought here filmmakers aiming for realism and authenticity.

'But don't be fooled by the rundown condition of the houses and the roads, sir ji,' he said. 'These homes might be old and lacking in amenities, but the people living in them have big hearts and are ready to serve sumptuous meals to perfect strangers any time of the day. The land here yields bountiful produce and the local cows and buffaloes never run out of milk.'

To prove his point, Baljit led me by the hand into one of the better-maintained homes. There, we came upon a dark-skinned senior citizen, seated in a reclining chair and supervising the construction of a compound wall. After introducing himself to the old man and explaining who I was, Baljit told him that we were on our way to Hussainiwala and would like to have some tea with him. The man, whose name was Satnam Singh, immediately asked his helpers to bring out a few chairs for us to sit on, while we waited for the tea to be served. Then he began recounting his experience of living in Chandiwala. A few minutes into the conversation, he began describing his experience of war in this region.

'While the first one was raging, the skirmishes would mostly take place on the other side of the border and failed to have much of an impact on us,' Satnam told me. 'But during the 1971 war, we experienced the trauma of bombing. Huge craters would open up where bombs had landed and they kept falling all over the village,' he went on, indicating various target points around his house. 'As Pakistani tanks rolled down the Hussainiwala–Ferozepur Road, the villagers fled to safety, crossing the Sutlej River to reach Ferozepur. While there were no human casualties, many of our cows and buffaloes were killed. Our homes were razed to the ground. We stayed away for two years, then returned to rebuild everything from scratch.'

Despite having the means to build a home with bricks and cement, Satnam's family decided to live in a mud house, keeping in mind the uncertainties of a border area, where military hostilities could flare up without warning and catch them unawares. They preferred to be ready for flight, abandoning their homes and possessions. And it was this mindset that had prevailed until recently.

'It is only now that we have begun to build proper homes in the hope that the army is keeping a vigilant eye on the border round the clock,' he said.

However, dread of war was not uppermost in his mind either. The raging Sutlej breaching its banks and flooding their village was a greater source of worry than the presence of armed Pakistani soldiers just a few kilometres from their homes.

After drinking a tall mug of tea prepared with fresh buffalo milk, I shook hands with Satnam Singh and bade him good-bye. Baljit and I resumed our journey on foot. The sun was shining brightly and I finally began to feel warm. A few droplets of sweat had even managed to break through and bead my brow. We had barely covered a kilometre and were hurrying through narrow lanes, when a tractor transporting harvested plants passed by.

Baljit asked if I would like a tractor ride. Even before I could respond, he had raced off after the tractor and brought it to a halt. Then he directed me towards the driver's seat and helped me climb onto one of the wheel guards covering the tractor's giant front wheels, before seating himself on the other one. And thus, we travelled the next few kilometres, taking pictures of the lush green countryside from our vantage point.

The tractor driver dropped us off at Gatti Rajoke, from where we set out on foot again. Before we could even cross the village, a passing biker stopped to offer us a ride on his Pulsar. But he too had to drop us off a good three or four kilometres short of Hussainiwala, as construction of the road was in progress. Baljit and I had no choice but to walk for more than half an hour along a gravel-topped road, even as giant trucks continued to offload gravel for the road-laying work, temporarily stalling all traffic.

Along the way, we passed several concrete bunkers, lying unused for decades. These sturdy structures, built by the Indian Army during the 1971 India–Pakistan war, each covered an area of less than 10 to 15 square feet and were camouflaged under huge mounds of earth, with tiny openings on all sides for soldiers to fire their weapons from. I stepped into one and clicked some pictures, before continuing with the journey. Several homes in the border villages also had bunkers built in the basement, I was told.

After some brisk walking that made me sweat even in that cold weather, we reached Hussainiwala by 4 p.m. – just in time for the retreat ceremony. While the actual show at the international border's Zero Point did not begin before 4.30 p.m., visitors were allowed past the BSF check post an hour earlier.

By the time I reached the venue, about thirty others – mostly members of large Sikh families, a few youngsters and some newly-weds– had already arrived and were seated in a large courtyard, where snacks and cold drinks were being sold. About ten minutes before the ceremony was due to begin, we were asked to proceed to a large gallery, with separate entrances for men and women. While all the men were seated on one side of the gallery, the women were sent to the other side that was supervised by female BSF personnel. Before us stood a tall pole from which the Indian flag was flying. Gathered under it was a small, imposing group of tall, well-built BSF jawans in khaki shirts and military green trousers, waiting for the parade to commence. Across the border, on the other side of Zero Point, stood an equally tall pole from which the green Pakistan national flag was flying. Half a dozen Pakistan Rangers, who bore a strong resemblance to each other, stood in military fatigues and turbans. A gallery meant for Pakistani visitors, like the one we were seated in, was visible on the other side as well. A few minutes before the parade was to begin, around a hundred visitors arrived from the Pakistani side and seated themselves, the men and women in separate galleries, waving little Pakistani flags they had brought along.

I could not help but feel a certain disdain for the entire parade, beginning with the way men and women had been segregated and confined to separate galleries, as if we were all still living in 1947. Young couples and families who had come to enjoy the event together were separated, with the women being sent off to sit in a gallery meant exclusively for them, while their men sat among total strangers. My derision was compounded by the fact that certain VIPS and influential visitors, along with those who had already booked seats, were allowed to sit with their families and children closer to the parade venue, while the rest of us were considered unworthy of sitting beside women. But this was only the beginning.

At exactly 4.30 p.m., one of the Indian soldiers, whose thick, twirling moustache extended all the way to his sideburns, blew a whistle and one of the most farcical shows I had witnessed in my life, commenced. The retreat ceremony took off with the soldiers on either side stomping their feet as hard as they could and trying to outdo each other in throwing up their legs as high as they would go without their khaki trousers splitting at the seams. Every time an Indian soldier stamped his boot hard on the concrete ground, the crowds on my side would cheer him. When a Pakistan Ranger did the same, the crowd of Pakistanis on the other side would cheer and wave their national flags with equal frenzy. This went on for a while, until the soldiers fell into some kind of formation and stood at attention, following which the show degenerated into a still more ludicrous spectacle.

The Indian soldiers now participated in a one-on-one exercise demonstration with their Pakistan Army counterparts. A soldier from each group stepped out and faced the other at Zero Point. Starting off with the Indian jawan, whose gestures the Pakistani soldier repeated verbatim, the duo stamped their boots, clenched their fists, twisted and shook their forearms in an intimidating gesture and beat their chests in the most flamboyant way possible, supposedly to convey their readiness – and, perhaps, even that of the army they represented – to initiate military hostilities against the enemy soldiers.

When the Pakistan Army soldier had completed his flashy routine, the entire crowd on the other side erupted in loud sloganeering. 'Pakistan *zindabad*! Pakistan *zindabad*!' they yelled, amusing me and several other people in the crowd of Indians on this side. For a brief moment, it was heartening to witness the maturity of the Indian crowd that had revealed decorum and common sense in resisting the temptation to boo the other side and cheer our own soldiers engaged in what was a meaningless routine in a mundane retreat ceremony.

It was at this moment that someone from the crowd behind me sprang to his feet and bellowed a loud 'Hindustaaaan zindaaabaaaaad!', drawing out the words as slowly as possible. It served as the catalyst to trigger off the madness on our side. From this point onwards, the crowds took over the show, with both sides screaming and cheering as hard as they could, whenever a soldier representing one country taunted his counterpart from the other by stamping his boots and clenching his fists in the now predictably confrontational routine.

The loud sloganeering reached fever pitch at one stage and I feared the Indian crowd might breach the flimsy barricades laid out in front of us and barge into the Pakistani enclosure for a full-fledged brawl, as it were, and thereby trigger off, perhaps, an international incident. But thankfully, that did not happen, at least not on this particular evening. The soldiers who had been relaxed earlier and were enjoying their role in this piece of international theatre grew tense as the crowds became agitated and vociferous. With things heating up, an Indian soldier, who had accidentally missed a beat in catching his rifle after flipping it up in the air, flushed with embarrassment when his momentary lapse invited a barrage of jeers and cusswords from the audience sitting with me.

Sitting there and watching this travesty of an official ceremony that seemed to go on forever only set me wondering as to who might have initiated it in the first place and to what end. From the little background information I could gather, this performance, formally known as the 'beating retreat border ceremony', had been introduced sometime in the 1950s as a far more dignified drill than it was today. Then the war of 1971, followed by the liberation of Bangladesh, took place and the situation changed; the show acquired a note of aggression.

The spectacle involving the armed forces of both countries has been criticized in several documentaries and newspaper articles. Yet, the drill continues to serve as the highlight of every evening in Hussainiwala, as well as on the Wagah border, with people from both sides turning up in large numbers to enjoy it. So much so that there have been demands for a similar spectacle on the India–Bangladesh border.

The only class act I witnessed in the entire ceremony came towards the end, with an Indian soldier moving to the Pakistan side to bring down the tricolour and his Pakistani counterpart crossing over to our side to retrieve their national flag, both men timing the moment with precision so as to ensure that their respective national flags crossed midway. Thankfully, the show ended on that decorous note, with no riots breaking out despite the provocation from the crowds on either side.

As I walked back from the venue of the retreat ceremony to the BSF check post, with cries of 'Hindustan *zindabad*!' and 'Pakistan *zindabad*!' still ringing in my ears, a comment made by an Indian Muslim friend came to mind. As the leader of a political outfit in Chennai, sometime before the 2015 Bihar elections when the BJP had gone all out to denounce the consumption of beef, he had confided in me about his decision to stop referring to our country as 'India' or 'Bharat' in his press releases. He had used the name 'Hindustan', instead, as he sensed that Muslims and other minorities no longer felt they belonged here. By shouting 'Hindustan *zindabad*!' to counter every cry of 'Pakistan *zindabad*!' at the retreat ceremony, the crowds who shared my nationality had automatically alienated nearly 200 million Indians from their homeland.

* * *

The next morning, I left for Gatti Rajoke, one of the oldest and largest Indian border villages located closer to Pakistan than any other. Living in this hamlet are over 2,000 families, mostly from the Rai Sikh community. Over a hundred of the farmers living here own land that lies beyond the international border fence;

every time they need to till their land or harvest the crops, they must seek BSF clearance. Gatti Rajoke is also home to some of the people most affected by Partition. The residents of this village are mostly migrants from Pakistan who had abandoned their ancestral homes during those turbulent times to flee persecution. Settling along the banks of the Sutlej River, these refugees, claim local journalists, were unfamiliar with the area's topography and started farming on whatever land was available, unaware that they were actually tilling the dry riverbed. They would discover, only too late, that when the Sutlej was in spate, this village, as well as its surrounding areas, would suffer from frequent floods. But despite such natural calamities, the tensions related to border strife and the absence of proper roads, health care or other basic amenities, including the supply of drinking water, several families have been living here for more than three generations.

Having passed through the village, the previous afternoon, on my way to Chandiwala and discovered the poor condition of the gravelled roads, I was in no mood to sweat it out again and had prepared for a smoother ride this time by renting an air-conditioned sedan from Ferozepur. The mounds of gravel dumped along the road the day before were now reasonably levelled, and we could reach Gatti Rajoke without much difficulty.

Like the other border villages, Gatti Rajoke was replete with mud homes. Mounds of cow-dung cakes lay on either side of narrow, unpaved roads and groups of men, with time apparently hanging heavy on their hands, squatted at street corners, playing cards, carrom and other games. In contrast to their seeming idleness, the fertile farmlands surrounding the village appeared to be a shining example of industry and devoted labour; they were abundant with wheat, mustard, potatoes, green peas and several other crops, harvested season after season.

Reaching the town centre, we asked for directions to the

sarpanch's house and were led to the home of another Makhan Singh, one of the village's two sarpanches.

While the sarpanch lived in a home that was a much-improved version of the neighbouring houses, with its cement walls, asbestos-sheet roof and well-laid flooring, it was, like the rest, yet another home that served simultaneously as living quarters and cowshed-cum-granary. When we arrived at the house, we learned that the sarpanch had gone to Ferozepur on an errand. His youngest son, Bahad Singh, lay on a charpoy in the shade of a leafless tree in the courtyard, reading a newspaper.

Unlike most other men in his village, who sported luxuriant moustaches and were proud of them, Bahad was clean-shaven and had thick, neatly combed hair. The 22-year-old was Makhan Singh's third son and the only one in the family to pursue a post-graduate degree after completing an engineering course. Bahad's two elder brothers, Shandu and Prem, had not been able to pass their matriculation exams and now helped their father in the fields. Bahad's family, among the oldest in Gatti Rajoke, had set up their home here some seventy years ago, when the place was just beginning to develop into a village. Originally from the Attari region in Amritsar district, his great-grandfather had lost everything he owned during Partition and settled on the banks of the Sutlej to start life afresh. In those days, the surrounding lands were unoccupied and people forced to flee from Lahore, Rawalpindi and other areas in what is now Pakistan set up their homes here and practised farming.

Despite being here for three generations, said Bahad, his family still had no ownership rights to the land on which they lived and worked. While they cultivated around five acres of agricultural land, his family had no documentation to prove it belonged to them. In fact, all the families which had settled on the banks of the river were in the same boat. A few years ago, the state government had come up with a proposal to hand over the necessary land documents for a nominal sum to those in temporary possession of the farmlands. But that project seemed to have backfired as the land mafia and the region's wealthy politicians exploited the opportunity and began usurping property from the poor villagers who could not afford even the token price demanded by the state. When the authorities discovered that the land mafia was grabbing most of these lands, pushing the hapless farmers into greater poverty, they put the project on hold.

'Such is life here,' Bahad lamented. 'The state government is least bothered about what goes on in these villages, because this is a border area.'

I understood the situation. With the area vulnerable to military offensives from across the border, the Indian government had chosen not to develop its infrastructure, thereby reducing the cost of potential damage from the enemy during times of political tension or even outright warfare.

Problems involving ownership of land were, in fact, just one of the many issues faced by residents of these perilous borderlands. Since Partition, the families living here had been uprooted from their resettled lives on more than one occasion, having to flee their village and leave behind their homes, possessions, livestock and crops, only to return later and start from scratch. The India–Pakistan wars of 1965 and 1971 had driven them away and they had been all set to flee again during the Kargil War, as the armies of both countries amassed troops near the border, readying themselves for battle.

'Whenever there is a bomb blast in New Delhi or Karachi, tensions simmer here in the village and we must pack our belongings and prepare to leave,' Bahad sighed. 'Everyone becomes unsettled all over again.'

In fact, the situation in these villages is such that just a few days before my visit, some villagers had spotted four or five suspicious-looking men roaming around in the vicinity and immediately alerted the BSF. A red alert was sounded in Ferozepur and its surrounding areas, army units were brought in and all dubious-looking persons were taken in for questioning.

'This was soon after the Pathankot terror attack and we could not risk taking any out-of-the-ordinary situation or movement lightly,' Bahad explained.

As he continued to narrate one incident after another to highlight the stress of living along the border, his brothers Shandu and Prem, along with a few other villagers, joined us and formed a little crowd around me. Prem brought me tea and Good Day biscuits and some of the more enterprising villagers, assuming I was a local reporter, shared their woes.

Growing up in such a remote village, one of the major challenges that youngsters faced was going to school and college. Until a few years ago, the sole school in Gatti Rajoke only taught till class VII and students who wished to continue their education had to go to either Ferozepur or Moga.

'With the roads being in such poor condition and buses plying rarely on this route, commuting to school and college regularly becomes impossible and most students are unable to continue their education,' Bahad told me.

Apart from the absence of proper road connectivity, the lack of work opportunities to enhance the meagre earning of farmers in this village had also dimmed the prospects of the local youth for pursuing higher education. This was obvious from Bahad's response when I asked him about the number of graduates in the village.

Counting them off on his fingers, he replied, 'Three.'

This included himself.

'Inspired by the example we set, four or five young people are doing their graduation now,' he added.

Another important reason for the lack of interest in education, claimed the villagers, was the absence of opportunities for those from the border region; in other words, members of the Rai Sikh community. The farmers here believed that the state government had systematically isolated them from the mainstream by branding them as smugglers and illicit arrack brewers.

'Besides, the local youth can only be inspired and motivated when they have successful people around them to serve as role models,' Bahad went on. 'Nobody of worth ever comes to visit these areas. Our children and their peers are so disconnected from the rest of the world that they are quite ignorant about the many professions that exist today. We don't have proper mobile-network coverage and the internet is still something of a novelty among the youth here. How do we keep pace with the rest of the world?'

As if such tribulations were not enough, those farmers whose lands lay on the other side of the international-border fence had to contend with additional woes. The border fence erected by the Indian government is not exactly on the international border (IB) but anywhere between 100 to 500 meters ahead of the IB which meant that several villagers had their farmlands on the other side of the border fence and had to get permission from the BSF officials to work on their lands.

Among them was Resham Singh, a tall, hefty man whose robust appearance belied the stories of need and deprivation I had been hearing so far. Forty-year-old Singh had been living in Gatti Rajoke with his family for several decades. One of the wealthier farmers in the village, Resham held 20 acres of land, of which 4 acres lay on the other side of the border fence beyond BSF Gate 3. Unlike other farmers in his village, Resham could not visit his farmland at will and had been given specific windows of time during which he could work on his land.

'Every time I cross over to the other side or return from there,

I am thoroughly frisked and not allowed to carry anything beyond the tools I need,' Resham told me. 'Sometimes, if my tractor or other equipment needs repairs, I have to get special permission from the Commanding Officer to take tools over to the land and get them fixed. If there are major repairs, then I bring the tractor over to Ferozepur. By the time I manage to do the needful, the crops have dried up and are of no use.'

Moreover, farmers like Resham, with land on the other side of the border, were apparently under army surveillance and forbidden to even speak to the owner of the adjoining plot in Pakistan.

'If the BSF catch me interacting with any of the Pakistani farmers, they will immediately seal my land and not allow me past the fence,' Resham said. 'Then I have to wait for several months to prove my innocence before resuming work.'

Given the hostile conditions in which men like him had to survive, I asked him if he ever felt fearful about going to the other side and farming in territory which was beyond the control of the Indian BSF. Did it not involve risks and had any farmer ever been shot?

'Fear is always present and we are quite uneasy about the whole situation, but no one has been shot in the last forty years,' he replied.

The problems for farmers like Resham had begun only in the late 1990s, when the Indian government erected barbed-wire fences along the entire stretch of the border. Until then, the border had been open and farmers could come and go as they pleased. With the erection of the fence, however, life had become much more complicated and land prices had crashed.

'The worst part is that I cannot even sell off that land to anyone else, as it would fetch no more than one-fifth the price of a similar plot of land on the Indian side of the fence,' Resham lamented.

'Despite suffering all these tribulations, we are still branded as smugglers by the Indian government. The BSF claim that we are acting as couriers for the smuggling of narcotics and other contraband, but in reality, all we do is suffer because of our lands that happen to lie on the wrong side of the fence.'

* * *

We left Gatti Rajoke later that afternoon and drove through Tendiwala, Chandiwala and other border villages, travelling along similar dusty dirt roads past the now familiar-looking ramshackle homes and wheat fields. We stopped to speak to farmers, village heads and whoever else we bumped into on the way.

In Tendiwala, we halted at the home of the Singh brothers – Dilip, Preetam and Jiggi – which was closest to the border. Now in their sixties, all three men had lived in this village since childhood, without ever stepping out to explore the rest of the country. Dilip, the oldest of the three, remembered his father telling him about their ancestral home in Rawalpindi and the acres of farmland they had owned before Partition.

'We lost everything during the country's partition and came here as homeless refugees,' he said.

The family occupied whatever little land was available when they arrived and rebuilt their lives. Several decades later, when the country's boundaries were redrawn and enclaves were exchanged between India and Pakistan, the Indian government set about regulating the use of land in this region, without handing over formal ownership documents to the farmers. Dilip's family was thus allotted five acres of land on the riverbed, where they were now growing crops.

'But it was a cruelly unfair deal,' he said. 'This piece of land lies on the riverbed and suffers from recurrent flooding. In addition to that, government officials rarely visit our villages, as we live in the border area. None of the subsidies or funds allocated for these villages ever reach us. Even if they do, they usually end up in the sarpanch's home.'

Tendiwala was also among those villages where one in every four farmers had land on the other side of the border fence. Often, their crops would be ravaged by wild pigs and other animals during the night, but there was very little they could do about it, as the border gates would close by evening, denying them access. Any claims for compensation were usually regarded with scepticism by slack government officials who rarely left their urban milieu to visit the villages and examine the situation for themselves. People here lamented that while the village had a primary and a secondary school, the appointed teachers were frequently absent from class. Similarly, doctors were rarely in attendance at the local, primary healthcare centre and the benefits of any scheme announced by the government barely trickled down to these distant borderlands, leaving the residents to fend for themselves.

As we visited many more such hamlets along the border, the same stories about lack of development, living in fear and government apathy were replayed to us by different village heads, farmers and students. By 4 p.m., I had decided to return to Ferozepur.

Unlike Baljit Singh, who had chattered incessantly all through the journey yesterday, the driver of the car I had rented that morning mostly kept to himself and rarely initiated conversation, although he would always stand by my side and act as my interpreter whenever I couldn't find anyone who spoke Hindi. I was, therefore, surprised when the middle-aged man from Ferozepur spoke up while driving back to his hometown along the expressway.

'Sir, did you believe everything those people said?' he enquired.

Taken aback by his words, I asked him to share what he knew about the border areas.

'While much of what those people claim is true, they aren't complete innocents either,' he declared. 'This border is infamous for the smuggling of narcotics, ammunition and all kinds of contraband items. Most of the villagers are involved in it and especially the ones who have land on the other side of the fence. At night, under cover of darkness, Pakistani smugglers bury the contraband in the fields cultivated by Indian farmers. Our people dig it up while working on those fields and bring it past the BSF gates, along with the crops they have harvested, without being apprehended. This smuggling racket is controlled by influential people and the villagers work for them and make good money. Besides, the entire region is infamous for the illicit liquor clandestinely brewed in every other home. And it isn't true that officials don't visit the border villages; on the contrary, it's the villagers who want to be left alone and resent outsiders in their midst, even government officials.'

* * *

When we returned to Ferozepur later that evening, the entire town was buzzing with activity, as the people geared up to celebrate Basant Panchami, the spring festival, in style. Terraces were being vigorously cleaned for hosting nightlong DJ parties, music systems with giant speakers were being erected on the roofs of homes and commercial complexes, while people on the street carried crackers, colourful kites of various sizes and spools of kite string to celebrate the arrival of spring. Vendors of hooting pipes, party masks, gas balloons and other toys stood at every street corner near the market where I was staying, their merchandise displayed on tall poles. The roads were clogged with two-wheelers, with many young pillion riders wearing masks and hooting as they sped past pedestrians.

By 6 p.m., loud Punjabi folk music started blaring out from the music systems. From the terrace of my hotel, I could see groups of well-dressed young men and women dancing to the pulsating beats. As night set in, the sky was lit up by hundreds of dainty floating lanterns that gently went where the mild breeze took them. Some children flew kites against the night sky, their spirit of competition high as they sought to best their rivals. As the night progressed, traffic increased on the streets, with an increasing number of young men criss-crossing the city on bikes, hooting all the way. Busy shoppers thronged the market, especially the kite shops, which were packed with customers even as late as 9 p.m. I went for a stroll in the market to soak in the ambience and found the road strewn with kite strings and shreds of kite paper. The loud music that blared from almost every other terrace added to the celebratory mood, while the street dwellers and the homeless huddled around little bonfires and hummed along.

I returned to my hotel, before the booze and its after-effects overflowed to the streets, to celebrate Basant Panchami from the confines of the bar. The partying continued through the night and into the following morning and businesses in Ferozepur remained closed through the day. Throughout that day, the number of kites in the sky and customers in the hotel's bar kept increasing and the giant speakers continued to blare loud music.

Since I was not particularly keen on going out in this frenzied merrymaking, I decided to catch up with the owner of the hotel-cum-bar. From the time I checked into the hotel, this tall, elderly man with the chiselled nose and thin grey moustache had been of immense help. He had facilitated meetings with local people and arranged for autorickshaws and taxis. He had even taken me out on his scooter once to a local taxi stand, where he negotiated with one of the drivers to take me to the border area for a reasonable sum of money. Every morning at seven, I would hear him yell at his employees in an attempt to rouse them from slumber and find him at the cash counter all day, dressed in a long, flowing kurta, with a black shawl wrapped around him. Throughout my weeklong stay in Ferozepur, I never saw him in any other garb.

By 6 p.m., he would settle down at the bar counter, with a full bottle of whiskey, savouring it slowly through the night, while his two sons managed the cash counter and the kitchen. Occasionally, old friends and business associates would drop by and sit beside him for a couple of drinks, before returning to their work. But this old man sat at the counter all by himself, until the bottle was empty. On that particular evening when I was confined to the hotel, I went and took the chair facing the counter behind which he sat drinking and asked him for an interview.

He looked me squarely in the eye and asked me what kind of book I was writing. I told him that I was writing about border towns and that Ferozepur happened to be one.

'Then please write in your book that this border needs to be opened up if Ferozepur is to progress in any way,' he said. 'Have you seen the Wagah border? There has been so much progress along that route, while we are left to languish here for so many years, despite being so close to Lahore.'

Pausing for a moment, he asked me if I had ever been to Lahore.

I answered that I had not.

'Oh, you should definitely visit Lahore. What a beautiful city it is!' he declared, his faraway gaze filled with nostalgia. 'I had been there once during the eighties to watch an India–Pakistan cricket match. I went to Delhi, got a visa and then travelled to Lahore. You remember that match where Abdul Qadir hit sixers? I was present in Lahore to watch that match. It's a wonderful city! People in Lahore are very different from those you see here. They are cultured and courteous and treat everyone with respect. Even a rickshaw-puller or beggar is treated with respect there. I stayed in Lahore for seven days and had one of the best times in my life. In the evenings, the entire bazaar lights up with the most spectacular *mujra* sessions. What a city!' A moment's silence followed. Then he turned to me and declared, '*Jinhone* Lahore *ek baar bhi nahi dekha, na, toh samjho ki unhe paida he nahi hona tha.*'

His statement that anyone who had never even laid eyes on Lahore was unworthy of being born was a strong one, indeed, and laid bare his passionate attachment to this vibrant city which was now in Pakistan.

With that, he returned to his yet unfinished bottle of whiskey. I also felt inclined to respect his moment of privacy and let him be.

* * *

On my last evening in Ferozepur, I went to meet educationist, and CEO of the DCM Group of Schools, Anirudh Gupta at his office in the sprawling campus of DC Model School near the Ferozepur Railway Junction. No other staff member was present on the campus when I arrived, except for his personal assistants and security guards.

Anirudh's family is among the oldest and most respected in town for their contribution to local education. His maternal grandfather, the late M.R. Dass, founded DC Model School in 1946, along with two British ladies, Mrs Spencer and Mrs Brown, both wives of British Army officers, to provide quality education to the residents of Ferozepur.

'In those days, Ferozepur had no school and local children had to travel far for a decent education,' Anirudh began, as we sat in his plush office. 'My grandfather was among the well-educated men in town and when he got an opportunity to serve society through the school, he gave up all his businesses and focussed entirely on developing the school, which has now grown into an iconic institution.'

After those early days, Anirudh's grandfather went through several ordeals, including the trauma of Partition, two major wars between India and Pakistan and epic floods, among others, that could easily have broken the spirit of an average individual. But DC Model School has gone from strength to strength and held regular classes all through, except during a brief period in 1947, one of the most tumultuous times in India's history.

'On learning that DC Model School had closed in the wake of Partition, the British Army officers insisted that it be reopened as soon as possible and, indeed, this was done in just two months,' said Anirudh, after reading an entry from the school's visitors' log dating back to September 1947.

The visitors' log is among the school's many preserved artefacts, along with several shields and medallions that were neatly showcased in the CEO's office.

As if the brutal shock of Partition was not enough, the school suffered again during the wars of 1965 and 1971, with the exodus from Ferozepur of great numbers of people to safer destinations. Then came the floods and the Khalistan movement, shaking the town's very foundations. Yet, DC Model School withstood the turmoil and actually outgrew it all to set up a world-class campus, probably the first of its kind in an area so close to the international border. While many educational institutions and industries have progressed sufficiently to assume a position of prominence, the DCM Group acquires significance as an entity that remained firm in the face of adversity, survived all odds, even as the town that served as its base was imploding from within.

When DC Model School opened seventy years ago, Ferozepur was a boom town and a major stopover destination for people and goods travelling to Lahore. Wealthy zamindars, businessmen and scholars lived in and around this army cantonment that was known for its prosperity. Following Partition, Ferozepur became a border town, abruptly losing its trade-route advantage. With diminished business prospects, a group of traders and businessmen preferred to move to other areas. Later, during the two wars, when Pakistan Army tanks – one of which is still on public display – rolled through the town's streets, more people decided to move out and businessmen shied away from investing in the boom town that was now in decline. To add to its woes, as the town was on the banks of the Sutlej it was subjected to periodic inundations. Anirudh still recalled how the entire school building had been submerged during the floods of 1988 and how much it had cost the management to set it back on its feet.

'Today, we are among the few influential families still living in Ferozepur. All the others have already settled in other cities and invested their money elsewhere,' Anirudh said. 'Due to all the adversities this town has faced, industrialization could never really pick up here. Even the few brave entrepreneurs who set up small-scale industries were forced to shut down, citing a dearth of business. So while the country and the rest of Punjab progressed, we went from bad to worse.'

To illustrate his point, Anirudh claimed that with the exception of the Indian Army and the railway headquarters, there was no source of employment in Ferozepur. Due to the lack of industry and the absence of other employment opportunities, youth born and raised in Ferozepur tend to move to other cities. As for the meagre influx into this area of people from other parts of India, it consisted solely of railway employees or armed forces personnel.

'Inevitably, a kind of stagnation has set in among the local population and the town's geographical location has become a curse for us,' Anirudh concluded.

Like most other residents of Ferozepur, he firmly believed that the only way to revive the town's fortunes would be to open up the Hussainiwala border and promote trade from Ferozepur to Lahore, as had been the case in the past.

'If the Centre can take such a decision, this town will get a fresh lease of life. Otherwise, I don't see how we can get out this mess,' he said with finality.

Though well aware of the many drawbacks of continuing to live in their hometown, Anirudh's family deserved praise for having gone ahead and built an international school mere kilometres from the border on the way to Hussainiwala.

'It was our way of paying back to the town that has given us everything,' he explained, 'and also to encourage others to put the trials of the past behind them and set up new business establishments along the border. Our dream is that sometime in the future, this border will open and students from Pakistani villages and towns will cross over to attend classes at our school every day.'

* * *

After a freewheeling chat that covered Ferozepur, the state of Punjab's politics, the problems of turning forty, the perils of constant travel – irregular or unhygienic meals, inadequate rest, exhaustion – and the merits and shortcomings of Bollywood's heroines among other topics that ranged from the serious to the succulent, Anirudh and I went down to the Ferozepur Club to wind up the evening with a few drinks.

Built during the British Raj, the club which stood a few kilometres from the school was among the handful in town patronized by affluent locals as well as army officers. Entering the lush grounds, we walked past the neatly maintained lawn and through a spacious visitors' lounge to the expansive, dimly lit bar. To our surprise, we turned out to be the first visitors on this Saturday night, although it was already ten minutes past nine. We sat down at one of the corner tables and drank Vat 69 with soda and water. In my twenty years of drinking, I had neither had an opportunity to taste this premium brand of whiskey from a bygone era nor seen a friend or acquaintance consuming it. My memories of Vat 69 were inextricably tied up with scenes from the Hindi and Tamil movies of the 1970s and 80s, where the story's villain, accompanied by his cohort of goons, would often be seen in a club, enjoying a titillating cabaret act, with the dark green bowling pin-shaped bottle of whiskey prominently displayed in front of them.

Half an hour later, an Indian Air Force officer came by to pick up some food he had ordered and decided to join us for a few drinks while it was prepared. With the entire staff serving just the three of us, we chatted for a while, putting away copious quantities of Vat 69 as we did so.

Well, this, it seemed, was clubbing on a Saturday night in Ferozepur. During our desultory conversation, I couldn't help but observe the general air of melancholy around me and ponder how delusional my initial impression of Ferozepur and rural Punjab, as the epitome of picturesque abundance, had been. But then, what more could I expect in a place subjected over the years to one ordeal after another that had left it teetering on the edge of so many uncertainties?

# 4

# Raxaul

The urge to flee from Raxaul was overwhelming, even before I had reached my destination. While my fascination for this shanty town on India's border with Nepal had been just as keen as my interest in our country's other borderland areas, it started dwindling the moment I began searching for accommodation online a few days before the proposed trip.

The few lodging facilities available in this sub-divisional town in East Champaran district – one of the busiest routes to Nepal – had received such negative reviews from travellers that a prospective visitor would have thought twice about spending a single day here. The words 'dirty', 'filthy', 'pathetic', 'rude', 'no service' and 'hell' came up with alarming regularity in reviews of every one of the hotels in Raxaul that I looked up online, hoping to book a clean room with basic amenities. Having failed to find any decent accommodation in this manner, I had willed myself to head for the border town and then decide whether to stay on or continue directly to the town across the border – Birganj in Nepal. The accommodation facilities there had received marginally better reviews. To put it mildly, I was not looking forward to this trip.

On a sultry summer morning, the Mithila Express, overflowing with passengers – mostly locals returning home from Kolkata and tourists on their way to Nepal – chugged into Raxaul Junction. For a major junction of the Eastern Railways, the station was surprisingly small, although it had a decent waiting hall and food court.

I alighted from the train and joined the crowd leaving the station. The scene outside was dismal, with not a taxi or autorickshaw in sight. The only motor vehicles present in the parking lot were private cars and vans, hired by tour operators and hotels in Birganj, to pick up and transport their guests. All other travellers arriving in Raxaul had to rely on cycle rickshaws which were parked in a long queue outside the railway station.

As we emerged from the station, the rickshaw drivers literally swarmed over us in their eagerness to get passengers. Those who preferred other modes of transport left the station, their faces shielded against the dust. There was a pervasive stench emanating from potholes filled with slushy, stagnant water that dotted the unpaved roads ahead. Outside the station's main gate, pushcart eateries, lined up on both sides of the road, sold jalebis, puris, kachodis and tea with biscuits.

Burdened by my huge, unwieldy backpack, I was easy bait for the cycle-rickshaw drivers. They almost mobbed me in their efforts to offer a ride to the 'best' hotel in town. After looking around for a while, I engaged a frail young rickshaw driver, asking him to take me to the cleanest hotel in town.

Soon, we were approaching a modest hotel on Block Road, just 300-odd metres from the railway station.

'This is a clean and decent hotel,' he announced. 'But if you don't like it, I'll take you to another place.'

I asked the rickshaw guy to wait outside, while I went in. Standing around in the reception area, engaged in conversation, were three tall, hefty young men. I approached them and explained that I was looking for a clean room. The tallest of the three said I could take my pick: a good non-air-conditioned room for ₹500 a night or an air-conditioned one for a little over ₹1,000 a night. I opted for a room with an air cooler that would cost something in between, but insisted that I would take it only if it was clean.

'Of course, sir. The room will certainly be clean,' the man assured me. 'And we will change the bed sheets, pillow covers and blankets whenever you ask us to.'

Surveying the rooms, I found them to be relatively neat, clean, habitable and quite unlike the descriptions I had read in the hotel reviews posted on travel websites. Relieved, I checked into a first-floor room with an air cooler and went downstairs again to pick up my luggage from the waiting cycle rickshaw. I asked the driver, who had become friendly by now, to return at 3 p.m. I explained that I wanted him to take me across the international border into Birganj. After we had agreed on a fare, I went back to my room and crashed.

But taking a nap during the day was not an option in that muggy weather, especially not in a town where an average of fourteen to fifteen-hour power cuts a day was the norm. The gigantic air cooler in my room spat out cool, peculiarly sticky droplets of water with a loud, grinding noise for barely thirty minutes at a stretch, before the next power outage silenced it, drenching me in a fresh film of sweat. A diesel generator ensured that the ceiling fan still worked, but it hardly provided any respite. Eventually, I realized that even lying on the bed in that heat was nothing short of torture and requested the management to move me to a room on the ground floor, which was not only much cooler, but also cheaper. There, I waited, counting the minutes until 3 p.m., when the cycle rickshaw would arrive, as scheduled, so that I could visit the border.

At 4 p.m., I was still waiting. The cycle rickshaw had not turned up and my lean, friendly rickshaw driver was nowhere in sight. Half an hour later, I approached the reception to enquire about the absconding rickshaw driver and was advised by Shiriram, a hotel staff member, not to expect him at all.

'People here promise much, but rarely keep their word,' he said frankly. 'Your rickshaw driver must have gone home by now. If you're keen to visit the border, you had better get yourself another rickshaw.'

There was no dearth of them on the streets, he assured me, and I would have no problems hailing one as soon as I stepped out of the hotel.

Braving the scorching heat, I set out, walking towards the railway station in my quest for a cycle rickshaw. Most of the rickshaw drivers I approached showed no interest whatsoever in taking me to Birganj and the ones that did quoted exorbitant fares, leaving me with no option but to walk all the way. Like most roads in Raxaul, the one leading to the railway station was narrow and unpaved. Puddles of stagnant water, accumulated from recent rains, added to the misery of pedestrians. They had to manage a balancing act between these, on the one hand, and the cycle rickshaws, bikes and occasional four-wheeler, they had to carefully maneouvre their way past, on the other, so as to avoid being run over. Passing the railway station, I headed to the market down a road that was wider, but extremely uneven and dotted with larger craters filled with more muddy water. Dozens of tankers and lorries were parked along the road, taking up so much space that pedestrians were forced to walk down the middle until the road had turned left towards a railway crossing. The dust and filth increased manifold as I approached the crossing, where dozens of horse carts, cycle rickshaws and motorized carts were parked, apparently waiting for passengers bound for Birganj. But for reasons I failed to fathom, none of the drivers seemed particularly interested in taking me across the border.

Beyond the railway crossing, a long queue of trucks, tanker lorries and other transport vehicles stood bumper to bumper, creating a traffic jam as they waited for customs clearance at the border check post. I walked past those vehicles and down a road which continued to be unpaved, despite being a national highway and an international border crossing, and made my way towards a bridge spanning a squalid, polluted river.

Crossing the bridge, I stopped by a roadside tea shop, drank a cup and paid for it. I was surprised when the tea-shop owner returned the change in Nepali currency. I asked for the change in Indian rupees, to which he retorted that I was now in Nepal.

'The other side of the bridge is India and this is Nepal,' he announced, pointing at the concrete bridge I had just crossed.

Unlike the India–Bhutan border, where the demarcation between the two countries is unmistakable, this particular international border bore no signs indicating where one country's territory ended and the other's began. The tea shop, its owner and clientele and everything else around me looked as Indian as could be. But it seemed that I was now in a foreign country.

I continued walking towards Birganj's Adesh Market, which is barely 2 kilometres from the border. At this point, the road had become wider, with a proper tar surface. About half a kilometre from the actual border stood a colossal gateway, faithful in all its details to the distinctive Nepali style of architecture. Due to the excessive heat and dust, its original colour had faded to a pale grey. Armed Nepali guards in military fatigues stood in groups and checked random vehicles and travellers for contraband.

Walking past the guards and strolling around the crowded shops for about half an hour, I saw little in Birganj that could set it apart from Raxaul. The dust, dirt and stagnant pools of muddy water I had come across on the Indian side were equally conspicuous by their presence here. The people in these two towns looked alike and communicated in the same languages – Hindi and Bhojpuri. The shops on this side looked no different from the ones in India and sported signboards in Hindi bearing their names, except for some which had their names painted in the Nepali script. I observed cycle rickshaws and horse carts transporting hundreds of people across the border in both directions, as I continued to walk until I was utterly exhausted.

Turning back to retrace my steps, I noticed little shops just beyond the India Customs House selling bundles of Indian and Nepali currency notes. To my mind, those bundles of Indian and foreign currency displayed on the road were the only indicators that I was somewhere in the vicinity of an international border.

* * *

I discovered on returning to my hotel that the electric supply had still not been restored. After that depressing cross-border walk, my urge to leave Raxaul was suddenly intense; the very thought of having to spend a few more days walking around in so much dust and filth and returning to long hours of power outage at the hotel seemed unbearable. The three men who had been present at the reception in the morning were back. They now sat on a sofa, engrossed in a melodramatic Bhojpuri TV serial. Earlier that evening, I had come to know from Shiriram that the three were siblings and jointly managed the hotel, along with a booming travel business in Nepal. Noticing me enter the reception area, the tallest of the brothers rose politely to his feet and asked if I had managed to cross the border and find whatever I was looking for.

I answered regretfully that of all the border towns I had visited so far during my travels across the country, this one had been the most disheartening. I vented my frustration, citing the heat, the power cuts and the general discourtesy of the locals as reasons for my adverse impressions of the town. Then I asked him if there really was anything of interest in Raxaul worth writing about.

'There really is nothing unique about Raxaul,' replied the youngest sibling from his perch on the sofa, 'except that it serves as a gateway to Nepal. Tourists spend a day here before heading to Kathmandu. Usually, nobody stays here for more than a few hours.'

'Then I might as well leave tomorrow or the day after, at the latest,' I told them. 'It's so hot here and there are power cuts most of the time.'

The two older brothers who had been listening to my rant now intervened. Rahul, the second of the Sharma siblings and also the one who had promised me a clean room in their hotel that morning, reassured me that while Raxaul was just another of Bihar's forgotten towns, there were still enough places and interesting people to keep me engaged for a few days, at least. He also offered to accompany me when I visited those places and met the people he had just referred to and was willing to generally help me out in every way possible during my stay. Surprised at the generosity of his gesture, I warmed to him and confessed how sceptical I had initially been about Raxaul after reading the series of negative reviews about its hotels and that things on the ground were actually not half as bad.

'I may well be in for a pleasant surprise,' I said hopefully, alluding to the prospect of visiting places and meeting local people in the next few days.

Rahul, however, dampened my enthusiasm somewhat by declaring that all that I had read in those reviews was, by and large, true.

'In fact, most of the hotel rooms in town are so squalid that you cannot step into them,' he said. 'But we are trying to change the reality that's responsible for the negative perception about this town and make it more appealing to visitors. You have come to the right place. We will show you whatever we think is important in Raxaul and worth visiting.'

Then he set about preparing a list of places I should visit and people I should meet over the next two days and also agreed to get a cab ready the next morning at seven to take me around town.

Back in my room, there was still no electricity and the speed of the ceiling fan, running on the hotel's generator, was barely enough to offer some respite from the stifling heat. Finally, unable to bear the situation, compounded by the presence of mosquitoes in the room, I stepped out of the hotel.

The town was shrouded in darkness. The only illumination came from the lamps glowing in eateries and in the few petty shops that were still open at 9.30 p.m. I walked down to one such shop opposite my hotel and bought a cigarette. Standing near me was a man in his early twenties. Uproariously drunk, he was busy calling his friends on his mobile phone, urging them to rush down to the shop and back him in the argument that had broken out between him and the shop owner over the apparently poor quality of *gutka* that was being sold. Equally infuriated, the shopkeeper was hurling abuses at the youth and challenging him to a fight, even as he attended to other customers. Near a pushcart eatery beside the shop, groups of young men, most of whom were inebriated, sat on parked motorcycles and chatted noisily, enjoying hot rotis and vegetable curry. A glance around made it clear that most of the people living in the locality had returned home, locked up for the night and turned out the lights, while the other neighbourhood shops had switched off their lights and downed their shutters. Still yelling into his mobile phone, the sozzled young man had now moved to his Hero Honda Splendour and perched himself on the seat, persisting in his efforts to convince his friends to come over and start a brawl. The atmosphere, fuelled by rage and alcohol, was so charged that I decided to stand in a corner and watch how the situation developed.

Even before I could finish my cigarette, however, Shiriram, the room boy from my hotel, ran across and urged me to return to my room immediately.

'I will get you whatever you need,' he said. 'It's just not safe to be out at this hour of the night. Too many drunks spoiling for a fight.'

Heeding his advice, I promptly returned to my room. Compared with the loud drunks outside, the mosquitoes here seemed quite harmless now.

* * *

While there are several entry points to Nepal from India, National Highway 28A, that passes through Raxaul and Birganj and leads to Kathmandu, is the most preferred route, especially for tourists and goods vehicles from Patna and Kolkata. According to the most recent census, Raxaul has a population of over 2.4 lakh, with the residents speaking Hindi, Bhojpuri and Nepali. A vast majority of them are businessmen who migrated from other North Indian cities and towns to set up shop here. The rural areas are primarily inhabited by farmers who have been living here for generations.

As an important transit point to Nepal, Raxaul Railway Junction had gained prominence several decades ago and is well connected with major Indian cities. The town also has an airport that was built in a hurry as an emergency landing ground for the Indian Army during the India–China war, but has since remained defunct and now serves as the office of Sashastra Seema Bal (SSB). Over the years, the border town has been in the news for all the wrong reasons. Raxaul has gained notoriety as a conduit for the trafficking of women and children. Hundreds of them, hailing from impoverished Nepali and Indian villages around Raxaul, have been lured away to big cities like Mumbai, Delhi and even Chennai with the promise of good jobs and a decent life, only to be forced into the sex trade or bonded labour in factories. Local NGOs with a strong network of informers have rescued several of these trafficked women and children from the Raxaul Railway Junction alone.

Moreover, owing to the porous international border between the two countries, Nepal has always been the favourite haunt of terrorists involved in hatching conspiracies against India. An intelligence report released a few years ago provided clear indications that Kathmandu was becoming a hotbed for funnelling counterfeit or fake Indian currency notes (FICN) into India, using Birganj as a channel. Police and intelligence agencies have, in fact, recovered several consignments of FICN from this town. The FICN menace is so rampant that no shopkeeper in Raxaul will accept ₹500 notes from customers. Raxaul has also earned infamy for its role in the smuggling of other forms of contraband.

Armed with this background information, I was up early next morning and waiting at the hotel reception at 7 o'clock sharp for Rahul to arrive with the cab that would take me around town. Until 7.30 a.m., the reception area remained deserted and even Shiriram, who had served me tea about an hour earlier, was nowhere in sight. A little after eight, the youngest of the Sharma brothers drove up on his Royal Enfield motorcycle and informed me that the cab was on its way. I asked him if Rahul would be accompanying me, as promised.

'No,' the young man replied, 'Bhaiya won't be coming. I have already instructed the driver as to where he should take you. So don't worry. Rahul might join you in the afternoon.'

This was the second time in two days here that a person had given me his word and gone back on it.

Half an hour later, a Mahindra Bolero SUV driven by Chottu, a young Muslim, arrived and we set out without further delay for our first destination – Barthamayi village, roughly 3 kilometres from Raxaul railway station and right on the international border.

Barthamayi comprises of five wards and has a total population of around 3,000, of which 2,000 have voter identity cards. People living here speak Bhojpuri, Hindi and Nepali fluently. The route to this nondescript village passes the Raxaul air strip, several narrow lanes cluttered with mud homes, and then moves on to a narrow dirt road, flanked on either side by tall, shady teak, almond and mango trees. Stretching away into the distance are vast tracts of farmland. A modest-sized pond stands between Barthamayi and the nearest Nepali *basti*.

On reaching our destination, we asked around for the village head and were directed to the sprawling two-storey home of Shambhu Das, the mukhiya.

Das was not at home when we arrived. Sitting on a tractor parked inside the compound were two of his workers who asked us to wait in the shade of an asbestos shed, where plastic chairs had been set out for visitors. While we waited, two young men drove up on a motorcycle and asked us if we were from the government. When I introduced myself as a journalist and expressed my keen interest in speaking to Shambhu about their village, the men assured me that he would be arriving in ten minutes.

About half an hour later, a middle-aged man with a broad build, a thick moustache and a loud, commanding voice, arrived, riding pillion on a friend's motorcycle. It was Shambhu Das. His demeanour suggested that he was among the wealthiest and most influential in town. His distaste for journalists was obvious from his dubious expression and his reluctance to agree to an interview. After persuading him that I was from down south, not from Bihar, and that I did not represent a newspaper or a television channel, Shambhu settled down for a chat. I asked him if I could address him as the mukhiya of Barthamayi village. He clarified that since it was a constituency reserved for women, his wife was the official head of the village. Ironically, I would never get to see her or any other woman, for that matter, in his home.

Shambhu lived in his ancestral home with his wife and six children. Like most of his fellow villagers, he was basically a farmer. He claimed that on account of the completely open border between the two countries, living in this particular Indian border village made no difference to him or to other residents of Barthamayi. They were free to cross over to the villages in Nepal without encountering any difficulty. It was only when crossing the border in a vehicle that an entry had to be made in the SSB registers. People living on both sides of the border actually belonged to the same communities, married into each other's families and shared strong, interpersonal relationships that went back several centuries. For generations, people in this region had been making a living by buying and selling goods across the border, as some of the items were cheaper in one country than in the other.

'For instance,' explained the mukhiya, 'we would buy wood from there and bring it here to Barthamayi to build our homes. Villagers from the Nepal side cross over to buy rice, sugar and other essentials that cost less here. We also take along some of this stuff for them when we go visiting.'

Most people in the region were apparently unaware, until very recently, that the kind of transaction Das had just described was a serious offence. As education made slow inroads into the area, its inhabitants gradually began to realize that they could not bring in goods from Nepal or send products there simply because of the price advantage.

'Nowadays, there is a lot more awareness about these things and most villagers have, therefore, stopped transporting goods from across the border,' Shambhu went on. 'Still, some exchange does take place, but it happens mostly because of ignorance, as most of our people are illiterate.'

Since this part of Bihar was among the most impoverished, men and women who did not own land and could not find jobs went to Birganj, as it was home to many more industries and other business establishments. Indian citizens did not require a permit to work in Nepal. Nor did Nepali citizens need one to work in India. This paved the way for skilled workers to get jobs easily in Birganj. In fact, Indians living in Raxaul preferred to cross over to Nepal even to watch a movie as Birganj had better theatres where all the Bhojpuri films released in India were shown.

Shambhu went on to explain how close-knit the people living in the border villages were and how a man-made boundary could never create a divide between the communities living on either side of it.

I gathered from my interactions with the mukhiya that most of the villagers from this area did not even realize that they were living near an international border. Other poor villagers I met in Barthamayi echoed Shambhu's views, acknowledging that they simply did whatever they could to eke out a living and if someone deemed it illegal, they could not really be bothered.

'We go to work in Nepal and if our employer wants us to take a few kilogrammes of sugar for him and is willing to pay a higher price for it than I would get in India, why wouldn't I help him out?' said Pavan, a young farmer from Barthamayi who had joined our discussion at the mukhiya's house.

When he rebuilt his home a few years ago, Pavan had apparently gone with some of his relatives to the interiors of Nepal's forests. There they had chopped wood and transported the logs to the border. During the rainy season when the water bodies were full, they had simply set the logs afloat and managed to bring them home to India in this manner.

Such activities, I would come to know, were common in these villages and largely coordinated and overseen by wealthy landlords who used poor, jobless farmers to smuggle in timber and other products that were cheaper in Nepal. Ignorant about the value of the goods they were smuggling across the border, those involved were usually paid a pittance for acting as couriers.

Almost everyone I interacted with in Shambhu's home admitted that they had smuggled goods across the border several times in the past, knowing full well that it was illegal. Their excuse was that given their impoverished circumstances, compounded by the lack of opportunities to earn a living in their villages, they were forced to engage in any activity that had the potential to bring in some money; they were in no position to judge what was right or wrong.

By the time I was ready to leave, Shambhu had warmed to me and noted all my contact details, exchanging phone numbers and promising to help me sort out any problems I might face during my stay in Raxaul. Before sending us off, he urged me to check out the new integrated check-post complex in Haraiyah village that was expected to change the face of this border. This check post was still under construction and turned out to be a huge complex covering several acres. It was being built along the new multi-lane national highway that was expected to replace the existing one. The integrated check post, which would be able to accommodate 700 trucks at a time when it became operational, was expected to clear the huge traffic jams that plagued this border between India and Nepal. Although work on the construction of the check post was still in the initial stages, land prices in and around Barthamayi had already soared; once the new highway came up, there was a possibility that Raxaul would lose its importance and be superseded by Haraiyah and the surrounding areas.

We drove around the new check-post complex, before halting at the Raxaul airport complex. Abandoned by the Airports Authority of India, the complex was being used as the makeshift office of the SSB Commandant. Separating the airport and the airstrip from the rest of the village was a neglected high compound wall. The airport building itself could probably have qualified as the smallest and most decrepit in the country. A proposal to upgrade the Raxaul airport so that it could handle small aircraft such as the ATR-72 was under consideration. If it was given the go-ahead, the airport runway could be increased in length, with the old building paving the way for a more modern one. Constructed during the 1962 India–China war as a base for IAF planes, this airstrip had been used most recently in the aftermath of the Nepal earthquake on 25 April 2015 to bring home Indian survivors stranded in Nepal.

We parked our SUV in the airport compound and went to the SSB Commandant's office to find out if he would be available for a chat. No airport official could be seen in the building. The SSB officer heading the unit was away and would not be available until the next morning. Disappointed, we returned to the hotel sometime in the afternoon.

At the reception, I enquired about Rahul. The manager informed me that he would not be coming in; both he and his elder brother had already left for Kolkata on some urgent work.

* * *

With the possibility of Rahul accompanying me on my explorations ruled out, I decided to go it alone. After lunch, Chottu and I took NH28A that would lead us into the interiors of Bihar. I intended to take a look at the rice mills and other agro food-processing units that I had heard were present here in large numbers. The condition of the road along this stretch of the highway was just as poor as it had been near the international border. Thankfully, however, there was less dust, as traffic on this highway was sparse in the afternoon. As we crossed one nondescript village after another, separated by large tracts of farmland, the first of the agro-processing units came into view. Basically, vast compounds dotted with giant sheds constructed from corrugated metal sheets, these factories churned out processed agricultural products which were supplied to eastern India, Nepal and a few other countries. Huge trucks from faraway destinations such as Haryana and Maharashtra were parked on the premises. Since it was late afternoon and most of the workers were indoors, busy at work, I could not really tell how many people were employed in these sheds, but the number of food-processing units increased the further we travelled from Raxaul.

About 10 kilometres from Raxaul we came across one of the largest rice-processing units in the area – Ripuraj Agro Private Limited. I asked Chottu to stop the car and went inside to meet the owner.

The processing unit had three large sheds, where thousands of sacks of polished and unpolished rice, along with bags of wheat, lay stacked. The actual processors had been installed behind the managing director's (MD) office, where about a dozen men could be seen working behind glass panels. I entered and was asked to take a seat in a modest reception area. After waiting there for about fifteen minutes, I was summoned to the MD's room.

Managing director of Ripuraj Agro Products, R.P. Gupta had just finished his lunch when I entered and was busy excavating the pulp from the orange-yellow skin of a fleshy mango. He had sunk his teeth into the fruit and was tearing out the skin with his thumb and index finger. Catching sight of me, the burly, middle-aged man with neatly parted hair and thick black moustache indicated the chair opposite his own for me to sit on. He ordered his staff to clear away the tiffin carrier and plate immediately and then went into the washroom. After he returned to his large chair, he fished out a pair of opaque sunglasses from his pocket, put them on, fussed a bit with his hair and looked up at me.

'So tell me, sir,' he said, 'what would you like to know?'

I started off by giving him a little background about myself. When he learnt that I was from Chennai, Gupta immediately intervened and reminisced about the two weeks he had spent there, trying to improve passenger amenities at the Egmore railway station.

'Nice city. Very hard-working people,' he remarked. 'If we had such people in Bihar, this state would reach the top.'

A native of East Champaran district, Gupta had been a farmer, before taking up agro food processing in a big way. Besides farming, he took a key interest in politics. Although farming was his ancestral occupation, as it was with most other landowning families here, Gupta's stint with the Indian Railways as an advisory committee member had taken him across the country and given him an opportunity to explore its industrial growth.

After completing his assignment with the railways, Gupta had returned home and set up Ripuraj with the latest imported machinery and state-of-the-art facilities.

Although he had established his firm only in the year 2013, investing a sizable amount of money in procuring the state-of-the-art equipment to process rice, wheat and other products on a large scale, Ripuraj had risen to become one of the top producers of quality rice in the region. Today, it polished around 500 tonnes of rice and other grains daily and had clients in faraway states like Tamil Nadu and Manipur. Gupta's brand of Basmati and other varieties of rice were sought-after products across the country.

'The agro-processing industry in Bihar is relatively young, when compared with the rest of India, especially the south. But in a short time, we have achieved significant growth, despite the shortage of labour and pathetic road-transport facilities,' Gupta declared.

He lamented the lethargic attitude of his employees as well as the lack of sufficient infrastructure development in the state. He felt that the state government had a lot more to do if it wanted to promote industrialization in Bihar, particularly in the East Champaran district.

While locals continue to suffer power outages of long duration, businessmen like Gupta have managed to secure uninterrupted power supply by flexing their muscles and offering the promise of employment to the hoi polloi. But the appalling condition of the roads remains the biggest impediment to the plans of Raxaul's industrialists.

Apart from Gupta, several wealthy farmers in the area have set up their own agro-processing units and meet requirements for polishing rice, wheat and other foodgrains of customers from across the country. Taking root only over the last decade or so, the industry has now usurped the role of the rice mills in nearby Birganj, where most of the rice produced in this region used to be sent earlier for processing. This is the outcome of the many incentives that Bihar's state government offered in an effort to bring industry to this backward district in response to the interest of local businessmen.

Yet, this industry hardly caters to the employment needs of the youth living in and around Raxaul.

'Biharis shy away from hard work,' Gupta declared frankly. 'If we could work as hard as the South Indians, we would probably capture the entire food-processing markets of Nepal and other South East Asian countries. All we need are quality workers and good roads to transport our products. With a little help, we could turn Raxaul into a hub for agro-processing.'

Before I left, Gupta also urged me to have a look at the rice-sheller machine-making units that had mushroomed as a separate cottage industry in the nearby village of Shitalpur, transforming this region into a major hub for rice-sheller machine-manufacturing units in the entire country.

* * *

Until a few years ago, Shitalpur in Kalyanpur Block used to be just another impoverished Indian village, indistinguishable from the ones in the surrounding areas, with their dirt roads, mud-walled thatched huts and landless farm workers. But when we drove through the village that afternoon, I was impressed by the number of homes that had been converted into mini workshops with rice-sheller machines of different sizes and colours on display. Almost every other family in Shitalpur was involved in the cottage industry in one way or another and had thus worked their way out of poverty.

Among them was Vasudev Sharma. Poverty had once forced his family into leaving their hometown to seek work in Nepal, but over the years, Sharma had succeeded in transforming Shitalpur into a mini industrial hub almost single-handedly. In fact, the origin of the local rice-sheller industry is inextricably linked to this man.

When Sharma was employed as a *maistry* (foreman) at a rice mill in neighbouring Nepal, he had an opportunity to work with rice-sheller machines imported from Japan. In those days, whenever a machine needed repairs, engineers from Japan would visit Nepal to fix the problem. The owners of the rice mill invariably sent Sharma over to assist the Japanese engineers, as he had a sound knowledge of the machines. On one such occasion, when an imported rice sheller broke down, Sharma informed his employers that he could fix the problem himself and there was no need to bring in engineers from Japan. As promised, Vasudev repaired the machine, thus saving his company a lot of money. He also assured the firm's owner that given an opportunity, he could manufacture a rice-sheller machine that would cost far less than the ones imported from Japan. Eventually, when Sharma managed to procure an order, he returned to Shitalpur and set up the region's first rice sheller-making unit. He employed local youth in his factory and even encouraged them to set up their own units to manufacture spare parts.

As news spread about the superior quality and affordable price of Vasudev's rice-sheller machines, more orders poured in. A time arrived when Vasudev had to pass on some of the orders to his workers, who started opening little factories in their backyards and built rice shellers of varying sizes. In that parched land, where farming had been the only occupation so far, rice-sheller machine manufacturing became a rage. More and more farmers began to give up agriculture to enter this cottage industry. Over the past few years, Shitalpur has been transformed into a hub for rice-sheller machines and farmers from far and wide come to this village to purchase them for polishing their rice. At least eighty to eighty-five units making rice-sheller machines and their accessories are based in Shitalpur. They employ over a thousand people. The fact that every other home in this village is a factory today is credited to Sharma. Shitalpur stands testimony to the change that just one person can bring about in a neighbourhood. To its residents, Sharma is no less than a hero who was instrumental in transforming their lives and the land they regard as home.

* * *

I returned to my room that evening after visiting Shitalpur, only to be informed by the hotel manager that they were expecting a special guest. A former Rashtriya Janata Dal (RJD) minister was scheduled to arrive later that evening and all the unoccupied rooms were booked. The politician was expected to stay overnight and proceed to a party meeting the next morning. The manager also offered to try and get me some time with the former minister.

By around 8 p.m., I could guess from all the commotion in the corridor running past my ground-floor room that the special guest had arrived. I was making notes, while waiting for an audience with the former minister, when I heard a loud rap on the door. The moment I unbolted it, an angry-looking man in his thirties, dressed in white cotton pajamas and matching half-sleeved kurta, shoved the door open and peered into my room without even a glance in my direction. His eyes scanned the room for a few seconds before he strode away, leaving the door ajar, as if I did not exist.

I stepped out into the corridor, wondering what was going on, and saw similar men, clad in the same white cotton kurtas and pajamas, striding up and down the length of the corridor, barging into every room and scrutinizing it. I approached the reception and asked Shiriram what was going on.

'Oh, don't bother about them,' he muttered. 'They are the ex-minister's associates and are furious that only he was given an AC room. They are now looking for other air-conditioned rooms in the hotel.'

None of the hotel's owners were in and both Shiriram and the hotel manager looked tense.

I returned to my room, bolted the door and resumed work. Within a few minutes, I heard the heavy thud of what sounded like running feet in the corridor and opened the door. A crowd had gathered at the entrance to the room next to mine and was anxiously peering in. Loud abuse poured out of the room. I joined the crowd at the door and peeped in. A bare-chested man stood on the bed, trying to wrench the ceiling fan off its moorings. Two others also stood on the bed, struggling to prevent him from doing so. Some of the minister's men stood around watching the developments and attempting to persuade all three to get down off the bed.

Shiriram came running and pushed me away from the crowd.

'I did tell you to leave them be, right?' he said, his face expressionless. 'Just go back to your room now, shut the door and bolt it securely. Do not open it until tomorrow morning, even if someone bangs on it or you hear a commotion outside.'

I could tell that he was scared and embarrassed about the goings-on in the hotel.

I bolted my room from the inside, called my travel agent and asked him to book me a return ticket on the next available train to Kolkata. Fortunately, I had eaten dinner early that night.

* * *

The ex-minister and his convoy had already vacated their rooms when I prepared to venture out the following morning. While I was waiting for Chottu to drive up in his Bolero, Rahul arrived on his Royal Enfield Bullet and parked the vehicle. As he came in, I told him how disappointed I had been on learning that he had left for Kolkata and would be unable to accompany me.

Apologizing for letting me down the previous day, Rahul promised to take me to the Raxaul market that afternoon and introduce me to local people who mattered.

'My elder brother had to accompany my mother to Kolkata,' he explained, underscoring the urgency of the situation that had kept him away. 'They drove all the way, as there was an emergency and we could not get either train or bus tickets.'

Having been stood up more than once, I had almost given up on Raxaul and its people's ability to keep their word. Rahul's assurances about taking me around town and introducing me to important people had rekindled my hope. My recent experience had taught me, however, to take nothing for granted.

As I had a morning appointment with the head of the SSB camp office at the old airport building in Pankota, I had Chottu drive me down. The Bolero, as expected, arrived at my hotel an hour later than the scheduled time. A young officer from south Bihar, the Assistant Commandant I was to see, had just emerged from a meeting with his seniors and seemed in an irritable mood. Requesting anonymity, he began speaking and moments into our conversation, brought up the subject of his four transfers over the past year. In fact, his posting in Pankota, the fourth one in less than a year, was so recent that the officer claimed he was still in the process of familiarizing himself with the terrain.

'We are never given enough time to familiarize ourselves with a region,' this young direct recruit said ruefully. 'By the time we are beginning to settle in, we are ousted.'

This officer and his team of men and women had been entrusted with the job of gathering intelligence from the border villages by mingling freely with the locals. They were to collect information about the illegal activities taking place along the border, assess the potential security threats to the nation and pass on the gathered information, along with the results of their evaluation, to other agencies. SSB personnel kept in regular touch with village heads and worked with their sources in the different villages to provide intelligence inputs to the defence forces. As the country's only intelligence agency whose staff members were expected to be in uniform during duty hours, the SSB naturally faced considerable difficulties in its intelligence work.

'We are uniformed personnel. How does one wear the uniform of an armed-forces agency and gather intelligence?' asked the SSB Assistant Commandant.

He pointed out that while his teams were trying their best to maintain friendly relations with those living in border villages, it was no mean task, considering the job requirements and the limited powers of the SSB officers.

'We are not empowered to be a prosecuting agency,' the Assistant Commandant went on. 'Which means that whenever our officers detect smuggling of FICN or other contraband across the border, they cannot take any action on their own, but must coordinate with local law-enforcement authorities, who are often hand in glove with the smugglers. Naturally, morale is low among SSB personnel, evident in the increasing number of suicides.'

As such, the true role of the SSB is a matter of debate, even among its senior officers, who feel that the force has increasingly been used as a backup unit for peace-time emergency operations such as flood or earthquake relief. The Sashastra Seema Bal was set up in 1963 as the Special Service Bureau (SSB) during the Sino-Indian war, when the possibility of India losing a full-fledged war with China and becoming an occupied territory seemed imminent. The SSB was assigned the task of mingling with the general public in border areas and forming insurgent units to engage the Chinese army in guerilla warfare. However, with the Chinese withdrawing their forces before a full-blown war could break out between the two countries, the SSB's role in this particular context became redundant. The agency's activities were then extended to cover other international borders that India shared with neighbouring countries. Recently, the role of the SSB was redefined as a peaceful border force and the agency has now been tasked with the responsibility of mainly guarding the country's borders with Bhutan and Nepal, apart from being the lead intelligence agency in these areas.

Speaking about his experience in Raxaul and other border villages, the SSB officer admitted that while there were organized gangs pushing in FICN and trafficking women and children across India's border with Nepal, the villagers themselves were mostly innocent of any wrongdoing. According to him, most of the smuggling and trafficking carried out along these borders had been going on for centuries and providing a livelihood for the people involved in them. To counter the induction of locals into these nefarious trades, SSB officers were being sent to the local villages to set up camps and conduct awareness campaigns which would enlighten the general public. Such campaigns, he claimed, had proved useful in acting as deterrents.

The officer wanted me to note, however, that despite the

limited intelligence-gathering skills of its personnel, the SSB posted on the Nepal border had detected, over the past few years, a steep rise in the number of madrassas along the border villages. They had even marked out specific areas where the number of madrassas were on the rise and shared the report with other Indian intelligence agencies. Like most newcomers to Raxaul, this officer also felt that the main problem with this border area was the apathy with which successive governments had treated it.

By and large, almost all Indian border towns are impoverished and neglected, presenting a poor image of the country in contrast to their sister towns or cities in neighbouring countries. Phuentsholing in Bhutan, for example, is a cleaner, safer and more sophisticated city than Jaigaon. Similarly, Raxaul is considered a dump as opposed to Birganj in Nepal, although only a few kilometres separate the two towns. The jobless travel from Bihar to Birganj in quest of employment and recreation, while towns on the Indian side of the border remain decrepit and singularly lacking in appeal.

The SSB officer firmly believed that if border towns could evolve into attractive destinations and provide a reliable source of legitimate income, the locals would be less inclined to engage in illegal activities.

'Besides, better-developed border towns would also enhance the country's image,' he declared. 'As things stand, a tourist visiting India from Nepal and crossing through this border area will form a very poor impression of the country as a whole.'

* * *

After two days of moving around Raxaul in a partially air-conditioned Bolero, battling extreme heat, terrible roads and a complete absence of civic amenities, the question uppermost in my mind was: how did things come to such a pass here?

Looking for an answer, I went off to meet Ashok Aggarwal, a prominent businessman and politician, at his retail outlet in the Raxaul market. The 51-year-old, who had been born and raised in this border town, was, at present, the town president of the Janata Dal (United) Party (JD–U) and also the councillor for Ward 11. Ashok's father, also a politician, had been a councillor since 1977. Their family had moved from Rajasthan three generations ago and now called Raxaul home.

Entering Ashok's shop in the market, I found him seated near a huge, annoyingly noisy generator that had been switched on to keep the lights and fans in his office functioning during a power outage. Unlike the other politicians I had seen the previous night at my hotel, Ashok was slim and neatly dressed in a blue checked shirt and khaki trousers. Nor did he seem prone to violence like the ex-minister's cohorts at the hotel. We settled ourselves near a table fan to get some breeze and Ashok began explaining why Raxaul was the way it was.

'Raxaul is a small place with hardly any development,' he began. 'Since it became an international-border town, it has gradually gained prominence. Some thirty or forty years ago, this place had a booming wholesale market and business used to be significantly bigger than it is now. In those days, there were no other markets anywhere within a fifty-kilometre radius and villagers from the surrounding areas had to come to Raxaul to buy and sell their goods. There were certain goods, like green cardamom, that you could only get in this market. I still remember how sacks and sacks of this spice would be sold out of our market and despatched to distant destinations, as it was not available anywhere else.

'But gradually, the wholesale market shrank in size and was replaced by a retail market catering mostly to Nepali citizens. Even people from as far away as Kathmandu would come down to Raxaul for their shopping. Trendy clothes, electronic goods and utensils, among other things, were mainly bought by Nepalis, as these items were not available in their own country. Many of them even came all the way to Raxaul to watch movies, as in those days, there were no theatres at all in Nepal. Back in the seventies, Raxaul had three movie theatres; it now has only two.

'Over the last five years, however, business in the retail market has also slackened,' Aggarwal went on. 'Many retail markets have now come up across Nepal, with the vendors stocking the latest products which they import directly from cities located in the interiors of India and from other countries like China. As a result, Nepalis no longer need to visit Raxaul.

'To make matters worse, the condition of Raxaul's roads has deteriorated considerably in the last decade or so, pollution from dust is dangerously high and the traffic situation is nightmarish. Traffic jams are so common in town and take such a long time to clear that travellers caught in them have no clue as to when they might reach their destination. Truck drivers whose vehicles get ensnared in stalled traffic at the border usually turn off their engines and step out for a day or so, returning later to discover that the traffic jam has still not eased. But if you are driving a private vehicle, you obviously cannot leave it and must spend a day or more just sitting in it. In Raxaul, nobody can ever be sure when he will reach his proposed destination.

'Despite becoming an international-border town, Raxaul has seen no development at all,' Ashok declared. 'There are no restaurants or bars here, not even a decent park. For anyone keen on a morning walk, the only option is to walk along the railway track. As for taking family or friends to a good restaurant, everyone has to head for Birganj across the border, where there are a number of them and even a few star hotels.

'The other big problem is rampant smuggling,' added

Aggarwal. 'Even rice, dal and other foodgrains are smuggled out in large quantities from this market and into Nepal on a daily basis, evading customs duty. Basic items like clothes, which are also dutiable goods, are smuggled across the border by carriers who undertake such work for a living. Smuggling on such an extensive scale has also been responsible for the collapse of the local market.'

As was the case with currency regulations along India's border with Bhutan, the Indian and Nepali governments too had enforced a ban on the free exchange of their countries' respective currencies. Until recently, businessmen in Raxaul could exchange Nepali rupees for Indian money through drafts. This practice had now been banned. In the absence of a robust legal currency-conversion mechanism, exchange of currency took place on the black market, with the commission charged going up, sometimes, to as much as ₹6 for every ₹100, thereby causing further inflation in the cost of goods.

According to Ashok, successive politicians who had been elected from this constituency to the Parliament as well as the State Assembly lacked political will and had completely ignored the needs of their constituents. No development had taken place during their tenure. Ashok believed that business would automatically pick up if even the roads were improved.

'But our politicians are incapable of bringing about even this one small change,' he sighed.

'During the regime of former Indian Prime Minister Atal Bihari Vajpayee, an initiative was launched by the central government to develop the border town so that it would match international standards,' Aggarwal continued. 'A budget estimate of ₹600 crores was also drawn up after a team from the Prime Minister's Office came down to Raxaul to conduct a survey. But with the subsequent change in power at the Centre, that project was shelved, leaving the Biharis here to grope in the dark. We tried to revive that project and ran from pillar to post to get it back on its feet, but nothing really happened.

'There is still a glimmer of hope in the four-lane highway project that is coming up and the integrated check post being constructed at Haraiyah,' Ashok observed. 'When these projects are complete, traffic jams will be a thing of the past and commuting will become so much easier. Those two changes alone could transform this region in a big way. Once the truck traffic and the related jams move out of town, it will be a huge relief for the general public, as well as for tourists. In addition, if the municipality were to plan a few parks and issue licences for quality restaurants and bars, we could also see a rise in the number of tourists choosing to halt overnight in Raxaul, instead of fleeing to Birganj immediately after their arrival here.'

Towards the end of our conversation, Ashok clarified that the problems he had mentioned so far were not limited to Raxaul alone, but common to Bihar in general. The entire state had hardly seen any development over the past few decades, a situation that was reflected in Raxaul's plight. The only consolation, if it could be described as such, for the local business community was Raxaul's relatively low crime rate, compared to that of other parts of Bihar. In fact, even during the worst period in the state's history, when crime had escalated to unprecedented levels, this region remained comparatively crime-free, enabling businessmen like Ashok and Rahul to set up their base in Raxaul.

* * *

By the time my discussions with Ashok Aggarwal and other senior businessmen at the market were over, I had formed a fairly clear impression of the factors that had proved to be Raxaul's undoing. It was heartening to know, however, that local people like Ashok had not given up on the town yet.

The end of my trip was drawing near, but for one final visit to a modest two-storey home in a residential neighbourhood, sandwiched between Block Road and the Raxaul market. On the ground floor of that home was the office of Prayas, an NGO working against human trafficking. Apart from the counterfeit-currency racket and smuggling of contraband, Raxaul was also notorious for human trafficking, especially when it came to children aged between nine and fourteen.

The NGO's Coordinator Sonelal Thakur was preparing to leave his office when I dropped in. For the past several years, this lean, energetic man had been working against child trafficking, forming a network of sources ranging from police officials and rickshaw pullers to *tonga* drivers that would help bust these rackets. On learning of the purpose of my visit, Thakur cancelled his plans for the day so that he could devote as much time as I needed for my discussion with him.

Until a few years ago, he declared, a stranger visiting one of the several impoverished villages in East Champaran district with the promise of providing a better life for the children there was welcomed as a hero or a 'god'. For poor farmers, whose very existence was in question, sending their offspring away to far-off lands, where greener pastures supposedly awaited them, was seen as a means of escape from the harsh realities of their lives in the village. Parents usually queued up eagerly to send their children off with these agents.

'Traffickers seldom used their real names and addresses,' Thakur went on. 'They deceived the farmers with blatant lies, claiming that their children would be trained in a technical skill and start sending home some of their earnings in a few years' time. To help persuade the parents, the trafficker also paid them a small sum as advance money, a clever incentive that made the criminal a hero among the villagers. Soon, trafficking began thriving here.'

The Raxaul railway station was, in fact, the most likely place to look for trafficked minors, as they were invariably taken to faraway cities by train. Contrary to popular belief that most trafficked children came from Nepal, Thakur had statistics at his disposal to prove that hardly 20 per cent of them were from across the border, while over 80 per cent were from East Champaran and its surrounding districts in Bihar.

Sheer poverty and the singular lack of opportunities were found to be the main reasons driving the trade. Traffickers targeted Nepali villages mainly for trafficking women. Over the years, Thakur had come across an alarming number of bizarre cases, in which women had even been trafficked to African nations and forced into marriage with wealthy black local men so that they could produce light-complexioned offspring. He recalled how his team had even rescued women who were being sent to Western countries to breastfeed newborn babies of affluent white couples, because their mothers could not spare the time to do so.

'Some of the cases are truly appalling,' Thakur remarked.

As always, lack of awareness among the villagers was the main reason behind this rampant trade. To win the confidence of the locals, Prayas regularly organized monthly meetings with the SSB, which played a key role in intelligence gathering, the Railway Protection Force, the Railway Police and village heads to keep tabs on suspicious persons visiting their villages. Despite the fact that the NGO had been working for several years and had established a strong network of informers, traffickers still managed to take local children away, because their networks were extremely well organized.

'Often, we receive calls from village heads, politicians and other influential people, directing us to release the traffickers already in our custody even as we are preparing to interrogate them,' Thakur confided. 'These criminals are so well connected that it is difficult to prosecute them.'

Despite the odds stacked against it, Prayas had, so far, rescued 1,050 children and sent at least a dozen traffickers to jail. Every day, Thakur kept track of the movement of traffickers through his contacts and police sources. He coordinated awareness activities and, if needed, was prepared to spring into action and rescue trafficked children with police support. Over the years, he had kept in touch with several of the rescued children, most of whom were now living in government homes run by responsible staff.

'These children have grown up now and are employed in different parts of the country,' Thakur announced proudly, sharing the contents of a photo album featuring him with the rescued children way back in the early years of the new millennium.

As we chatted, two adolescent boys, neatly dressed in shirts and trousers, entered the room to clear away the files that Thakur had taken out for my benefit. After they had left, he revealed that these boys had also been rescued when they were less than ten years old. Now they attended school in Raxaul and stayed in a government hostel, helping Thakur out with his work in the evenings.

On my way back from Prayas, I wondered about those parents who had sent their children off with a stranger, dreaming of a better future for them. And I couldn't bring myself to blame them. After spending just four days here, I could not wait to get back to civilization – in other words, a place where I could at least get into a taxi and go to a decent restaurant whenever I wanted to.

* * *

Although two days had gone by since I had seen everything there was to see in town and spoken to anyone who mattered, I simply could not get out of Raxaul. Every morning, my travel agent would desperately try to book me a train ticket to Kolkata through the Tatkal scheme and miss a confirmed ticket by mere seconds. He would then call and apologize for the wait-listed ticket, which would invariably get cancelled two hours before the train's scheduled departure. I spent that period of anticipation in my hotel room, suffering the scorching heat all day and the mosquitoes that came with the long hours of power outage at night.

After my second Tatkal ticket got cancelled, I was overcome by the feeling of being trapped forever in that godforsaken town and driven to check out alternative modes of transport. I approached Rahul for help. He said that while a train journey was the most reliable and comfortable way of reaching Kolkata, I could also take one of the two air-conditioned Volvo buses that left for Patna every night and then proceed to Kolkata from there. While buses were available between Raxaul and Patna throughout the day, he considered the regular vehicles too unreliable and uncomfortable to travel in.

I asked him to book me a ticket right away on one of the Volvo buses leaving for Patna that night and gave him the required money. After the ticket had been confirmed, the hotel manager insisted that I check out by 12.30 p.m. or pay an additional day's charges, although all the other rooms were lying vacant. So I checked out by one o'clock, dumped my luggage at the hotel reception and decided to spend my last day in Raxaul alfresco.

Like most small towns and villages across the country, this town practically shuts down in the afternoons. At the hotel, nobody was around, except Shiriram, who lay on the three-seater sofa, watching Bhojpuri soaps on TV. I tried reading a book and when that made me drowsy, I even made an effort to watch the Bhojpuri serials, but the long afternoon just would not come to an end. Fed up, I asked Shiriram for directions to the nearest cinema hall. My plan was to enter one, take a seat and sleep in cool comfort until the day waned and the heat became more bearable.

'You won't be able to sit in the theatre at this time of the day. It will be just too hot,' he warned.

Was there no theatre with air conditioning, I asked. Shiriram laughed and heaved himself off the sofa.

'Theatres here don't even have electricity most of the time and you're asking about air conditioning? Why don't you just lie down here?' he suggested, pointing to the sofa.

Then he went to the storeroom behind the lobby, pulled down a mattress, settled himself on it and went off to sleep.

As I lay down on the sofa in the reception area and watched a Bhojpuri serial in which a heavyset woman sobbed loudly, the thought struck me that I had never returned to the international border after that depressing first visit and decided to check it out once more. Besides, I had been told only too often that Birganj was more hospitable than Raxaul.

I set out again, heading for the railway station, and climbed into a rickshaw in true Bihari style. Over the past few days, I had noticed that most prospective passengers just climbed into a rickshaw's passenger seat before even specifying their destination. The reason was not hard to find; if you mentioned the destination to the rickshaw driver before boarding the vehicle, his invariable response was to turn you down. So it was only after I had made myself comfortable on the seat that I asked the driver to take me to Birganj.

'Birganj *mein kahan*?' he enquired.

'Bazaar,' I replied.

'Market?'

I nodded and he grasped the vehicle's rusted handlebars and guided it towards the road before climbing on to the driver's seat. Crossing the dusty border and manoeuvring your way through a perpetual traffic jam while seated in a rickshaw that was moving at a brisk pace was infinitely preferable to navigating it on foot. Twenty minutes later, we had reached Birganj's Adesh Market.

Barely three or four kilometres from Raxaul, the Adesh Market area had wider, well-paved roads and well-maintained pavements. The shops and eateries were cleaner than the ones I had been going to in Raxaul over the past few days. The market had a number of clothing outlets, fashion boutiques, footwear showrooms and exclusive shops for caps, mufflers, cosmetics, jewellery and every household item one might need. At the far end stood the fresh-produce market, which was also well maintained. And for the first time in a week, I would see traffic police regulating vehicular and pedestrian traffic. Glad to have returned to civilization again, I walked around Adesh Market all afternoon, buying clothes and other items.

Returning to the hotel at 6 p.m., I found Rahul and his younger brother back from their afternoon break. Shiriram and the manager were at the counter and a few new guests, businessmen from Rajasthan, had checked into two of the other rooms. Rahul approached me and insisted that I join him for a few drinks in one of vacant rooms, since it was my last day in town. I was not particularly keen on a drinking session with him, especially a few hours before my departure, but try as I might, I could not persuade him to leave me be. Eventually, after my packing was done, I found myself joining him in one of the rooms that he had been regularly reserving for drinking sessions.

Rahul opened a bottle of whiskey and mixed his drink with soda and water. For every drink of mine, he would gulp down three glasses of whiskey. After the first few drinks, he simply could not stop talking. He described his childhood and narrated anecdotes from the few years he had spent doing a Merchant Navy course in Chennai, going into the details of how he had been cheated by someone he had paid a huge sum of money to get him a course-completion certificate. He also dwelt on his struggle to make it big in the tourism industry. All through, I kept darting glances at my mobile phone to check the time and ensure that I would not miss the bus.

At around a quarter to nine in the evening, Rahul's younger brother entered the room with a friend and announced that the bus would be leaving in another fifteen minutes. They reminded me that I was yet to have dinner and offered to pack some food for me. I assured them that I was not hungry and asked them to arrange for a rickshaw to take me to the bus terminus. While Shiriram was being instructed to summon a cycle rickshaw, Rahul insisted on taking me to the bus stand on his bike and personally ensuring that I boarded my bus in time.

As is the case with most friends when they are drunk, Rahul was so insistent about dropping me off himself, supposedly because I was in his care, that an argument broke out between his brother and him on the mode of transport I should avail of to reach the bus terminus. Since my opinion did not seem to matter at all to the Sharma brothers, I just waited for them to arrive at a decision.

Eventually, Rahul prevailed over his younger sibling. It was decided that I would ride pillion on his Bullet, while my luggage was brought in on another bike driven by his friend. Setting out, we drove through narrow, bumpy roads past dimly lit homes and reached the terminus just in time for me to catch my bus.

The place turned out to be a dark, vacant ground, where a few buses were parked at the far end. Two men, seated on a bench near the vehicles, were filling in a register by the light of a hurricane lamp. Rahul approached them, showed them my ticket and proceeded directly to a non-air-conditioned Volvo sleeper bus, with us in tow, as the AC unit in the air-conditioned bus covering the same route was reportedly not functioning. The bus was almost full and its driver was standing beside it, next to the right front wheel. As the lights inside had not yet been switched on, I could not make out how many of the seats were still vacant. We boarded the bus and found my seat, which turned out to be by the aisle. Rahul turned to his friend and gave him a firing for not booking me a window seat.

'Okay, no problem,' he murmured to me and turned his gaze on a hefty youth in his late teens, who was sitting by the window. Pointing to the aisle seat I had been allotted, Rahul told the boy, '*Abe, tu idhar baitke ja.*'

The boy nodded, got up from his seat and moved to the aisle seat.

Rahul turned to me and said, 'Now go and make yourself comfortable in that window seat, my friend.'

I squeezed myself through to the window seat and slumped into it. Rahul's friend, who was also quite drunk, made futile efforts to wedge my backpack into the rack above my seat, before it dawned on him that the bus was a sleeper coach and there was a passenger lying on the bed he had made on that rack. Dumping my backpack and duffel bag on my lap, Rahul's friend then shook hands with me and said good-bye. So did Rahul. Then the two men left together.

I looked around. The bus stand was engulfed in darkness. The only sources of light were the hurricane lamp near the bus operators' desk and another lamp in a little shack further away that sold water, cigarettes and other snacks. Groups of people stood near the bus, chatting loudly. Women and children arrived in cycle rickshaws and boarded the bus, accompanied by male family members. Everyone seemed to be loud and sweating profusely.

About ten minutes later, the engine of our Volvo bus roared to life and the vehicle rolled out of the Raxaul bus terminus. Soon, we were on NH28A, bumping and bouncing past thatched huts, palm trees and the occasional concrete building that loomed up, mere silhouettes on a night submerged in total, power-deprived darkness. The bus halted at several villages along the way and took in more passengers. During one such halt, a fight broke out between the bus conductor and a young man seated two rows behind me. Though the youth had bought a ticket for a bus to Patna, due to leave only at 10 p.m., he had boarded our bus, instead, which had left on schedule an hour earlier. Since he was now occupying a seat on the wrong bus, another passenger with a valid ticket for this bus had been deprived of a seat. The conductor insisted that the youth get off, but the fellow refused to comply and threatened him by calling up his friends in Patna and urging them to gather next morning at the bus terminus there to teach the man as well as the transport service he worked for a lesson they would not easily forget.

Gazing out of the window as I listened to the heated exchange, I suddenly realized that I had forgotten to collect my ticket from Rahul. I had not even thought of checking if the ticket they had bought for me was meant for this bus or the next one or if it was at all a valid ticket. With little time in hand before my departure from Raxaul and the commotion caused by Rahul at the very last minute, it had not occurred to me to question the two burly six-footers who were so keen to see me off safely. I had followed them without a thought and boarded the bus they indicated. The bus had long left Raxaul and my fellow passengers were now beginning to doze off, one after another. Whenever the semi-sleeper coach stopped to take in more passengers, I would close my eyes and pretend to be fast asleep, afraid that I might be thrown out for travelling without a ticket. Sometime during the night, the alcohol I had consumed worked its way into my brain and I passed out.

A few hours later, someone shook me awake. I stared blearily at the teenager who stood before me.

'*Thanda pani, thanda pani chahiye*?' he asked.

At least a dozen one-litre bottles of drinking water, strung together with coir rope, hung from both his hands. I glanced around and noticed that I was now the only passenger on the bus; the others had long alighted. Even the engine had been turned off. I bought a bottle of water from the boy and asked him where we were.

'Patna *aa gaya*,' he replied, confirming that I had reached my destination.

# 5

# Gangtok

It was on a Tuesday afternoon that I arrived in Gangtok after a long, exhausting journey from New Jalpaiguri (NJP) Railway Junction. Although the distance between the station and Gangtok is hardly 120 kilometres by road, the bumpy, uncomfortable ride in a shared Tata Sumo had taken six long hours.

Getting a seat in a Sumo available for hire on a shared basis is an extremely tricky endeavour, I had discovered, if one is travelling alone and especially during the peak tourist season. The problem began right in the parking lot of NJP Junction, where I was shunted out of two such Tata Sumos in quick succession, despite being offered a seat initially, because a large family had come along at the last minute and its members insisted on travelling together. In the third vehicle I approached, I was offered a window seat in the last row, to which I clung like a bat to a wall. As had been the case with the other two SUVs from which I had been summarily ejected, a large Bengali family from Guwahati, consisting of a newly married couple, the bride's mother and her two siblings, arrived moments before we were due to set out and insisted on boarding the vehicle.

The driver flicked me an apologetic glance, expecting me to cede my place. When I flatly refused this time, he made the young couple occupy the passenger seat next to his own, while the bride's mother, her brother and her sister sat in the last row with me. Since the boy was bent on occupying the window seat, his plump, middle-aged mother insisted on squeezing herself into the narrow space between her attractive daughter and me, thereby acting as a sort of buffer. And thus, we left for Gangtok.

After chugging along flat, dusty roads for about twenty minutes or so, the SUV began its ascent up the lower slopes of the Himalayas along a winding road flanked by thick vegetation on one side and deep, picturesque valleys on the other. Flowing below us were the muddy waters of the Teesta River. Parked along the kerb around almost every sharp bend were dozens of SUVs and private luxury cars, their occupants, travel-weary tourists, having stepped out for a snack or a refreshing cup of tea between taking photographs of the river and the landscape around it.

During the first two hours of the journey, the middle-aged woman and I were engaged in a silent tug of war in reverse, trying to make inroads into each other's seat space as the Sumo navigated hairpin bends and bumpy, potholed roads. Whenever the SUV swerved to the right, the woman would lean towards me, making silent but determined little forays into my seat space and wedging me a little further against the window. I reciprocated in kind, encroaching on her seat space every time the driver swerved the vehicle to the left. As we navigated one bend after another along the winding mountain road, we became increasingly aggressive players of the game, until a sudden and violent swerve to the left made the woman turn and glare at me with a look that members of her sex reserve exclusively for perverts. It was then that the thought struck me: she had suspected all along that my efforts to wrest more seat space for myself were just a pretext for touching her inappropriately.

For the rest of the journey, I clung to the rusted metal frame of the Sumo with such tenacity that a portion of my right shoulder was actually jutting out of the vehicle's back-seat window. When the journey was nearing its end and we were about to drive into Gangtok, the woman turned towards me and said something in Bengali. I had no clue what she meant, but those two words did sound rather sympathetic.

As vehicles with out-of-state registration numbers are not allowed within the city limits, I was dropped off about two kilometres from Gangtok's city centre. From there, I had to hire a local cab to reach my hotel, located just a flight of stairs above Mahatma Gandhi Marg or M.G. Marg, as the town's nucleus of attraction is popularly known. Tired and sleepy, I did not venture out of my room until late in the evening.

Unlike other borderlands I have visited so far, Gangtok is not a border town as such, but the capital city of a beautiful Himalayan state that became a part of India only in 1975. It lies around 55 kilometres from the international border that India shares with China and is the most prominent and populous town in Sikkim, the landlocked state that shares its western border with Nepal, has China on its northern and north-eastern border, Bhutan to the east and the state of West Bengal to the south. The town – in fact, the whole of Sikkim, with a population of around 6.5 lakhs – is so remote and detached from the rest of the country that it feels like a vast borderland caught between two strong, imposing nations.

Gangtok looks like any other hill station hugging the Himalayas, with ugly, featureless concrete structures sprouting from everywhere and uneven, potholed roads whose kerbs are strewn with refuse like used polythene bags, torn paan sachets and empty packets of potato chips. But the scene changes dramatically when one reaches M.G. Marg, the hotspot of this little town perched on a ridge at roughly 5,500 feet above sea level.

All tourist routes in Gangtok eventually lead to M.G. Marg, where a beaming statue of the Father of the Nation greets visitors. This tiny stretch, hardly a kilometre or so in length, is unlike any other in India and probably the first and sole pedestrian-only thoroughfare in the entire country. It is also, perhaps, the only one that I know of with storm-water drains running along both sides.

When I stepped out of my hotel that evening, refreshed and

more receptive to my surroundings, I was pleasantly surprised to note that the street was neatly paved with gleaming black tiles, while the pavements had been laid with granite slabs. In the centre median stood tall metal lamp posts that branched out at the top, with ornate antique lanterns hanging like fruit from each branch. Sitting between these lamp posts, equidistant from each other, were giant pots of neatly trimmed ornamental ferns. In smaller pots placed between the ferns were rose shrubs, their vibrant, colourful blooms lending the entire stretch a vintage European charm against the backdrop of the Himalayas.

Flanking the street on either side was a chain of shops selling goods as diverse as paan, traditional Buddhist artefacts, designer wear and products from well-known brands. Karaoke bars, restaurants and pretty much everything that Gangtok has to offer lined the street.

This was easily the town's most attractive tourist destination, with visitors beginning to flock here as early as 8.30 a.m. and the teeming crowds not dispersing until nine or ten in the evening. Trendy, smartly turned out Indian couples, large families and groups of single men and women thronged the promenade all day, licking ice creams, munching on vegetable and chicken rolls or simply lazing on the many benches set out by the city corporation, as they watched the world go by.

But while the ambiance here was informal and relaxed, the anything-goes mentality was certainly not in evidence. A ban on smoking was in place and, from what I could gauge, it was effectively enforced. I could not spot a single smoker on the street and was even warned that should I indulge in a smoke and be caught by the cops, I would have to pay a fine of ₹500. This was also the only stretch of road where the pavements and building walls were unsullied by paan stains, as spitting was banned here and, more importantly, the ban was strictly enforced.

Liquor shops were aplenty and almost every other bar had a karaoke facility, with scores of Hindi and English soundtracks. During the peak tourist season, like the Durga Puja holidays when I happened to be there, one could hear the refrains of untunefully rendered Bollywood numbers wafting out of almost every karaoke bar. Come 7 p.m. or thereabouts and groups of youngsters would put their vocal chords to the test after priming them with whiskey or rum.

Bollywood too seemed to have staked its claim almost everywhere on this fashion street, with local businessmen using the titles of legendary Hindi films and the names of memorable characters who had featured in them to promote their enterprises. A hotel-cum-restaurant on M.G. Marg, for example, went by the name of Babumoshai, an unforgettable character played by Bollywood icon Amitabh Bachchan in *Anand*, a blockbuster hit of the 1970s. Another restaurant across the road, serving non-vegetarian meals, had plastered its walls with huge posters featuring yesteryear Bollywood actors Amjad Khan and Amol Palekar, among others, and famous quotes from their movies just to spice up the ambiance which the general public seemed to love.

I was so lost in the magic of M.G. Marg on my very first evening out in Gangtok that I found myself strolling back and forth endlessly along the promenade, merging with the milling crowds of window shoppers and tourists who would hang around the city centre until the town shut down for the night. Here, finally, I told myself with satisfaction, was a walkway that made me feel proud to be Indian and I could see the same pride reflected in the eyes of almost every *desi* tourist out there that evening.

* * *

The next morning, I went back to M.G. Marg, wondering if there was anything more I could add to what had already been put on record by hundreds, if not thousands, of bloggers about this beautiful little town with a showpiece of a central boulevard, crowds of happy tourists and cheerful shopkeepers. It was just a little past nine, but tourists had already started flocking to the place.

I sat for a while on one of the benches near the central median and indulged in some people watching. When I got bored with that, I walked into the state government's Tourist Information Office at the far end of the road to check out the availability of shared trips to Nathu La, the gateway to China. To my disappointment, I learnt that permits to Nathu La were not being issued for a week as government offices were closed due to the holiday season. In fact, even those who had already obtained permits through travel agents were not being allowed to visit the pass due to certain political developments. I was advised to check with private tour operators if they could accommodate me on one of their scheduled tours to the other tourist attractions en route, such as Sherathang and Baba Mandir, a few kilometres from the border. Accordingly, I visited each and every one of the several travel agencies on M.G. Marg, but received the same response: they were fully booked for the holiday season.

In sheer desperation, I went to a news mart near the tourism office to check out the local newspapers of the day. While the *Times of India*, the *Telegraph* and a few other national dailies did reach Gangtok, none of the major newspapers had a city edition and the only ones that carried exhaustive news reports of Sikkim were local publications which, I was told, served mostly as a government mouthpiece.

The man who ran the news mart was a third-generation Bihari businessman, whose great-grandfather had, allegedly, beaten up an Englishman back home in the 1930s and escaped to Sikkim shortly thereafter to escape the inevitable repercussions.

He lamented the state of the local press and the tendency of the mainstream media to confine its focus to the touristy M.G. Marg, never moving beyond its glitzy surface to probe and discover the real face of Sikkim. I asked if he could suggest the name of someone with whom I could engage in in-depth discussions about the Gangtok that lay beyond its attractive façade of trendy hotspots, majestic mountains and lakes and colourful religious festivals.

After pondering over my request for a while, the shopkeeper pointed to an old man in a light jacket and a balaclava or monkey cap basking in the morning sun sitting on one of the benches near his shop. He looked to be in his sixties and sported a grey stubble.

'You see that man sitting there?' the shopkeeper said. 'He is the best person to tell you all about Gangtok and its politics. Don't be fooled by his innocuous appearance. He can make anyone the chief minister of Sikkim, if he so chooses, or even topple the state government. He has succeeded in doing both in the past. His name is Prem Goyal. Just go and talk to him.'

I approached Goyal and greeted him. Then I expressed my keenness to know more about Gangtok than I had managed to so far and delve deeper into its history and politics. I added that his name had been mentioned to me and he had been described as the most appropriate person to talk to in this connection.

The senior citizen rose from the bench, shook hands with me and asked, 'So what do you want to know from me?'

I told him how impressed I was with M.G. Marg and Gangtok, in general, and how different it was from other Himalayan towns.

'You think everything is fine and lovely here?' Goyal shot back. 'It is all fake. You cannot imagine how much filth lies behind this beautiful promenade. Every shopkeeper here is apprehensive and uncertain about his future, but no one dares speak of it. This showcase of a town is meant to fool visitors and VIPs arriving from Delhi into believing that Gangtok has evolved phenomenally over the last forty years since it became a part of India. But it is all a big lie. We were so much better off as subjects of the king.'

Goyal invited me to sit beside him in the sun if I was not in a hurry. I immediately obliged, took out my recorder and notepad and listened attentively, as forty years of history slowly unfolded before me. From the moment Goyal started speaking about Sikkim, he appeared to become a different person; his feeble voice acquired a new timbre, sounding stern and forceful, his hunched shoulders straightened and he was transformed into the ruthless political activist that he had been for the better part of his life.

Prem Goyal was born in October 1946. His parents, who were originally from Haryana, had moved to Darjeeling in search of work soon after his birth. Later, sometime between 1954–55, Goyal Senior found employment in the kingdom of Sikkim and the family moved to Gangtok. Prem remembers spending his childhood and youth in this picturesque hill town, insulated from the rest of the country. Life under the king was peaceful and fulfilling. All citizens were treated as equals and there was no communal tension whatsoever.

'But all that is not important,' he said. 'What is important is the series of events that unfolded after 4 April 1973. For that was when the revolution began in Sikkim.'

For the past several centuries, Sikkim had been an independent Himalayan kingdom with a predominantly Buddhist population. Dynasties came and went and the country, like its neighbouring kingdoms, had to deal with its fair share of invasions and wars. With the British taking over peninsular India, Sikkim became a protectorate state of the Raj in the nineteenth century. But its king continued to enjoy a greater degree of sovereignty than the rulers of other protectorate kingdoms and was able to discharge his duties with minimal interference from the country's colonial rulers. When India became an independent nation in 1947, Sikkim refused to join the Indian Union and opted, instead, to become a protectorate state of India, with the latter taking control of its defence, foreign policy and communications.

Since the days of the British Raj, New Delhi had looked upon Sikkim and Bhutan as twin Himalayan kingdoms and dealt with both the regimes in an identical manner. Both were Buddhist kingdoms and their royal families were also related to each other. But unlike Bhutan, which continues to remain a strong and fiercely independent country, Sikkim's monarchy failed to win the confidence of its subjects.

Experts in the region attribute this failure to the huge surge in migration that had taken place in Sikkim over the years. As of now, the state's population comprises Nepalis (70–75 per cent), local tribes (20–25 per cent), including Lepchas, Bhutias and Sherpas and Indians from the mainland (2–3 per cent). While there were hardly any Nepalis living in Sikkim until the nineteenth century, the community is now the largest in the state, thanks to the British, who encouraged their migration to Sikkim, as they found it easier to put them to work than the less pliant natives.

With Sikkim's racial composition undergoing drastic changes over the past century, a revolution was inevitable. On 4 April 1973, Gangtok erupted in protests against the Chogyal (monarch), as agitated mobs surrounded the palace, demanding his abdication and the end of monarchy. While there had been widespread discontent against the king and his rule ever since he married Hope Cooke, a 23-year-old American who was his second wife and consort, the situation worsened in early 1973, after the Palace was accused of rigging local elections in favour of a party floated by the throne. The general discontent among the public was ignited by local political parties who spearheaded the revolution, allegedly with the blessings of the Indian government.

Two years later, in May 1975, Sikkim had joined the Indian Union as its 22nd state, its abolished monarchy replaced by an elected legislature. All the subjects of the erstwhile Himalayan kingdom were automatically granted Indian citizenship and allowed free access to the rest of the country. To quell possibilities of unrest, instigated by rumours making the rounds that Sikkim's new status was not quite the outcome of a merger, but of brute force exercised by the Indian Army at the behest of the Indian government, the Centre doled out a long list of special privileges to appease the newly inducted citizens. For Prem Goyal, an aspiring politician in his early thirties at the time, and his contemporaries, the Indian government's apparent partiality towards its new citizens of Sikkimese origin was an unmistakable sign of discrimination.

The problems, however, for those who had moved from mainland India to the Himalayan kingdom in search of better prospects began much earlier, in 1950, when the Indian government signed a treaty with Sikkim's monarchy, taking charge of the kingdom's defence, foreign affairs and communications. As per the conditions of the treaty, citizens of Indian origin were not allowed to purchase agricultural land in Sikkim, but could own trade and business establishments which they themselves had set up there.

'This was the first sign of discrimination against us and it would continue even after Sikkim merged with the Indian Union,' Goyal recalled.

But Prem and other migrant Indians like him had failed to anticipate the ways in which the special privileges granted by the Indian government to its citizens of Sikkimese origin might affect their community. In those days, he was officiating as Party Treasurer for the Sikkim Janata Parishad, headed by Nar Bahadur Bhandari. Kazi Lhendup Dorjee was the ruling party's chief minister and the Sikkim Janata Parishad was the most powerful opposition. Being an active young politician, Prem wanted to enter the State Assembly as a legislator, but was told that he did not have the right to contest. Of the thirty-two Assembly seats in the state, sixteen were reserved for the Lepcha–Bhutia community and the other sixteen for Nepalis.

'I came to know from the chief minister himself that while Indians like me, who had been living in the state for so long, had the right to vote in Sikkim, they had no right to contest as a candidate,' Goyal recalled. 'I was also asked not to meddle too much in Party policies, as I was ineligible to stand for election. It came as a shock, not just to me, but to the entire community.'

Challenging the unfairness of the system, the migrant community soon took to the streets and garnered public support against total reservation of seats in the State Assembly. It was Goyal's first major plunge into political activism. Over the next few weeks and months, he, along with his supporters, would take up the issue with the then Prime Minister Moraji Desai, leading politicians like Jayaprakash Narayan and even the President, highlighting the injustice meted out to ethnic Indians who had no right to contest in a poll in Sikkim, despite the latter's status as an Indian state.

'We were finally able to persuade the PMO to give due credence to our grievances,' Goyal went on. 'An ordinance was introduced, whereby sixty per cent of the seats were placed in the open category, while the rest were reserved for the state's indigenous people. Since Nepalis no longer enjoyed the privileges of reservation, the disgruntled community leaders appealed against the ordinance and moved the Supreme Court. The apex court, however, upheld the reservation quota prescribed in the ordinance through an Act of Parliament.'

By now, the sun was directly overhead and I welcomed its

warmth. Prem was fervently narrating one incident after another from his political life, when an elderly man in a grey suit stopped by to greet him. He turned out to be a retired Secretary from the state's Energy and Power Department and a former IAS officer who had wielded much authority in his time. Soon, several other prominent members of the migrant Indian community stopped by, fell at his feet and sought his blessings at regular intervals. When these interruptions grew too frequent for Prem's liking, he suggested that I accompany him to his home which stood right on M.G. Marg.

Goyal led the way across the street to a shopping complex on M.G. Marg. I discovered that he owned it and had rented out all the space, except a one-room flat at the far end, where he now lived with a servant. From the time his wife passed away in the late 1980s, Prem had been living with his only son, who had, however, subsequently got a job in the United States and settled there with his family.

We went up a narrow flight of stairs to a spacious room on the second floor. This was where the political activist lived. A table and three chairs were set out at the entrance. Further inside stood a bed on which a thick mattress had been laid. Behind the bed was a bookcase crowded with books, magazines and newspapers that protruded in an untidy jumble. Beyond the bookcase lay an open kitchen equipped with a kerosene-pump stove and a handful of vessels and utensils. I could not help commenting on his Spartan lifestyle, to which Goyal responded that he was now too old to crave luxury. Turning on the stove, he set about preparing tea for the two of us. I sat near him on a little stool in the kitchen and turned my voice recorder on again.

The next major issue Goyal chose to take up on behalf of Sikkim's Indian residents involved yet another form of discrimination that would manifest itself with the resurgence in 1989 of the Sikkim Subject register. Sikkim subjects, that is, those residents of Sikkim who had been subjects of the king before 1975 and held a certificate identifying them as such, were entitled to government jobs and educational scholarships and even exempted from income tax, whereas the rest were denied these benefits despite living in Sikkim for generations. Migrant Indians like Goyal's ancestors had refused to become Sikkim subjects during the king's reign, preferring to retain their Indian identity in acknowledgement of their ethnic roots. Ironically, with the resurgence of the Sikkim Subject register, the quest to assert their own identity had been the cause of their undoing, turning them into targets of yet another form of discrimination.

Bringing up this issue now, Goyal contended that while even the Chogyal (king) had not discriminated against persons of Indian origin during his reign and granted them equal access to opportunities in the kingdom, the Indian government was now overtly favouring Sikkim subjects, who had become Indian citizens only in 1975.

The issue triggered protests and led to market shutdowns, highlighting the plight of a few hundred families of Indian origin who sought to challenge the injustice of being denied important benefits, because they had declined the offer of becoming Sikkim subjects during the Chogyal's rule. Prem Goyal filed a petition in the Rajya Sabha, seeking protection of the interests of bona fide Indian nationals who had been residing in Sikkim prior to its merger with India. In his petition, he claimed that Indian nationals living in the state were being treated virtually as second-class citizens for no fault of theirs and demanded that they be treated on par with Sikkim's indigenous residents.

After much effort, the activist and his supporters managed to get the Parliamentary Committee to recommend that all citizens of Indian origin living in Sikkim be granted the rights already enjoyed by its indigenous population. In 2013, the committee urged executive action on the government's part to ensure that all Indian citizens and their descendants residing in Sikkim from before 26 April 1975 be treated as Sikkimese Indians and brought under the ambit of Income Tax Exemption, a privilege hitherto granted exclusively to the state's indigenous people.

But nothing had really changed on the ground.

'This is Sikkim's plight,' Goyal sighed, as we sat in his apartment overlooking M.G. Marg. 'Nothing has changed. We continue to be treated like second-class citizens and keep having to pay income tax, while our brothers from the local tribes, who grew up with us, enjoy all the benefits and exemptions denied to us. If I question this state of affairs, I am branded an anti-national. How can you expect a common citizen to be happy in a state that practises such blatant discrimination?

'This is why I keep repeating that we were much more contented under the king. He ensured that all his subjects were treated equally. Even after governing this state for forty years, India has failed to guarantee the same degree of equality for all. And now, all because of these discriminatory practices, there is so much anger and mutual distrust between the Nepalis, the indigenous Lepcha–Bhutia folk and residents of Indian origin like us.

'Don't be fooled by the glitter of M.G. Marg,' was Prem Goyal's parting shot. 'It is just a façade. Look beyond this street and you will discover the truth about Sikkim.'

And so I did. After leaving Goyal's home, I headed for the potholed, congested Tibet Road that turned right from M.G. Marg and went uphill. I came across more crowded roads and bylanes, where damp multi-storey buildings stood cheek by jowl. Thousands of Sikkimese lived in these congested little blocks and made a living working in hotels, restaurants, bars, travel agencies and other outlets that had mushroomed along M.G. Marg over the past decade. But although I tried to initiate a conversation with them, these people simply would not talk to me; they were either too busy with their work or too drunk for their conversations to make any sense, although it was just late afternoon in the lower Himalayas.

After wandering around for a while, I hailed a taxi and went directly to Lepcha Cottage, a home for destitute children run by Ms Kipu, one of the city's most respected social workers. She was apparently among the few influential members of the Lepcha community – one of Sikkim's two main indigenous tribes – and an authority on its present situation.

Lepcha Cottage is located in Chanmari village, about five kilometres from Gangtok. It stands in a modest grassy compound and consists of a main office and a central playground, surrounded by lodging facilities for about a hundred children between ages five and seventeen. For the past 25 years, the organization has been taking in children who were either orphaned or whose parents live in such abject poverty that they are unable to take care of their offspring. The home provides the children with food, lodging and education, until they are able to stand on their own and fend for themselves. Some of its former inmates have even earned engineering degrees and are on their way to a lasting career in Sikkim and elsewhere in India. Having started off as a temporary shelter for six or seven children who were raised under the personal care of Ms Kipu, Lepcha Cottage is now a respected institution in Sikkim and has recently tied up with the state government for future projects.

When I arrived at the place, most of the children were away, having gone off to their village homes in the mountains for the Puja holidays. Just thirty-odd tiny tots remained and I watched them happily playing with one another, unmindful of a stranger in their midst. These innocent and cheerfully noisy little children who screamed in delight and seemed to have not a care in the world, despite being separated from their parents at a tender age, were precisely the Sikkimese citizens I had been seeking to interact with. Their parents were mostly illiterate, with no notion at all of the value of education and, therefore, devoid of any motivation to send their offspring to school. Ms Kipu and her volunteers had taken on the responsibility of identifying such children and bringing them to Chanmari, where they were given a formal education and training in vocational skills.

When I asked to see her, I learnt that she too was away at a month-long meditation camp in the plains, leaving the institution in the care of Ms Pasang Amu, who had been with Lepcha Cottage for the past 15 years. Despite having worked for so many years with Ms Kipu, Pasang, I discovered, did not understand English and was not at ease speaking Hindi either, although she did understand the language.

As I struggled to explain to her that I needed to talk to some of the home's older students and residents for a clearer understanding of the community, another young woman who had arrived with her five-year-old daughter began helping me out by translating my words for Pasang's benefit. The visitor turned out to be Dr Namgay Donka Bhutia, a physician from Gangtok who had come to celebrate her daughter's birthday with the home's young residents.

Dr Bhutia, who worked as a respiratory therapist at the government hospital in Gangtok and lived in the city with her lawyer husband, liked to visit Lepcha Cottage whenever she was dispirited, as the place filled her with hope and inspiration. She spoke English, Hindi and Nepali, apart from her native Bhutia language, and between us, we somehow managed to persuade Pasang that it would be all right for me to interact with a couple of her senior residents.

Pasang Amu left the visitors' room and returned, fifteen minutes later, with two of her senior residents Asanmit Lepcha and Jiki Lepcha in tow. Dr Bhutia joined the gathering as well and the five of us sat in a circle in the visitors' room and chatted. The physician would translate my questions into their native tongue and render the girls' responses in English for my benefit. And so, on that fun-filled evening spent together, enlivened by laughter and warmed by steaming cups of tea – a custom apparently prevalent even in the poorest of Sikkimese villages – I understood a little more about life in the erstwhile Himalayan kingdom.

Asanmit, who had recently completed her graduation and worked as a teacher, had been with Lepcha Cottage since class VI, while Jiki, who had just completed class XII, had been in Ms Kipu's care for the past seven years. Both the Lepcha girls had been brought here from remote mountain villages, as their parents could not afford to take care of them, let alone send them to school. The girls were initially very shy in my presence and would not utter a word, until Dr Bhutia put them at ease by urging them to speak freely and express their views.

'The problem with these girls is that they hardly ever meet outsiders and are unaware of what is going on around the world,' Dr Bhutia explained.

It struck me that this could possibly be the reason why both Asanmit and Jiki expressed their hope of becoming teachers when I asked them about their future plans. They rarely had the chance to meet people from any other profession and were clueless about the kind of education one might need to become a lawyer, a journalist or even a chartered accountant. Living in a kind of cocoon, many of these these girls and boys were not even acquainted with the Internet or YouTube and unaware of the existence of Facebook, Twitter and other social media that were not entirely unknown even in remote villages across the rest of

India. Even on a distant island like Minicoy, largely cut off from the mainland, I had seen people use Facebook to communicate with each other, while here in Chanmari village, located just five kilometres from a bustling town like Gangtok, the girls lived in ignorance of the social-media revolution sweeping across the rest of the country. Thanks, however, to the state government's preference for Sikkim subjects as candidates for government jobs, the two girls were likely to get more stable employment and would probably lead better lives than their parents and grandparents had. And hopefully, their children would catch up with rest of the country.

On the other hand, the slim Dr Bhutia, with her sculpted features and smart outfit of black fitted trousers and matching woollen jacket, was a classic symbol of the changes that had swept over Sikkim in the past forty years. Dr Bhutia's parents were illiterate. As a Sikkim subject, her father had managed to get a job as a policeman in Gangtok and support his family on his meagre income, while her mother stayed home to take care of the children. But in spite of being unlettered, both parents had insisted on Dr Bhutia and her siblings attending school regularly and doing well in their studies.

'I am a product of the government,' Dr Bhutia told me proudly. 'I studied in a government school in Gangtok. After passing out of school, I gained admission to the government medical college in Sikkim. When I had obtained my MBBS degree, I went off to Madhya Pradesh and did my Masters before returning to Sikkim to work.'

It was while practising medicine in Gangtok that Dr Bhutia would meet her future husband, a lawyer. They dated each other for a while before deciding to get married. Even after having children of her own, Dr Bhutia continued to support her siblings financially, claiming that as the eldest, it was her responsibility to do so, as both her parents had passed away.

'Out here, women are a lot more independent than in other parts of India,' she explained. 'We decide on how we will spend our earnings and lead our lives. Our husbands do not interfere. I take care of my siblings and am proud of it.'

Young women like Dr Bhutia were a source of inspiration for the older residents of Lepcha Cottage like Asanmit and Jiki. While there were many in Gangtok who were resentful about the government favouring Sikkim's indigenous tribes by doling out freebies and jobs to them, Dr Bhutia, Asanmit and Jiki were living examples of these efforts bearing fruit, for without government support, young Sikkimese subjects like them might have remained trapped forever in their anachronistic world in the Himalayas. Of course, these women are among the lucky few; there are thousands of youngsters still living in faraway mountain villages busy helping out their mothers and grandmothers in basic chores like raising yaks, making cheese and butter and waiting for someone like Ms Kipu to find them and lead them to warmer climes and a more promising future.

While we sat in the spacious visitors' room and chatted, the sun began to set on the western horizon and cold winds blew over Chanmari. The onset of dusk meant that it was time for evening prayers at Lepcha Cottage and the thirty-odd children who had been happily playing were summoned and made to stand in queues, one behind the other. Pasang, Dr Bhutia and the two older girls who had been present during our discussions excused themselves and went out to the corridor to chant along with the children. A few minutes later, I heard the words ring out:

'*Losa Maasa Budhasa, Buddham Saranam Gacchami, Sangham Saranam Gacchami, Dharmam Saranam Gacchami...*'

* * *

For a small tourist town, Gangtok has a vibrant nightlife, which includes a casino located barely six kilometres from its outskirts, three posh night clubs that come alive on weekends and dozens of karaoke bars and cocktail lounges. As in other north-eastern states, booze flows freely here and every fourth or fifth shop or restaurant either has an attached bar or is a liquor outlet.

On my second night in town, I ventured into a little restaurant-cum-bar on Tibet Road, very close to M.G. Marg, but off the tourist radar. I had heard someone singing the familiar lyrics of a song from a Bollywood film and stepped in to check out the place. I discovered, to my surprise, that the bar was crowded with locals, mostly in their early twenties, singing and dancing to karaoke music. The bar and its ambience, even the smell of the room freshener, evoked powerful memories of my stay in Phuentsholing, a town situated on Bhutan's border with India.

I ordered a local brew called 'HIT' and chose a corner table for two that faced the bar counter. As was the case in Bhutan's bars, young girls, drinking and partying, were present here in much larger numbers than the men accompanying them. A glance around told me that I was the only 'original Indian' (the term commonly used in Gangtok to address non-Sikkimese, non-Nepali persons of Indian origin) at the lounge and was attracting quizzical looks from everyone there.

Probably out of pity – or was it curiosity? – a fair-complexioned young man of less than average height approached me and asked if he could join me at the table. I nodded. I noticed that despite his flabby upper arms, he was wearing a sleeveless brown t-shirt with a round neck. His thick hair was neatly combed back and he sported a wispy, barely-there moustache which was untrimmed. From his distinctive features, it was apparent that he was either a Bhutia–Lepcha or belonged to one of the other indigenous tribes.

After sitting opposite me for a while and quietly sipping HIT beer – the same drink I had ordered – from a coffee mug, the man asked me where I was from. I replied that I was from Chennai.

Thanks to the movie *Chennai Express*, starring Shah Rukh Khan and Deepika Padukone, I no longer had to answer absurd questions about the city's location or the meaning of its name. The one weird question I did get asked from time to time was: 'So how far is Chennai from Madras?' To which I always replied, 'Oh, don't you know? They are both located in the same place!'

Now leaning a little closer, the man at the Gangtok cocktail lounge introduced himself as Lemka, the owner of the place. I was mildly surprised. He looked like a kid just out of school and had he visited a bar back home in Chennai, he would surely have been questioned on suspicion of being underage and asked to show his ID. Here, in Gangtok, he actually owned the cozy little bar.

Over a couple more beers, I came to know that Lemka was 28 years old. He had opened the bar a year ago, investing ₹10,00,000 in the business. He had also insisted that his wife, who used to be in government service, quit her job and take over as the bartender in his little restaurant-cum-bar. Here was yet another reason why I found Sikkim to be so unlike the rest of India; nowhere else in the country was a man likely to persuade his wife to give up her secure government job and work as a bartender in his business. But this had, it seemed, worked well for Lemka. With his wife keeping track of the customers' accounts, he could relax and start drinking from around seven in the evening and go on till the bar closed for the night.

Lemka's clients were mostly locals who congregated at the bar, drank beer, chatted with friends and joined in singing their favourite songs. Some of them even danced for a while after getting high on liquor. But they all went home only after they had paid their bills without argument. Drunken bar brawls were rare in these parts.

The young bar owner confided that he earned enough to make the business worth carrying on with.

'Besides, this is what I love to do. I don't want to do anything else,' he said simply.

Lemka's dream was to own bars all over India, especially by the beach in Goa, and become a bar tycoon. Owning a seaside bar there and partying every night had also been my dream for a long time, until I found out about the presence of Israeli and Russian mafias. Since Lemka and I had got along so well, I suggested that we should meet again when he was sober so that I could write about him. Could I return the following evening for a chat, I asked.

'No, I'll be busy all day tomorrow,' he replied. 'It is the Durga Puja holiday, na? I have some work to do.'

I would subsequently discover that the 'work' he referred to involved sitting down to gamble with friends. On every public holiday, Lemka and his friends apparently got together in one of their homes, a boys' day out, as it were, and gambled from dawn to dusk, sipping beer and munching on their favourite snacks. Missing one such daylong gambling marathon on a government holiday meant that the concerned person would be out of the loop for the next marathon. When I asked him if I could join in, Lemka replied that I was welcome to do so – but on one condition.

'To enter the private residence where we gamble, you will need to bring at least ₹30,000 in cash with you,' he said. 'That is the minimum entry fee. Booze and food are on us.'

I thanked him for the offer, but politely declined, explaining that I couldn't afford the fee.

Apart from these private gambling marathons on government holidays, Lemka and his friends also frequented the casino down the hill once a month. In fact, it was from him that I would come to know about the casinos of Sikkim, which are among the rare few in the country and hardly publicized by the state. Speaking of his monthly visits to the casino near Gangtok (the other one was down south) where he spent an entire day gambling, Lemka justified them by saying, 'That's my only entertainment, buddy. Otherwise, it is work all the time.'

* * *

Having spent the last few days roaming in and around Gangtok, I couldn't wait to get out of town and take the ancient Silk Route to Nathu La, one of the two border trading posts between India and China. After the 1962 war with China, the pass, situated at an altitude of 14,140 feet above sea level was closed. It was reopened several decades later, during the regime under Prime Minister Atal Bihari Vajpayee, to boost trade between the two countries and was now a popular tourist spot.

I had originally planned to visit Tsomgo Lake, the Sherathang border market and Baba Mandir on my way to Nathu La. With the Puja holidays over now, tourists were heading back home in huge numbers every day, but curiously enough, I found it impossible to manage a seat on a shared vehicle bound for Nathu La. Finally, I was forced to negotiate with a local cab driver and managed to persuade him to take me to the pass for a slightly lower fee than was usually charged. The driver, a Nepali called Suraj Chetri, agreed to get my permit ready for the trip and pick me up from my hotel at 7.30 a.m. the following day.

Chetri failed to turn up at the scheduled time. My call to his phone number went unanswered. Half an hour later, I called him again. This time, he answered the call, explaining that he was stuck in the tourism office, as there was a huge rush for permits. He also informed me that the authorities were not issuing permits for Nathu La and that I could only go up to Baba Mandir. I waited for another hour outside my hotel, but Chetri did not turn up.

Tired of waiting interminably, I made my way to the tourism office that was located just behind M.G. Marg, a ten-minute walk from my hotel. The state-government office where tourist permits were issued resembled any Regional Transport Office (RTO) in Chennai, with dozens of young men clutching a bunch of papers in their hands as they carried on frantic conversations over the phone, while pasting photographs on documents and verifying the names and ages of the tourists who had applied for the Inner Line Permits deemed mandatory for visiting restricted areas in Sikkim. Like most middlemen across the country, these tourism-department staffers all seemed adept at multi-tasking. A huge crowd of tour operators and cab drivers waited outside the window, where duly filled-in application forms for tourist permits were accepted by Sikkim government officials, to find out if permit documents for their clients had arrived. I managed to spot Chetri in that crowd and asked him about the status of my application for a permit. Pointing at the chaos ahead, the driver replied that although my application had been among the first few to be submitted that morning, my permit had not come through yet.

I hung around for another half-hour and observed the crowds. I realized after a while that the similarities between the tourism office in this hill town and an RTO in Chennai were not limited to the crowds and the hectic activity; the Gangtok office was apparently just as prone to corruption, with policemen and other agents entering it with a bunch of papers and emerging in minutes with complacent smiles and the permits they had applied for. Having noticed this, I shared my misgivings with Chetri, expressing serious doubts about obtaining the permit, unless he had a source in the office he could tap.

'If you're willing to shell out a couple of ₹100 more, I can get the permit soon,' he said confidently. 'I know someone here.'

I agreed to fork out the extra sum and thirty minutes later, we were on our way, climbing up the winding road to Nathu La, along with hundreds of other cars, SUVs and huge army trucks manufactured at the Vehicles Factory, Jabalpur.

The majestic valleys and the moist, rocky slopes of the Himalayas, dotted with shrubs displaying the crimson, orange and yellow hues of late autumn, stretched out invitingly like the colourfully draped contours of a curvy woman. Despite my efforts to resist the temptation of taking too many photographs, I found myself asking Chetri to halt at a dozen spots, a least, to capture the breathtaking scenery along the way. All through the roughly 53 kilometre journey, we came across army settlements and tiny hill villages that catered to passing tourists with souvenir shops, a few eateries offering steaming-hot momos and chow mein and shacks selling jackets, sweaters, other winter clothing and goods imported from China through Nathu La.

Two and a half hours and several army check posts later, we had covered a mere 40 kilometres, but ascended to an altitude of 12,310 feet. Before us lay Tsomgo lake, whose crystal-clear waters, formed through snow and ice melt from the surrounding peaks, usually remained frozen all through winter and early summer. On the sunny afternoon of my visit, the water was as limpid as a mirror, reflecting every detail of the steep mountains surrounding it, but for the gentle ripples that an occasional stone, tossed into the lake by playful tourists, would create on its surface. I lingered there for a moment, admiring the lake's pristine beauty and observing the shaggy-haired yaks that had been trained to take tourists for a short ride, before resuming my journey. Twelve kilometres away lay Sherathang.

The Sherathang Trade Mart was opened in 2009, three years after bilateral trade relations between India and China had resumed through Nathu La. The town was marked as the customs and excise check post for vehicles arriving from China. The market remained open from Monday through Thursday between May and November every year, with Chinese trucks, laden with goods authorized for import, arriving in the morning and returning home with Indian goods later in the day. As I had visited Sherathang on a Friday, the trade mart, one of the highest international markets in the world, was deserted, with just a few army trucks parked inside for shelter. Driving around the mart, we couldn't find a soul, except a young jawan from Haryana who informed us that the market was closed till Sunday. When I asked him if there was a chance of meeting Indian dealers who bought regularly from the market, he advised me to visit Kupup village.

'It is beyond Baba Mandir and you can get there without a permit,' he informed me helpfully.

We left Sherathang and headed towards Nathu La, about eight kilometres away. A little further on, the road split into two, with the one turning away to the left leading to Nathu La. At the entrance to this road stood a check post; only vehicles with a valid permit to visit the border were allowed beyond this point. Without such a permit to allow us access, we had to continue our journey towards Baba Mandir. From this point onwards, the number of Indian Army camps would increase dramatically and notice boards planted at regular intervals alerted us that we were under surveillance from Chinese military observation posts.

Nathu La had last witnessed serious military action in 1967, when the Indian Army was erecting a fence along the international border to avoid routine skirmishes between the two armies. On 11 September 1967, Chinese officers objected to the Indian authorities fencing the border and a minor scuffle ensued. Subsequently, the Chinese soldiers returned to their bunkers, while the Indians resumed work on the fencing. Not long after, the Indian soldiers faced heavy machine-gun fire from the north shoulder of the pass. The group of army men involved in the fencing work was caught unawares and thus suffered heavy casualties. The Indian Army soon retaliated with heavy firing, resulting in casualties on the Chinese side as well. The artillery exchange would continue non-stop for the next three days, before the situation was brought under control.

The brave action of the Indian soldiers and the pictures of the martyrs had been documented and put up for tourists at the point where the road bifurcated towards Nathu La, warning them of their proximity to the Chinese border.

As we approached Baba Mandir, there were more signboards informing us that we were under Chinese observation and should exercise caution. About six kilometres beyond the entrance to Nathu La, a winding road led to Baba Mandir, a shrine built in memory of a young Indian soldier who had died near the pass while posted there. The locals have a fascinating story to tell about him.

Sepoy Harbhajan Singh was born to a Sikh family on 30 August 1946 in the Sadrana village of Gujranwala district (now in Pakistan). On 9 February 1966, he was recruited for service in the Punjab Regiment of the Indian Army. Exactly two years later, a natural disaster in Sikkim and North Bengal claimed thousands of lives in both states. The sepoy, who had been posted in the upper reaches of the mountains, is remembered for his laudable efforts in rescuing and helping the survivors. On 4 October 1968, while escorting a mule column from Tuku La, his battalion headquarters, to Donguchui La, Harbhajan accidentally slipped and fell into a fast-flowing nullah and drowned. It is said that the strong current swept his body away, carrying it about two kilometres further downstream from the site of the accident.

On the fifth day after his disappearance, his colleague and friend Pritam Singh apparently had a dream in which Harbhajan conveyed to him the news of his tragic death and also mentioned the location of his body, buried under a heap of snow. According to Pritam, Harbhajan also expressed a desire to have a samadhi built in his memory.

While Pritam did not pay much heed to his dream initially, he was stunned when Harbhajan's body was recovered from the very place mentioned in the dream. To honour his wish, a samadhi was built near Chhokya Chho, the area where the sepoy was originally posted, located at an elevation of around 13,123 feet. However, the fact that they had to climb fifty steps to reach the bunker seemed to discourage tourists and a new, more easily accessible shrine was eventually built along the highway.

Locals believe that even today, a rug routinely laid out in the shrine by the soldiers posted near the Old Baba Mandir is found crushed and wrinkled the next morning, suggesting that Baba Harbhajan's spirit still visits the old shrine and spends the night at the bunker, guarding his country against the enemy. It is also widely believed in the surrounding villages that the holy water obtained from the shrine has curative powers and heals many ailments.

As we approached Baba Mandir, the weather changed suddenly. Dark clouds hovered over the valley ahead of us and little snowflakes drifted on to the car's windshield, only to be demolished by the blades of the wiper. I could not believe, at first, that it was actually snowing and asked Suraj to stop the car so that I could step out and enjoy the experience. Within a few minutes, however, the folds of my jacket had trapped so many snowflakes that I was compelled to rush back to the vehicle to warm up. We set off again, hurrying along a narrow dirt road towards the remote Himalayan village of Kupup, barely a few kilometres from Chinese border posts. Within five minutes, we were approaching a kind of plateau, flanked on three sides by mountain peaks, where more army camps had been set up. To the right of the camps was a signboard indicating that we had reached Kupup.

This remote village was little more than a cluster of a dozen-odd cabins, built almost entirely of logs of wood stacked one on top of the other, with strong pillars supporting the floor and a corrugated metal sheet serving as a roof to shield those living in the cabins from sun and snow. At the entrance to the village was the marketplace, where a series of cabins, converted into shops, sold groceries, alcohol, cigarettes, clothes and winter wear.

We reached the village to discover that there wasn't a tourist in sight. The shops were full of soldiers stocking up on booze and snacks to last them through the night ahead that had turned bitingly cold with the season's first snowfall. I walked into one of the liquor shops and explained to the shopkeeper that I was looking for someone who traded goods with China through Nathu La. He immediately directed me to Sonam's.

Sonam's Stores was situated at the far end of the village market. Like other shops in the village, it was built almost entirely from logs of wood and doubled as a home for the family that ran the store. At the portico of the cabin was the liquor shop, where different brands of rum, whiskey and brandy were neatly arranged on varnished shelves. To the right of the liquor shop was a larger room stocked with colourful shawls, sweaters, mufflers, monkey caps and smart jackets exclusively for women, made of leather, suede and even fur.

Ti Bhutia, who ran the shop, lived in the cabin with her husband Sonam Gyatso and their two sons. As soon as I entered the store, she welcomed me with a bright smile and asked me to look around and choose whatever caught my fancy. When I informed her that I was a writer and keen on interviewing her, the middle-aged woman made no effort to hide her indifference and asked me to wait, as she was busy with customers.

'Are all these products made in China?' I asked her.

'That's right,' she replied. 'They come from across the border. Where else would we get them from?'

Before I could formulate another question, Ti was asking me

to wait for her in one of the rooms behind the store; she would be ready to give an interview only when there were no more customers to attend to. By then, it was snowing heavily and bright white patches had formed strange patterns on the metal rooftops, along the rough edges of rocks and on roadside curbs. Despite the weather, at least half a dozen private vehicles had arrived in Kupup and its passengers were heading straight to Sonam's.

Spotting the huge influx of customers, Ti rushed out to greet them, leaving me to wander from one room to another. Right behind the clothing store was the Bhutias' living room, which also served as their bedroom. I paused here and peered in. At the far end of the living area were two bedsteads with thick mattresses arranged next to one another. A pile of half a dozen woollen blankets, neatly folded, lay on the beds. In the centre of the room was a giant Tibetan-style metal fireplace, with a tall chimney that allowed smoke to escape through the roof. A few feet from the fireplace stood a two-seater sofa; settled comfortably on it and warming his hands was 15-year-old Tenzin. It turned out that he was also a native of Kupup village and a classmate of Ti Bhutia's second son Thuptin, who was studying in class X at a private school in Gangtok.

I introduced myself and asked him what he was doing at Sonam's.

'I just came by to help my friend Thupkin and his family with the store,' Tenzin replied in fluent English. 'It is awfully cold here.'

He looked too young and small for his age, but seemed more enterprising than anyone I had met so far in Kupup. Tenzin told me that his father worked as a contractor with the army, coordinating labour in road-building projects and other civic activities in Kupup. His mother was a homemaker.

In a remote village like this one with few sources of income generation and even fewer luxuries, the relations between the Bhutia, Lepcha, Sherpa and other Nepali families were harmonious and peaceful, unlike in the bigger towns. Until the international border at Nathu La was thrown open for trade in 2006, there were few visitors to the village and the families living here had not had much of an income.

'Now we get a steady flow of tourists and that brings in more money,' Tenzin said. 'When the pass closes for the winter months, we go down to Gangtok where we also have homes.'

As I chatted with the boy, Ti Bhutia's son Thupkin entered and offered me black tea. Taller and more mature-looking than his classmate, he informed me that while his mother ran the shops, his father Sonam and his elder brother kept shuttling between China and India to bring goods from there at an advantageous price.

'In fact, even as we speak, they're off to the market to buy winter clothing and other goods for that season, as the pass will close in a month's time.'

For the next half an hour, the two boys shared everything they knew about Kupup. Ti's family was among the 100-odd ones who called the remote Himalayan village their home. Unlike other villages situated at lower altitudes, cultivating the land in these parts was not possible due to the extreme weather conditions. Locals mainly depended on rearing horses and yaks to make a living. The village market in Kupup consisted of those few businesses that had prospered since the trade route was reopened. Until then, Sonam's used to be one of the few shops in Kupup that sold mostly booze, rum in particular, to soldiers posted at the camps nearby.

After trade resumed between the two countries and the Sherathang market came up, Ti and her family had begun to make good money by importing clothing and other accessories from China. Tourists who came to Nathu La and Baba Mandir usually stopped by to purchase authentic Chinese stuff at lower prices than were available elsewhere. Thupkin's father Sonam Gyatso was among the few Indian traders who had the licence to cross the border and import goods from the Chinese markets in Yadong county, located about 30 to 40 kilometres from Nathu La, where he purchased goods in bulk and brought them to this side of the border. Apart from their country home and shop in Kupup, Sonam and Ti also owned a shop in Gangtok, where they sold the bulk of their goods to visiting tourists.

I asked Thupkin if he was interested in their family business and would like to be actively involved in running it when he grew up.

'No way!' came the emphatic reply. 'It's too cold out here. I want to become a software engineer and work in Delhi.'

Tenzin also felt that Kupup was too cold and remote a place for him to settle down.

'I will probably come here and settle down when I grow old,' he said. 'But while I am still young, I would like to travel across India.'

I asked him if he would like to go to China which was so close to their village.

'No way! Not to China,' he replied.

Outside, snowfall had intensified and owing to the wind chill, the temperature had dropped by at least ten degrees. Suraj came running into Sonam's and announced in an urgent voice that we would have to leave immediately. There was some danger of the road getting snowed in. If that happened, we would have no option but to spend the night in his car. After waving a hurried good-bye to the two boys, I ran to the car with Suraj and we set out on our return journey.

Meanwhile, more tourists were arriving in Kupup in their Sumos, Tata Innovas and other luxury cars to shop at Sonam's. But it was clear that they would not be able to linger for long in such weather. When they departed, the locals and soldiers camped out in Kupup would huddle under piles of blankets or squeeze themselves into sleeping bags to make it through the night's bone-chilling cold. Thupkin and Tenzin would soon retire to their bedrooms and continue to stoke the fire to keep warm, while the cold winds blew over their log cabins and more snow fell on their metal roofs. And this would be the relentless routine, night after night, for the next six months.

# 6

# Jaigaon

The most indelible experience from my brief but memorable stay in Jaigaon, a congested little town perched on the banks of the Torsa River in West Bengal along the country's eastern border with Bhutan, is of waking up in my hotel room every morning, setting out to cross the international border and hike up a hill in Bhutan, as if the foreign terrain were just a joggers' park in my neighbourhood, before returning to India for breakfast – that too with no border checks or requests for identity documents on either side, no queues and the access gates for the border crossing wide open round the clock!

I would step out of my hotel on N.S. Road at around 6.30 a.m., turn right towards Bhutan Gate, an ornate structure in the typical Bhutanese-*dzong* style of architecture that stood about 200 metres away, walk through the international-border check post to the left of Bhutan Gate, past two armed Bhutanese guards, who greeted me with a curtly polite 'Good morning', and enter Phuentsholing, the town on the Bhutan side of the border. The entire exercise took me less than ten minutes.

Even at that hour, Jaigaon was bustling with life. Buses, tourist cabs and autorickshaws available for hire on a share basis clogged the arterial N.S. Road, scouting for passengers, while pushcart eateries, where fresh puris and parathas were being rolled out, fried and served with hot *sabzi* to hungry customers, claimed the remaining space. The pavements were abuzz with vendors selling tea, coffee, biscuits and cigarettes out of their bicycle carriers and tourists waiting with their luggage to board long-distance buses.

On the other side of Bhutan Gate, the scene was usually far

more tranquil. The roads were wider, cleaner and less congested. The vehicles visible at that hour were mostly private cars in which upper middle-class Bhutanese parents were taking their children to school. Most of the shops still had their shutters down. The first batch of officegoers – generally middle-aged Indian men and women, who lived in and around Jaigaon, but worked in various offices in Phuentsholing – crossed the border, along with me, and headed to their workplaces.

It took hardly a couple of minutes for me to reach a four-way junction, with a majestic view of the Himalayas. Although I was less than a half a kilometre from the Indian side of the border now, I felt as if I were far away in a more prosperous country.

At the junction, I turned left, as usual, and walked towards a bridge that straddled a mighty river. When it turned turbulent during the monsoon, this great watercourse, carrying snowmelt from the Himalayas, would spray the bridge with pristine droplets, leaving its road surface slippery-wet. Standing right next to the bridge was a green notice board, which stated: 'Welcome to the Himalayan Kingdom of Bhutan. Dorti Khola is sacred and the lifeline of Phuentsholing. Let us join together in protecting it.'

Crossing the bridge, I passed a Buddhist *gompa* on my left and the Phuentsholing Bus Terminus to my right as I took the winding hill road that ascended steeply to a school run by the Bhutan government. On the way, I passed the offices of two major hydroelectric power projects in Phuentsholing: the Punatsangchhu–II Hydroeletric Project and the Mangdechhu Hydroelectric Power Project.

By now, more people were joining me on the road: Indian men in plain, full-sleeved shirts and dark trousers carrying colourful backpacks; Indian women in sweaters worn over bright saris and salwars, leather handbags slung over their shoulders; Bhutanese men in denim jeans and jackets, Bhutanese women wearing bright red lip gloss to set off their national costume – the many-hued *kira*, a figure-hugging, ankle-length dress, worn with a light outer jacket called a *tego* slipped over a *wonju* (blouse). Constrained by the sleek lines of their *kira*, these local women took small, dainty steps as they climbed uphill with ease, chatting with their friends all the way. Hurrying past these women, I, on the other hand, would be gasping for breath, as if I had an urgent appointment at the hospital; and by the time I reached the entrance to the government hospital at the top of the hill, I would be dripping with sweat, despite the nippy air. From that vantage point, the view of the river cutting across the grey, densely populated plains was so breathtaking that I never tired of spending time in that spot, although I had been going there every single day and should have grown accustomed to it.

In less than thirty minutes, I would be back at Bhutan Gate and ready to enter India, my lungs filled with the pristine mountain air, my muscles toned after the long, tiring walk, my skin wearing a healthy sheen after flushing out all kinds of toxins and my brain soothed through a release of endorphins.

Walking past the guards of the Royal Bhutan Police, I would enter Jaigaon, only to be greeted, a few feet from the check post, by a middle-aged beggar suffering from acute elephantiasis, his right leg so swollen and its skin so ruptured that I had to turn my eyes away in revulsion from the festering sores after barely a glance. Ignoring the unfortunate man, I walked directly to a roadside cigarette shop on Link Road, where I bought a Gold Flake Kings cigarette. Lighting up, I inhaled the smoke, turning again to gaze at the Himalayas, knowing quite well that I could smoke with impunity on this side of the border. In Bhutan, however, both smoking and the sale of cigarettes were banned and violators of the law were punished with a hefty fine. While the smoking ban seemed perfectly justified on the other side of the border, releasing a little carbon dioxide and nicotine into the Indian air did not, somehow, seem like a sin on Jaigaon's Link Road, where the dust and pollution were as natural as the sight of a beggar with a diseased, monstrously swollen leg.

By this time in the morning, Jaigaon was truly awake. All the retail outlets were open and the endless trail of Maruti Omni vans, Tata Sumos and autorickshaws available for hire on share basis plying from Jaigaon to various destinations had almost completely blocked N.S. Road. The dust rising from the poorly paved roads as buses and other heavy transport vehicles sped to different parts of India was nearly choking. I placed my usual order of four rotis and some *sabzi* from a roadside pushcart vendor for ₹40 and had a very satisfying meal standing there on the pavement, before returning to my room by 9 a.m.

I did nothing else during the first few days of my stay in Jaigaon. The brisk morning walks, followed by a cigarette and the usual roadside breakfast, almost seemed like work, considering what I would be doing for the rest of the day. After returning to my room, I spent the next few hours surfing TV channels, dipping into a few pages of the novel I had not been able to finish reading even after a fortnight and taking a little nap before heading out to Bhutan Gate again in the afternoon. By then, the bars and liquor shops present almost everywhere in Phuentsholing would be open. After downing a couple of Druk beers at one of the cheap restaurant-cum-bars, I enjoyed a quiet siesta on the bench of a neatly maintained park attached to a Buddhist shrine.

In the evening, I returned to Jaigaon and took a stroll along the busy market area, going back to Phuentsholing later for a few more drinks before hitting the sack. Needless to say, I loved every minute of my stay in this particular border town. I felt like I was finally getting a grip on the Bhutanese pursuit of Gross National Happiness (a term coined in the 1970s by the fourth king, Druk

Gyalpa (Dragon King) Jigme Singye Wangchuk who abdicated in favour of the current monarch, Druk Gyalpa Jigme Khesar Namgyel Wangchuk, in 2006) in place of a focus on the Gross National Product.

* * *

On the third day of my stay in Jaigaon, the manager of my hotel called me to enquire when I planned to check out. My blissful state and aimless wanderings had obviously worried him.

'No tourist stays in Jaigaon for more than a day. Indian tourists spend a night here and then leave next morning for Thimphu and Paro. Similarly, Bhutanese tourists on their way to Kalimpong, Dharmasala and Darjeeling halt here for just one night and leave early the following morning. The only reason I asked you about your plans was because it's unusual for us to have tourists spending more than a day here,' he said apologetically. 'You can stay here as long as you like.'

I could hardly blame him for doubting my intentions. I had to do better than just go for morning constitutionals, have beer lunches and get sloshed in the evening, I told myself. It was not as if I followed this routine mechanically, oblivious to the town I was in or to the people around me. While Jaigaon had initially seemed to me like any other town in rural India, with its unpaved roads, paan-stained pavements, aggressive beggars and noisy shopkeepers, I had sensed the subtle differences that lent this border town a more cosmopolitan vibe. And the process of awareness had begun well before my arrival.

The Bamanhat–Siliguri passenger train is usually crowded even before it reaches Dinhata railway station on weekday mornings. More officegoers, college students and villagers board the train at Dinhata, leaving the coaches packed, until it reaches New Cooch Behar (NCB) Junction, where most of the passengers alight and the train practically empties out.

Painfully crushed in the crowd until the train reached NCB station, I was thankful for a single seat by the window and travelled comfortably through the rest of the journey, enjoying the rural Bengal landscape, resplendent in all its lush and fecund beauty after repeated nocturnal monsoon showers. My fellow passengers now were mostly poor villagers and small-time vendors on their way to the state's less prosperous northern parts. I was probably the only passenger in the entire train in shorts and t-shirt, with a flashy backpack in tow.

When the train reached Alipurduar Junction at around noon, the profile of the passengers began to change. On that sultry afternoon, the station was teeming with groups of trendily dressed young girls and boys who boarded and alighted from the train at will and kept moving restlessly from one coach to another. Around fifteen minutes after the train's arrival in Alipurduar, a young woman entered our coach and took the single seat opposite mine. A little on the plump side, she had large, attractive eyes and must have been in her early twenties. She wore a denim skirt with a red top and her hair was neatly tied back in a ponytail. From the time she sat down, facing me, we had caught each other's eye. Though I felt a little strange doing it, I continued to gaze at her. She stared right back at me. I wanted to say, 'Hello,' just to ease the awkwardness of the situation, but refrained from doing so, as I felt most Bengalis from this region were not comfortable with the Hindi language. Meanwhile, the train had remained motionless at the junction due to some track fault. The woman and I kept staring at each other, occasionally turning to look out of the window for a break.

Sometime around 12.30 p.m., three more girls, younger and leaner, entered the coach and surrounded the woman sitting opposite me. Two of them were in jeans and tight tops, while the third – the most petite one – wore a black skirt with a khaki shirt.

All four giggled and chatted among themselves for a while, then quietly got off the train before it left Alipurduar station. When the locomotive finally started moving out of the station, I noticed that the girls were still on the platform. In fact, there were several such groups of pretty young girls and restless teenage boys roaming around aimlessly at most of the railway stations that we passed through after Alipurduar.

At the Hasimara railway station, I boarded an autorickshaw plying on share basis to Jaigaon. As the vehicle passed the Hasimara market area, my attention was drawn, once again, to groups of trendily dressed young boys and girls, their hair streaked in different shades, hanging around street corners. They looked shockingly out of place in their impoverished surroundings, which seemed caught in a time warp.

The road from Hasimara to Jaigaon is flanked on both sides by tea estates, where thousands of migrant Nepalis are employed. Most of the passengers who share the autorickshaws plying this route are workers from these plantations; tourists and visitors on official government work usually hire private cabs. Midway through my autorickshaw journey, a middle-aged Nepali woman passenger got off and handed the driver 20 ngultrums (the Bhutanese currency). The man happily pocketed the fare in foreign currency and continued with his journey. Surprised at the sight of Bhutanese currency changing hands in India, I asked the driver if he accepted ngultrums as well as Indian rupees.

'Oh, it's no problem,' he replied. 'In the border areas, it is a common practice for people to use both currencies. I go across to the other side every day. I'll use the ngultrums in Phuentsholing.'

When I reached the bazaar area in Jaigaon, I was taken aback by the number of Bhutanese men and women shopping on a weekday afternoon. They happily purchased Indian products and paid for them in their own currency, before returning to their country across the border without being subjected to any kind of checking. I saw little Bhutanese boys, dressed in their traditional *gho*, cross Bhutan Gate and enter their hometown Phuentsholing, after attending school in India. The pavements around the bazaar were lined with mobile eateries selling piping-hot momos, vegetable and chicken rolls, chow mein, rotis and parathas which, I discovered, the Bhutanese relished. Within a few hours of my arrival, I knew that I was in an exciting place.

These, however, were no more than casual observations. I had not yet engaged in conversation with a local. So breaking away from my usual evening routine of pointless window shopping at the Jaigaon bazaar, I went to a swank coffee shop in Phuentsholing, close to the Zangtho Pelri Lhakhang shrine. I had been keen on going there from the day I first set eyes on it, for it was easily the most chic café in the Jaigaon/Phuentsholing area. It had tastefully decorated interiors, a pastry bar, with an arrangement of chairs and tables on the ground floor, and a plush restaurant-style set-up upstairs. In keeping with the ambiance, the menu too was truly international, offering a wide range of dishes and beverages, from masala chai to pizzas, burgers and even some Italian delicacies. I ordered a cappuccino and savoured it as I listened to soft classic rock. The soothing ambiance, subtle lighting and friendly staff made it such an enjoyable experience that I could not help expressing my appreciation to the young waitress at the pastry bar. She pointed at once to a middle-aged woman outside the café who was chatting with her friends and said, 'The owner would be really pleased to hear it from you personally.'

I stepped out, approached the lady, introduced myself and complimented her for opening such an elegant café in a small town like Phuentsholing. I added that I was keen on finding out more about her and the town where she lived. The woman turned to exchange a glance with her friends and burst out laughing.

Then she introduced me to the clean-shaven, sophisticated, middle-aged man sitting next to her, adding that he might be a more appropriate person to answer my queries.

Jigme Tsering was 55 years old and had been living in Bhutan for the last 47 years. Jigme's parents had moved from Darjeeling to Phuentsholing when he was just a year and a half and his father took up the job of an accountant with the Bhutan government. Barring a brief period in between, the family had been living in the Himalayan kingdom since then. After introductions and an exchange of visiting cards, Jigme and I went off to a restaurant nearby so that we could chat without any interruptions. Over the next half an hour or so, the hotelier took me back to a time when Phuentsholing was just a frontier village and he himself was a mere toddler clinging to his mother's hand.

In those days, this yet-to-develop Bhutanese town was the only entry point to India. Jigme remembered his parents saying that the town of Phuentsholing had only come into existence sometime in the 1950s, after the Bhutan government decided to build a road connecting this point of the country's border with India to the Bhutanese capital of Thimphu.

'It was the only road connection with India at the time and the biggest office in Phuentsholing belonged to the highway-construction department,' he said.

Having failed to find sufficiently qualified people among their own citizens, the Bhutan government had employed several Indian citizens from Darjeeling, Kalimpong and the surrounding areas to work on the highway project. The road-construction department staff and the labourers hired to work on the road needed groceries, clothes and other essentials, which brought the first traders to Phuentsholing from mainland India. Mostly from Bihar, these men set up shops in the border town and imported goods from the larger Indian cities to be sold here. While Jigme's father took up a post with the road-construction department, his mother and grandparents ran a shop that sold horseshoes, household utensils and sandals, among other items.

'We lived in the middle of town and our shop stood at the entrance to our home. Back then, I remember Phuentsholing being a cluster of no more than nineteen shops, including the one owned and run by my family,' Jigme reminisced.

His family, along with their fellow traders, had been living here for decades, with the second and even third generations continuing to run the business set up by their forefathers.

With no officially demarcated land boundary existing between India and Bhutan in those days, it would not even have occurred to the original traders who had settled here in the 1950s and 1960s that they were living in a foreign country. The road connecting India with Bhutan was constructed sometime during the mid-1960s and a diminutive check post, built of bamboo, on the Indian side would be the only indicator of an international border, until the majestic Bhutan Gate came up a decade later.

While there were at least nineteen shops at the time in Phuentsholing, Jigme went on, continuing with his account, there were barely any traces of a town in the area where Jaigaon was now located. It was only in 1974, during the construction of the Chhukha Hydropower Project, the oldest mega power project in Bhutan, that Jaigaon would begin to develop as a town. It would expand further in another few years while work on the construction of the Tala Hydropower Project was in progress. Since those engaged in the construction of the two dams were Indian nationals, all the wholesale and retail shops set up in Jaigaon were primarily intended to cater to their needs, supplying hardware, utensils, electrical items and other goods necessary both for the power projects and for those employed to execute them.

During his early years in Phuentsholing, Jigme did not perceive it to be any different from the area on the other side of the border and would freely shuttle between the two places with his friends, completely oblivious to the fact that they were living in a border town. When the children were old enough to go to school, Jigme's parents sent him to a boarding school in Kalimpong. He would visit the family only during vacations. There were no schools at the time in Bhutan providing quality education on par with some of the convent schools in Darjeeling and other hill stations patronized by the children of India's British rulers and most Bhutan-based children of Jigme's age attended schools in India. If the child happened to be a Bhutanese citizen, it was the King of Bhutan who often sponsored his or her school education.

'If you talk to Bhutanese citizens in their fifties or sixties,' Jigme said, 'you will discover that they all received their schooling in India, as the education system in Bhutan was still in its nascent stage.'

After graduating in hotel management in India, Jigme returned to Bhutan and settled in Thimphu, joining its fledgling hotel industry and doing well enough to soon make his way to the capital's top star hotel, where he would work for over sixteen years, interacting with some of the most influential people in the kingdom as well as dignitaries from across the world. During this period, Jigme got married and fathered a son. As custom dictated, the boy was sent off to a boarding school in India when he reached school-going age. When Jigme's his son completed his schooling, the hotelier returned to his birthplace Darjeeling in 2001 with the intention of settling there permanently.

Meanwhile, the quaint little town that had taken baby steps into the world with the construction of the Thimphu–Phuentsholing Highway had grown significantly over the years as the only accessway for goods being transported to Bhutan from

India. With business thriving, Phuentsholing was about to become a major trading hub. Gradually, the number of tourists arriving in Bhutan also increased, making Phuentsholing an important overnight halt both for Indian tourists and visitors from faraway countries seeking to explore the kingdom. In fact, Pasakha, one of the largest industrial towns in Bhutan, is just 17 kilometres from Phuentsholing and most people living in the border town are associated with the industrial town in some way or the other. Phuentsholing is also home to Tashi Commercial, one of Bhutan's biggest corporations, and to several other private firms providing employment to thousands of Bhutanese citizens.

The twin cities of Phuentsholing and Jaigaon that developed around the same area on either side of the border now present an interesting phenomenon: Indian nationals looking to spend quality time with their families or interested in buying quality products prefer to patronize restaurants and shopping outlets in Phuentsholing, while thousands of Bhutanese citizens from Phuentsholing flock to the busy market area in Jaigaon, firm in the belief that quality products are available on the Indian side of the border at more reasonable prices.

While Phuentsholing was coming into its own, Jigme and his family, having lived for several years in Bhutan, were finding it impossible to adapt themselves to Indian living conditions in Darjeeling.

'I simply could not settle down,' he admitted. 'India was so polluted and life there was so hectic. Besides, the competition was cut-throat and running a business in Darjeeling was far more difficult than it would have been in Bhutan. Also, the standard of living is, in general, much better in Bhutan. So after a stint of about eight years, I returned to Phuentsholing and settled here.'

Jigme was now working as a consultant in the hospitality industry and helping young entrepreneurs set up hotels in and around Phuentsholing. He enjoyed the quieter life that Bhutan offered. However, it was unlikely that the country's stringent citizenship laws would allow him to become a Bhutanese national in his lifetime; he would have to continue renewing his work permit to live and work there. He claimed, nevertheless, to be content living in the border town, getting the best of both worlds.

* * *

The next morning, I went out in search of some of Jaigaon's oldest residents, keen on learning if they were as content and satisfied with their lives here as Jigme seemed to be with his across the border. My quest left me shuttling between N.S. Road and M.G. Road at least a couple of times, before I eventually landed up in front of the outlet of textile businessman Pushkar Ojha in the basement of a shopping complex on N.S. Road. When I informed him that I was writing about Jaigaon, the lean, slightly stooping middle-aged man with a pencil-thin moustache and oiled, neatly parted hair immediately invited me in and settled down for a chat.

Pushkar recalled how he had come all the way to Jaigaon from his native village in Rajasthan in search of a livelihood. A cousin who had preceded him and set up a business invited Pushkar to join him. In 1981, the year of his arrival, the bazaar hardly comprised of 25 shops along N.S. Road and M.G. Road, the town's two arterial thoroughfares. These retailers mostly dealt in electrical goods and hardware. There were also 200-odd hawkers who had set up roadside shops along the highway, catering to the needs of cargo vehicles on their way to Bhutan or returning from there. Bhutanese farmers brought potatoes, onions, beetroots and other crops they had harvested in the hills to sell them in the market here; on their way back, they would purchase clothes, shoes, electronic goods and other items with the money they had earned in Jaigon. The growth of Phuentsholing, Pasakha and other towns close to the border infused fresh life into the market in Jaigaon. Pushkar's family was among the first few to tap into this demand. With business booming, they were able to establish themselves in a matter of years and settle down to life in this border town.

In those early days, there were just two or three concrete homes in all of Jaigaon; the rest of the dwellings were little cabins built out of logs of wood chopped from the forests in the hills nearby.

'We faced any number of problems,' Pushkar recalled. 'Unavailability of potable water was the biggest of them all. In those early days, we had to cross over to Bhutan to fetch water from the river for drinking, cooking and so on. The fact that people had to travel long distances to collect water discouraged many from settling here with their families.'

In 1985, local panchayat leaders installed hand pumps in two locations, from where the general public could collect water for drinking and cooking purposes, providing much-needed relief for locals who had been going all the way to Phuentsholing to collect water. A few years later, the local body also built an overhead water tank in Mangalwadi and began supplying water from it to all homes in the area through pipes, thereby solving this critical problem for good. With regular water supply assured, more shops began coming up on N.S. Road and M.G. Road. By 1988–89, a number of Indian businessmen had come down to invest in Jaigaon, thereby setting it on the road to further development.

Due to the availability of clean water, cheap land and quality educational facilities, people started flocking here and soon, Jaigaon's population and that of its surrounding areas grew manifold. Sometime during that period, Pushkar and his two brothers, who had already established their business by then, decided that it was time to bring their families down from

Rajasthan. Jaigaon's growth and development were, in fact, so rapid that many of its available civic amenities could not match the pace and began falling short. But Jaigaon still continues to be, primarily, a trading centre for Bhutanese farmers whose dealings constitute 80 per cent of the business in the market, while tourists and locals generate the remaining 20 per cent.

Over the past few years, though, businessmen in this border town have been an aggrieved lot. The biggest problem their community currently faces in Jaigaon is related to currency exchange between the two countries. The ngultrum, the Bhutanese currency, is officially pegged to the Indian rupee and freely exchanged all over Bhutan for Indian currency, with the exception of ₹500 and ₹1000 notes. Until 1974, Bhutan had no national currency to speak of and with most of the Himalayan country's industrial development and trade being carried out in collaboration with India, the Indian rupee was used for all transactions. As of now, the ngultrum is in circulation in denominations of 1, 5, 10, 20, 50, 100 and 500, all of which can be readily exchanged for Indian rupees and vice versa on both sides of the border. With an open border between the two countries and the currencies of both accepted by shopkeepers on either side of it, my own wallet was full of Bhutanese currency, as it was rare for people to return change in Indian rupees in the border areas.

Until recently, Indian traders accustomed to receiving payment in ngultrums from their customers enjoyed the privilege of opening accounts in Bhutanese banks where they could deposit their earnings in the Bhutanese currency. Subsequently, they were allowed to avail of a banker's draft in Indian rupees of the money in their accounts so that they could freely use it in banks across India.

The situation, however, changed a few years ago, according to Pushkar, when the Bhutan government withdrew this facility, preventing Indian businessmen from opening accounts in Bhutanese banks. Moreover, the draft facility was no longer available to those Indians who already held accounts in these banks.

'Now the situation is such that if we accept payments from our Bhutanese clients in ngultrums, we cannot deposit the money anywhere,' Pushkar explained. 'Nor can we exchange it for Indian rupees. The trouble is that our clients only carry money in ngultrums and we have no option but to accept it.'

The traders' association had apparently contacted the governments of both countries to sort out the issue amicably and had insisted on a currency-exchange counter being opened, where they could legally exchange the Ngultrums for Indian rupees.

'If the government does not do something about this soon, trade will come to a standstill and the market in Jaigaon will shut down,' Pushkar warned.

Confronted by this impasse, the traders had apparently gone back to the barter system by which Bhutanese farmers would sell their produce to Indian wholesalers who extended them credit, thereby enabling them to buy whatever they needed from other shops on the Indian side of the border.

'But trade thrives only in an open environment,' Pushkar went on, 'and if the [Bhutan] government imposes restrictions on the currency we use and does not provide us with the facilities to exchange it, many shops will be forced to shut down and their owners will set up the same business elsewhere.'

The issues, however, were not always related to the currency-exchange matter. Pushkar claimed that lately, Indian traders were facing other hurdles in doing business in the Himalayan country, because the Bhutan government had become less generous about granting them the necessary permits.

'Now the government has put a number of restrictions in

place that prevent us from supplying goods even to a client based in Thimphu or Paro, unless he first sends us a formal invitation letter,' Pushkar elaborated. 'If a businessman who has sent goods to customers in Bhutan wishes to visit the country for collection of dues, the only way he can have an entry pass issued to him is to disclose the names of his clients and submit the dues-collection bills to the [Bhutanese] immigration authorities. We are expected to produce copies of our trade licence every time we visit Bhutan. All these new rules are creating major hassles for Indian traders from Jaigaon. Our main grouse against the Bhutan government is that while their citizens are allowed free passage to any destination in India, there is no reciprocal arrangement for our own citizens who wish to travel to Bhutan. Why should Indians alone be asked to apply for a permit? Why should so many restrictions be imposed on our businessmen?'

He added that while Indians were allowed to live in Phuentsholing and its surrounding areas, extending up to three-odd kilometres from the border, travelling beyond that point was prohibited, except with a permit issued by the Bhutanese immigration authorities at the border.

On a personal level, however, the situation was heartening. According to Pushkar, Indian businessmen shared an excellent rapport with the Bhutanese. In fact, he personally knew so many who had chosen to live in Jaigaon, while working in Phuentsholing, as rent was lower in India. Likewise, Indians craving a little peace and quiet preferred to live in Phuentsholing, despite the slightly higher rent, because the quality of life in the Bhutanese border town was superior.

I asked Pushkar if he was happy about living in Jaigaon and would want his children and grandchildren to continue doing so.

His reply was emphatic. 'No, I want to go back to Rajasthan when I retire,' he declared. 'In fact, my children are pursuing their higher education in other cities. While members of my generation have somehow managed to make Jaigaon their home, given the present circumstances, I don't think it would be wise for the younger lot to invest in this place and settle here. The situation is no longer what it used to be and even if it were, this is, after all, a border area and much depends on the nature of the relations between the two neighbouring countries. It's best not to get caught up in these things.'

* * *

Like the mornings, my evenings in Jaigaon too followed a steady routine from day one. Within an hour of checking in, I had found out from the hotel room service that there was neither a bar nor a liquor shop anywhere in town. One had to go to all the way across the border to Phuentsholing to buy booze legally or even to unwind over a drink in a decent bar. Obviously, I found no reason to linger in Jaigaon after sundown.

On my first night there, I left for Phuentsholing at around 7.30 p.m., although the skies had opened up and rain pounded the border town, bringing some respite from the heat. Unfurling my large black family-size umbrella that looked sturdy enough to withstand the force of even Himalayan rain and wind, I walked straight into a seedy little bar in the basement of a shopping complex close to Bhutan Gate. I had spotted this place earlier that evening, while out on a stroll along the streets and lanes of Phuentsholing to take stock of all the watering holes in town. I had found that every third establishment had a 'Bar Open' sign prominently on display. However, most of these bars were no more than disreputable extensions of dingy homes, equipped with a couple of tables and about half a dozen chairs, where a few popular brands of liquor were sold. The slightly more respectable-looking ones had flashy neon name boards that proclaimed DJ nights and karaoke music as added attractions. I chose the one that was tucked away in a corner along the highway to Thimphu, simply because it was secluded.

Reaching the four-way junction on that rainy evening, I heard female voices giggling outside the karaoke bar. Glancing in that direction, I noticed at least four young girls huddled together outside the bar's large front entrance, sharing a cigarette. In their late teens at the very most, they were smartly dressed in denim jeans or short skirts, with tight tops in dark hues that glittered under the lights. The fact that they could flout the local ban on smoking so openly intrigued me and I headed directly for the bar's entrance, furling my wet umbrella and placing it out of the way in a corner. Having smoked their cigarette, the girls returned to the bar.

What surprised me when I stepped inside was the size of the establishment. Although tastefully done up and illuminated, the single-room lounge could not have measured more than 15 feet by 10 feet. There were three tables in all, wedged into different corners of the room and standing perpendicular to one another. Three sofas were grouped around each of the tables. A wide-screen TV was mounted on the far wall and to my right stood a compact bar counter, where two young women were busy serving drinks to the customers. Sitting close to each other at the table nearest the bar and drinking Druk beer was a group of seven or eight men, all in their late teens or early twenties. The girls I had seen earlier occupied the table parallel to it. The third table at the far end, closer to the TV, was unoccupied.

As I made my way to it, one of the young men, clutching a mike, was belting out a number from the 1980s Bollywood movie *Disco Dancer* to loud cheers from his friends. '*Yaad aa raha hai tera pyar*,' he sang, in sync with the words that appeared on the TV screen. In fact, he sang it so well that I too couldn't help cheering him when the song ended and everyone present broke into loud applause.

Then another youngster grabbed the mike and asked the bartender to key in the code for yet another number from the 1980s – these boys seemed to know even the codes by heart! – and burst into song, even as the group of girls giggled and booed him.

Once the second song was over, one of the girls asked for the mike and launched into a romantic English number. The boys ordered more Druk beer and chicken tikkas. For a while, the mike remained with the girls who kept singing the same song over and over again. Yet, no one seemed exasperated by the repetition. I was somewhat surprised to note that none of the young men present ogled the girls or made lewd comments, let alone make a pass. All they did was drink beer, enjoy their snacks and wait for their turn to sing their favourite songs.

By around 9.30 p.m., all the girls had left. The places at their table were taken by two slightly older couples, who asked for the mike as soon as they came in and tried, with a singular lack of success, to sing Bollywood duets together. The boys were all so drunk by now that they chatted loudly and made no further attempts to sing.

Around ten, when I paid for my drinks and walked out, the two couples and the group of boys were still there. Outside, I could see young men and women in trendy outfits standing together in corners or walking back home in groups. Some of them hitched rides with friends who had cars, while the rest made it on foot.

I walked back to Bhutan Gate and proceeded to my hotel in Jaigaon, amazed at how different this town was from Phuentsholing, though the latter lay just across the border. Even back home in Chennai, a much larger city, I had never seen a group of girls go out on their own, unescorted by male companions, and have fun late into the night without being accosted or harassed by strange men. Girls down south were present in groups at posh pubs and night clubs, but would never have been found in little bars such as this one, especially so late in the evening. In this Bhutanese border town, groups of girls simply walked into a bar, enjoyed their drinks, sang songs and generally had a good time, without having to fear censure or harassment.

Back in Jaigaon, the shops and restaurants had shut down for the day. The roads were deserted, except for random groups of tourists smoking and chewing paan and policemen patrolling the pavements, lathi in hand. I could not spot a single woman out on the streets.

* * *

The next evening, I visited the same bar a little earlier and found myself to be the very first customer. The lights on the neon signboard had just been turned on and the two young female bartenders of the previous night, it seemed, had arrived minutes ago. As I entered the place, the two were setting out cocktail glasses and arranging the liquor bottles in place. The girl who had been serving drinks last evening gave me a smile of instant recognition.

'Would you like to repeat the same order?' she asked.

I nodded and went directly to the table at the other end of the lounge where I had sat earlier. The girls turned on the karaoke system, checked both the mikes by humming their favourite tunes for a while, turned on the air-conditioning units and sprayed lavender-scented room freshener all over the place before serving me my drink.

When they seemed to have settled down, I approached the bar counter for a chat. The two, who were in their early twenties, introduced themselves as Dorji and K.T. (the girl explained that her real name was too complicated for non-Bhutanese to remember and suggested that I use its abbreviated form instead, to address her). While Dorji was lean and pale, with a sharp nose, delicately sculpted lips and shiny black hair, K.T. was broad-shouldered and on the heavier side, with gleaming, yellow-toned skin, a stubby nose and thick lips coated with red lip gloss. She came across as the friendlier of the two. The girls confided that they preferred to work as part-time bartenders in the evenings, simply because they both loved Hindi film songs and working in karaoke bars gave them ample opportunities to sing. During the day, Dorji attended classes to complete a beautician's course as she aspired to have her own salon. K.T., on the other hand, said that she dreamed of being a singer some day. Assisting the two women in the kitchen was a five-man team of support staff which also served in the capacity of bouncers in case of trouble at the bar. The owner of this facility had three other bars in Phuentsholing and made occasional visits to ensure that everything was running smoothly. Otherwise, Dorji and K.T. were in charge.

Like other Bhutanese youngsters I encountered in Phuentsholing, K.T. and Dorji spoke little English, but were fluent in Hindi and Nepali. They watched Bollywood movies, listened to Hindi film music and were addicted to the never-ending soaps that Indian TV channels dished out with relentless regularity. Dorji even declared that *Kyunki Saas Bhi Kabhi Bahu Thi* was a bigger hit in Bhutan than in India and I had every reason to believe her, as every time I peeked into a shop in Phuentsholing, Zee TV or some other Hindi channel would be telecasting a soap and there was an avid audience for it. Popular contestants in super singer reality shows were household names here and songs rendered during the live singing competitions were a big hit in karaoke bars across the Himalayan kingdom. Both Dorji and K.T. confirmed that most local youth religiously followed these programmes and frequented the bars primarily to sing Hindi songs exactly the way they were sung in such contests. Bhutan was probably the only foreign country where Shah Rukh Khan and Deepika Padukone were more popular than Brad Pitt and Angelina Jolie. While film productions in Dzongkha, the national language, were on the rise, they were not as popular as Bollywood fare, as most local movies were cheap imitations of Bollywood melodramas from the 1980s and 1990s.

Since both Dorji and K.T. loved to sing and I was still the only customer around, I requested a few songs from them. The women happily obliged, choosing '*Aap jaisa koi meri zindagi mein aaye*' from the 1980 hit film *Qurbani*. The two sang so well together and their voices were so perfectly synchronized with the music that the karaoke system gave them a score of 9.8 out of 10, with some loud applause to round it off. By then, more customers had started to trickle in and I returned to my table to sit and enjoy some retro Bollywood music. Couples and groups of young men dropped in, ordered Druk beer and went for the karaoke mike. There were more performances of Hindi and English songs and an increasing number of empty beer bottles began accumulating on the tables. There were fewer girls present this evening, but some Indian customers did stop by.

A large sardar ji, who looked like a giant next to the petite Dorji and K.T., came in at around 9 p.m. After drinking a couple of rounds of whiskey, he sat near the bar counter and asked for the mike to try a Kishore Kumar number. Realizing, however, that none of the other customers were particularly impressed by his performance, he stopped midway. The mike went, once again, to a Bhutanese couple, while the sardar ji gulped down a few more drinks and left. All the while, I enjoyed my drinks and listened to retro Bollywood. When it was time to leave, I tipped the girls lavishly and promised to return the following evening.

Work held me up over the next two days and on both days I

visited the bar a little later in the evening. After 8 p.m., the place was really crowded and the two girls I had befriended earlier were so busy serving drinks, communicating food orders to the kitchen staff, selecting songs on the karaoke system and shuttling between the kitchen and the bar counter that they hardly had any time to talk. Yet, Dorji and K.T. welcomed me with broad smiles and my preferred drinks were served without my having to utter a single word. I already felt as if I had been a regular there for ages and the girls, especially K.T., seemed friendlier by the day. She would gaze at me while singing songs, occasionally sit at my table, as there were rarely other customers sharing it, to enquire about the quality of the food and service and generally seemed to be warming up to me. While bartenders are generally expected to be friendly with their customers, K.T. seemed a little too solicitous, almost flirtatious. Having spent several solitary weeks travelling on my own, K.T.'s tender smiles and attentive gaze had drawn me to her and I longed to see her more often. But I hardly got to spend much time with her, as she was busy until the bar closed for the night.

To make up for my lack of conversation with K.T. over the past few evenings, I set aside all my other work the following day and landed up at the bar at 7.30 p.m. sharp. K.T. and Dorji had just arrived and were cleaning the bar counter and setting up the glasses and liquor bottles as usual. Other than the two girls, there was another man behind the bar counter. Bald, clean-shaven and muscular, he wore a black leather jacket with denim jeans.

I approached the girls and greeted them. They reciprocated with their lovely, welcoming smiles, before turning to the bald man and introducing him as the owner of the place. Then K.T. introduced me to him as the 'uncle' from Chennai, 'you know… Chennai, of *Chennai Express*'. Highly excited by my association with that city, the bar owner asked me if Chennai really was the way it had been shown in the movie. I answered that I hadn't seen that film and wouldn't know. After that evening, I stopped visiting the bar.

* * *

Towards the end of my stay in Jaigaon, I decided to go on a day trip to Thimphu. I had read and heard so much about this beautiful city nestled in the Himalayas and come so close to it that I did not have the heart to return home without visiting it once, even if it were only for a day. As I have mentioned earlier, visitors intending to visit Bhutan and proceed three kilometres or so beyond Phuentsholing must apply to the immigration office near the border for a travel permit. For Indian nationals, a valid identity document and a photograph are enough. So armed with a passport-size photo and a copy of my voter identity card, I set off for the immigration office late on a Thursday evening.

Finding the office closed, I approached the extension counter next to the main office that remains open for tourists intending to travel to Bhutan outside business hours. After filling in the necessary form and attaching a photocopy of my voter identity card to it, I went to a counter where three young men sat browsing the Internet. They ran their eyes down my form and directed me to another room, where an official of the Bhutan government, dressed in a mustard yellow *gho* with a colourful muffler wrapped around his neck, sat behind a large desk, staring at a computer screen.

He scrutinized my application and said, 'So you want to go to Thimphu?'

'Yes sir,' I replied.

'And why do you want to go there?'

'Oh, no particular reason, actually. I was visiting Jaigaon and thought of going on a day trip to Thimphu.'

'Where is your family?'

I replied that I was travelling alone.

'So you're travelling alone to Thimphu. Why would you do that? We don't issue permits to single travellers.'

I asked the officer how it would matter to the Bhutan government whether I travelled alone or had a partner accompany me. But the officer remained adamant, firm in the conviction that there could be no legitimate grounds for single men to visit Thimphu. The more I tried to reason with him, the more annoyed he seemed to become. Besides, his Hindi was not easy for me to comprehend.

So leaving the situation at an impasse, I returned to my hotel room, picked up my passport and brought it right back to the immigration office to show the recalcitrant official how many countries I had visited so far, just to prove that I had better things to do than travel to the Bhutanese capital, find a local girl and settle down there with her. The official still would not budge from his position. It was only after I had presented my Press Card and handed over a photocopy of the same did he agree to issue me a tourist permit for visiting Thimphu and Paro. On my way out with the coveted permit, I learnt that I could have spared myself all the trouble with a simple fib: I could apparently have told that official that my family members had already left for home or were arriving a day later.

The next morning, with the permit document safely tucked inside my back pocket, I boarded a Coaster Bus for Thimphu from the Phuentsholing Bus Terminus. Other than a few honeymooning Indian couples and myself, the passengers were all Bhutanese nationals returning home to the capital for the weekend.

The road from Phuentsholing to Thimphu offers breathtaking vistas of high mountains, mist-filled valleys, dense forests and gushing waterfalls and rivulets all through the journey. But after the first halt at the immigration check post, where I had to present my permit for inspection, a thick fog obscured the view so that all I could see was a few white clouds clinging to the mountain slopes. Occasionally, the fog cleared and I could spot small villages consisting of clusters of shabby log cabins and government offices built in the traditional *dzong* style, with bright-hued walls and a roof that perched atop the building like a colourful fisherman's hat. Buddhist prayer flags and poles planted on the edge of steep, rocky cliffs enhanced the overall air of mystery in which the country seemed shrouded.

It was evening when the bus cruised into Thimphu. I checked into a hotel in the centre of town, near the Thimphu Clock Tower, and immediately returned to the streets to fit in some souvenir shopping, before the usual nocturnal showers began. A casual visit to any of the shops in Thimphu would have been enough to reveal why Jaigaon was so popular with the Bhutanese. The prices charged here for goods were unreasonably higher than they would have been for products of similar quality in India. An ordinary souvenir like a fridge magnet, for instance, cost a minimum of Nu. 300, while a key chain that would have been available for less than fifty bucks in India didn't come for less than Nu. 200 in Thimphu. Even a bottle of drinking water cost a great deal more here.

I was casually walking in and out of several art and crafts shops and gift outlets, searching for an appropriate souvenir, when I first spotted them. At first, I mistook these smooth, elongated toys for some cute Buddhist artefact. Only on closer scrutiny did I realize that these long, smooth, pinkish objects were actually penises carved out of wood. It appeared that after fridge magnets and key chains bearing scenic photographs of Thimphu and the Himalayas, the penis or phallus was the most popular Bhutanese souvenir in every local gift shop! They were available in different sizes too: big ones that could be mounted on the wall, table-top phalluses or phalluses meant to serve as paperweights and even little ones made of sandalwood, rosewood and ivory that could be attached to key chains.

Having recovered from the initial shock of seeing so many representations of the male organ on public display, I picked up a little pink phallus attached to a key chain and asked the saleswoman about the significance of this organ in their country. She explained that it was a symbol of fertility in Bhutan and was popularized by a crazy saint called Drukpa Kunley. Known as the 'Divine Madman' for his unorthodox ways of teaching Buddhism through the use of songs, humour and outrageous behaviour with sexual overtones, Drukpa is also alleged to have advocated the use of the phallus as painted symbol on the walls of Bhutanese homes to drive away evil spirits.

'Weird, isn't it,' the saleswoman remarked. 'You want to take it home?'

There was a naughty smile on her lips as she assessed my discomfiture at such a question.

Eventually, I chose not to buy it, as I could well imagine the reaction if I gifted such a toy to a family member or friend. I also did not relish the prospect of being caught back home in Chennai – or anywhere else but Bhutan – with a toy or souvenir of this kind in my wallet or luggage. But I think it was at that moment that I fell in love with the Bhutanese for their simplicity and honest approach to life, traits we Indians, who have been worshipping the phallus or *lingam* for so many centuries, seem to have lost.

Like Phuentsholing, Thimphu also seemed very much like a partygoer's paradise, with bars, snooker parlours and pubs spread across the city. Apart from these regular watering holes, at least a dozen or so posh night clubs came alive only on weekend nights and on select days of the week for the diehard party crowd. Since I was there on a Saturday night, I could hear music thumping past the apparently sound-proof halls of sports bars and lounges as early as 7 p.m.

I was returning to my hotel room on Norzim Lam Road, when I heard loud strains of unfamiliar music coming from the corner of a dilapidated building. I decided to check out the source, as there was no signboard outside and the place didn't seem like a regular pub. A rustic wooden door with its outer plywood sheet half peeled out opened into a dimly lit hall, where low tables and benches were neatly arranged. A tall young woman dressed in a maroon *kira* was standing on a stage giving instructions to a DJ, while a group of even younger women, mostly in their late teens, sat next to each other on a bench near the entrance. To the right of the stage was a little bar.

As I entered, the smell of cheap perfume mingling with the musty odour of an ageing godown overwhelmed me. Before I could even approach the bartender, a slender woman, neatly dressed in a navy blue *kira* with gold embroidery, her face plastered with make-up, came up, held my hand and began talking to me in Dzongka. Although I did not understand a word of what she said, I could now hazard a guess as to the kind of place I had entered. The woman pulled me closer and led me to a table near the bar where the two of us sat down. I noticed that I was the only customer present and presumed the place to be some kind of a hostess club. I ordered a couple of Druk beers for the two of us and tried talking to the woman in Hindi. My companion, who went by the name of Kino, replied in broken English and urged me to request a song for which I would have to pay so that she could dance. I could not understand why I had to pay money for a woman – that too a fully-clothed one – to dance on stage.

Even as I argued the point with Kino, another young woman

came up and sat down next to me. Telling me that I could address her as U.T., she began explaining in slightly better English than Kino's how the bar operated. I finally understood that I was in a club where men paid anywhere between Nu. 100 and Nu. 300 for a lady dancer of their choice to perform on stage to their favourite song from a Dzongka film, while enjoying their drinks. In other words, it was a dance bar, except that the girls would perform only if the customers paid for each dance.

U.T. coerced me into paying Nu.100 to the club manager so that she could dance to a Dzongka song with which I was completely unfamiliar. The song, a slow number similar to a Bollywood melody, was played and U.T. went up on stage, faced me and started dancing. With her *kira* tightly wrapped around her body, she could just about manage to bend her knees, shake her hips a little and rotate her wrists – all in the name of dancing. All through the song, she stood at the centre of the stage, moved her wrists and fingers, occasionally bent her knees and shook her head, a big smile directed at me. I felt the whole thing was nothing but a rip-off.

After the song was over, the other girls crowded around me as well, trying to get me to pay for another song. I walked up to the manager, who spoke decent English, and announced that I was not interested in the dancing.

'What is it that you actually do? Is this a pick-up joint?' I asked him.

Realizing that he had not quite grasped the meaning of my words, I asked him more explicitly if a customer was allowed to take any of the girls home with him.

'Oh,' he said. 'I'll check with the girls and let you know.'

I returned to my seat, finished the beer and hurried out, for by then, the girls were becoming really persistent. As I was leaving the club, however, the tall woman who had been issuing instructions to the DJ earlier, approached and asked me to return at around 11 p.m., by which time, she promised, there would be a crowd. She also informed me that a new night club, the most happening one in town, apparently, had opened across the street. It would open at 10 p.m. I thanked her and stepped out into Thimphu's lashing rain.

A little after ten that night, I returned to the club I had visited earlier, as the tall, pretty woman had suggested – but not before ensuring that I had removed my identity cards, credit and debit cards and other important documents from my wallet and left them behind in my hotel room. I was expecting the young women at the club to swarm all over me again.

When I entered this time, a modest crowd of around thirty young men had gathered to drink and watch the dancers perform. To my surprise, none of the girls who had pestered me earlier approached me or even smiled at me, although I recognized most of them. I stood for close to ten minutes at the entrance, waiting to be invited in, but the waitresses and dancers seemed to avoid me purposely. So I went up to a table where a chair was vacant and sat next to a group of young Bhutanese men who were busy drinking and chatting among themselves. Another ten minutes went by and still none of the waitresses had approached to take my order. Finally, I got up and went to the club manager to complain that I had been waiting for half an hour at the table without a single person turning up to take my order.

He looked at me and laughed.

'Oh, you're back?' he said. 'If no one's gone up to take your order, it's probably because I told the girls what you'd asked me about them earlier.' Then he winked.

I returned to my table with a beer. A young man with bushy hair who was sitting next to me introduced himself as Kimzong and asked if I was from south India. When I told him that not only did I belong to that region, but was from Chennai, his face lit up.

'I lived in Chennai for four years and studied at the Alpha Engineering College' he said enthusiastically. 'I have good friends there and love the city.'

After completing his engineering course, Kimzong had returned to Thimphu. He now worked for the Bhutan government. He was 25, still single and lived with a group of friends in Thimphu, while his parents lived in a village not too far from the capital. Kimzong confided that he and his friends partied at least three or four nights in a week. I could not help asking him why they had chosen to come to this bar, in particular, and pay good money merely to watch these girls just stand there and twirl their wrists and fingers animatedly to Dzongka movie songs.

'These girls are poor, no?' he countered. 'They do this for a living. If we don't give them money and encouragement, what will they do? But this is not the only place we frequent. After spending some time here, we will go on to other pubs.'

I remarked to Kimzong that he and his friends were very nice people, indeed, and left the dance bar.

By now, Thimphu's nightlife had gathered steam and groups of young men and women were out on the streets. Most were dressed in tight-fitting black shirts, tops and jackets. I walked past the partying crowd to the new night club the woman from the dance bar had recommended. The place was located across the narrow street.

The bouncers at the entrance allowed me in after frisking me and collecting a cover change of ₹350, which included two complimentary drinks. Although it was a little past 11 p.m., there were at least two dozen local women on the dance floor, shaking and rocking to the latest pop music. In comparison, there were fewer men at the club at that hour. The average age of the guests was less than twenty-five. The only ones who were around thirty-five or older were Indian men. They were trying hard to impress the Bhutanese women with their fake smiles and the awkward, jerky manner in which they swayed their hips. It was quite obvious that these men, who all belonged to my age group and probably had a wife and kids back home like me, were not there just to dance.

After watching them for a while, I went to the bar, gulped down my two free drinks and left. On my way out, I met Kimzong and his friends, who were getting the fluorescent stamp on their hands that would permit them to enter the club. We greeted each other again and he advised me to be careful while walking back to my hotel.

'It's not very safe here at nights,' he warned. 'You know…crazy guys. In Chennai, my local friends would protect me from crazy guys. Now, it is my turn to return the favour.'

I thanked him for his words of caution and walked back to my hotel. On the way, my thoughts turned to the Bhutanese official at the immigration office who had made it a policy to refuse permits to single male Indian travellers. It had annoyed me then, but in retrospect, I couldn't help feeling that he had a point.

# 7
# Tawang

I arrived in Tawang on a cold October night when this little Himalayan town, perched at nearly 10,000 feet above sea level in North-West Arunachal Pradesh, lay shrouded in darkness. The roads and pavements were deserted, the shops all shuttered and locked for the night and the homes indistinguishable from one another, with not a sliver of light escaping through their windows. There was nary a soul in sight.

After fumbling around in the dark for a while, I spotted a policeman on patrol near the Old Market area who directed me to the hotel where I had booked a room.

I walked into the hotel's reception area and was filling in my particulars in the guest register under the pale glow of an emergency lamp, when the owner of the establishment, a young man who looked to be in his late twenties or early thirties, informed me that there was a power outage scheduled every evening between seven and nine. Apologizing for the inconvenience, he assured me that the power supply would be restored in an hour.

It was extremely cold. The first sensation I became aware of as I reached the room assigned to me was the numbing chill that seemed to not only cut through my denim jacket, but also my skin and bones. I had expected Tawang to be cold, but this teeth-chattering experience, especially indoors, was not something I had prepared myself for. To add to my misery, none of the rooms in the hotel had any kind of heating equipment. So all I could do was crawl under the bed's neatly laid covers (a pair of comforters and a woollen blanket), without removing my jacket or shoes, and lie there immobile for more than an hour until the power supply was restored at 9 p.m.

It had been a long, exhausting day. The muscle-crunching journey from Tezpur in Assam's Sonitpur district had begun at 5.15 a.m. The tour operator from whom I had purchased a ticket to Tawang on the previous afternoon had informed me that the Tata Sumo would leave at 5.30 a.m. and urged me to be ready at least fifteen minutes ahead of the departure time. He had also agreed, in lieu of some extra cash, to arrange for my permit document to visit Tawang. Shortly after five, I got a call from the driver of the Sumo and I was sitting in the middle row of the vehicle, along with two other men, fifteen minutes ahead of schedule. After picking me up, the vehicle roamed around Tezpur to pick up more passengers from various locations and all the seats had been filled up by the time we left town.

The distance of 320-odd kilometres usually took fourteen hours or more to cover because of the winding, badly maintained mountain roads that we had to navigate for much of the stretch. Until a few years ago, the state government had operated a regular commercial helicopter service between Guwahati and Tawang through Pawan Hans Helicopters Limited, allowing tourists and locals, who could afford the hour-long trip, easy access to the border town. However, following a series of helicopter crashes in 2011, including the one that killed the state's chief minister Dorjee Khandu and four others on 29 April that year, the services had been suspended. They were briefly resumed in 2013 in some sectors, only to be discontinued again because of renewed safety concerns. With no access to Tawang by air, tourists as well as locals had to endure the arduous journey to reach the scenic hill town.

Our first scheduled halt en route was at Bhalukpong, a small town located on the Assam–Arunachal Pradesh border around 52 kilometres from Tezpur. The tour operator had informed me when I boarded the vehicle in Tezpur that my permit – without which I could not enter Arunachal Pradesh – was with Ravi, the driver. As we were approaching Bhalukpong, I asked Ravi for the all-important document. His response was to bring the Sumo to a halt about 50 feet from the barricaded check post and suggest that I cross the border on foot.

'If they ask to see your permit,' he said, 'just tell them it is with the driver and that you will be able to show it to them after having breakfast. Your permit will be ready by then.'

It turned out that I was the only tourist among the Sumo's passengers. So I stepped out of the vehicle alone and walked past the barricade and into Arunachal Pradesh, unnoticed by the soldiers manning the border check post who were busy going through the papers of the occupants of another SUV.

As advised by Ravi, I had my breakfast and returned to the Sumo, which had, by now, crossed the border into Arunachal with its local passengers. I asked him for the permit again. The driver now informed me that since we had already crossed the border, I no longer needed a permit, as nobody would ask to see it. At this, I protested vehemently, refusing to get back into the vehicle and resume the journey until he handed over my permit – for which I had paid ₹200 extra to boot. Ravi then made a few calls from his cell phone. After a twenty-minute wait, a motorist arrived with my permit. Now armed with the document, I got back into the Sumo and we were on our way.

The road beyond Bhalukpong followed the course of the Kameng River, a major tributary of the Brahmaputra, and passed through hilly terrain dotted with colourful little hamlets comprising of a few dozen homes, some grocery shops and a handful of eateries. The condition of the road deteriorated markedly as it climbed, with certain stretches stripped of their tar surface almost entirely and scarred with potholes. Further impeding our progress were the long convoys of army trucks from the Vehicle Factory, Jabalpur, that moved so slowly uphill that our driver, frustrated by the delay, began yelling at the army drivers for not giving him right of way.

Other than Ravi, there were ten of us packed into the Sumo which was now bumping and creaking its way past Bomdila, Dirang and other hill towns. Two young women sat in the front, four of us occupied the middle seat and another four were in the rear seat – all belching from the undigested, oil-soaked puris and potato curry we had eaten that morning. All along the road were memorial stones laid by the Indian Army for the thousands of soldiers who had either lost their lives in combat and in road accidents or had simply succumbed to the region's harsh weather conditions. The names of the deceased officers and jawans inscribed on those stones ranged from that of K. Karuppaiah, a man from the south who had been part of the 4 Corps Operating Signal Regiment and had lost his life on 17 October 1999, to that of Jaswant Singh Rawat from Punjab, who had been awarded the Maha Vir Chakra for his exemplary valour during the 1962 war with China and in whose name a war memorial had been erected about 14 kilometres from Sela Pass. The heavy militarization of the region was also evident in the number of army units and regiments we passed on our way. Besides the army and the Sashastra Seema Bal (SSB) (formerly, the Special Service Bureau) other paramilitary units had also set up their camps along the hills.

Despite the distance we had to cover and the poor condition of the roads, the charming Buddhist villages and the panoramic vistas of mountains, valleys, forests and river ensured that the journey seemed less monotonous and gruelling than it actually was. While dense shrub forests carpeted the lower slopes along the course of the river, offering breathtaking glimpses of numerous little waterfalls, the vegetation became sparse as we headed closer to Tawang, where the soil was reddish brown, with the occasional rocky patch gleaming in the evening sun. The only green cover we saw on the upper slopes consisted of clusters of army tents erected close to water bodies.

We climbed all the way to an elevation of roughly 13,700 feet, reaching Sela Pass at around 4.30 p.m. Ravi halted the Sumo here for a little while, with the tranquil Sela Lake as a backdrop, for us to don our woollens and drink some piping hot tea to fortify ourselves against the biting cold. The crystal-clear lake that mirrored the surrounding mountains and their rugged, snow-capped peaks was also known as Paradise Lake, with justification, for the visual feast that lay before me seemed marked by a certain timelessness, as if nothing had changed here since prehistoric times.

As we carried on to Tawang and the sun began its descent, the temperature started to dip rapidly. By the time we had reached the Old Market in Tawang, another three hours later, the temperature had plunged to a single digit and wind was blowing in powerful gusts.

As promised by the hotel owner, the power supply was restored at 9 p.m. sharp. Despite the numbing cold, I jumped out of bed and rushed to the bathroom for a wash after the long journey along dusty roads. I switched on the geyser and waited by the hot-water tap, divesting myself of all clothing as I kept checking if the water was warm enough for a comfortable bath. At precisely that moment, the power supply went off, plunging the town into darkness again. I was left naked and freezing in that icy bathroom, before the water had even had a chance to heat up.

Ditching the idea of a bath altogether and cursing the Arunachal Pradesh power department, I rushed back into the room and put on the thickest winter clothing I had brought with me. Then I rushed downstairs, determined to go out and find the nearest bar, where I could gulp down enough whiskey to keep myself warm. On my way out, I sought suggestions from the guy at the reception. He recommended a lounge bar just outside the hotel, the only bar, apparently, that would still be open in Tawang at the unearthly hour of 9.30 p.m.

I hurried out of the hotel, crossed the road and raced to the lounge bar, only to discover that the owner had just locked up and left for the night, as no customer had turned up since 8 p.m.

Disheartened, I went back to my room, consumed the meal of chicken chow mein I had ordered, sipping on warm water in between, and went to bed, burying myself under three thick blankets and ensuring that neither head nor toe was uncovered. And that was how I spent my first night in the sleepy little town near China.

* * *

The first thing I did the next morning on waking up at around ten was to turn on the geyser in the bathroom after making sure that the electricity supply had been restored. Fortunately, the power supply remained uninterrupted and I was able to manage two buckets of hot water and enjoy the luxury of bathing in peace and relative comfort. Outside, the eastern sun shone bright above the rugged mountain slopes, turning them orange brown, while the dark pine trees below turned sepia green in the early morning light. The air was crisp and cool, with an occasional mild breeze.

By the time I stepped out of the hotel, Tawang had already bounced back to life. Dozens of Maruti Omni vans were parked at the Old Market Square opposite my hotel. Their drivers stood around, chatting in little groups. All the shops in the market area that had been shut last night were now open and doing brisk business. A board put up by the local body outside the market carried a map of Tawang town. Next to it, a signboard warned would-be transgressors that driving vehicles without a licence plate was an offence punishable by law.

Inside the market, several old Monpa women sat on an open platform, surrounded on all sides by colourful brick walls, with a Buddhist shrine at one end, and sold fresh vegetables, fermented cheese balls and other farm produce.

The Old Market ended where the relatively new Nehru Market began. The latter consisted of fewer shops, beyond which the road turned downhill towards residential neighbourhoods. Buddhist monks, Indian Army soldiers, tourists and permanent residents of this scenic town that offered a spectacular view of the surrounding mountain ranges walked up and down the narrow pavements of these bazaars, shopping for essential items and generally enjoying the warmth of the afternoon sun. The market area, as well as the town, in general, were distinguished by an abundance of liquor shops. One in every five stores was either a liquor outlet or a regular shop that sold alcohol, along with other provisions. The market area was also dotted with a number of small eateries serving mostly traditional Indian food, besides chow mein and momos, and trendy bakeries that displayed cakes and pastries in different colours, shapes and sizes. There was also a sizeable number of stores specializing in army supplies that catered to the large population of soldiers stationed in and around the town.

While I considered the presence of armed forces personnel in significant numbers an invasion of privacy where the residents of this quaint little tourist town were concerned, the locals themselves seemed to be least bothered. Soldiers of different ranks roamed the streets of Tawang as if it were a part of their camp. One would find them at the cobbler's, in hairdressing saloons and even at street corners, where they stood around chatting in pairs or trios. Apart from the soldiers and ethnic Monpas, several migrants from the plains had also settled in Tawang in recent years to cater mostly to the tourist crowd. In fact, most of the shops in the Old Market and in Nehru Market were run by migrants from Assam and other parts of India.

The town, along with the district of Tawang, was predominantly inhabited by members of the Monpa tribe. Of the 50,000-odd Monpas in Arunachal Pradesh, more than 95 per cent lived in the Tawang and West Kameng districts. Apart from their presence in these areas, there was a significant Monpa population in China (or the Tibet Autonomous Region, as it is known). In fact, the tribe was listed as one of China's 56 recognized ethnic groups. Devout and spiritually inclined, the Monpa were followers of the Gelug or Gelugpa sect of Tibetan Buddhism of which the current Dalai Lama is the religious head. Buddhism seemed to be firmly entrenched in Tawang and unlike in other northeastern states like Mizoram and Meghalaya, where religious conversions had taken place in large numbers in days gone by, a church or a mosque was hard to come by here.

Since it was my first day in town, I spent all afternoon strolling down the streets aimlessly, getting some suntan and giving my limbs adequate exercise after having spent the previous day cramped inside an SUV. Barring a few smiles and nods of acknowledgement exchanged with the locals, I did not get an opportunity to interact with anyone, although everyone in Tawang seemed to speak fluent Hindi. By around three, dense clouds obscured the sun and the temperature began to plunge. Purchasing enough snacks and booze for the night, I returned to the hotel by 5 p.m., well before sundown, and decided to stay put.

Later that evening, I would meet Tenzin Dorjee, the owner of the hotel, at the reception again. He was busy poring over the day's accounts. I remembered him checking me in the previous evening when I had arrived and assuring me that the power supply would be restored by 9 p.m. I stopped by now to share my unhappy experience of trying to take a shower last evening and nearly freezing to death.

For a hotelier and a man of thirty, Tenzin looked awfully young and the spontaneous chuckles that broke through his shy demeanour every couple of minutes made him seem younger still.

'The power situation here is really bad,' he admitted, apologizing for the inconvenience it had caused me. 'What's worse is that the supply is erratic. Usually, after power is restored following the scheduled outage, it remains for some time, but yesterday, the situation was worse than usual.'

Along with his two brothers, Tenzin, the second oldest of the siblings, managed the hotel and a few other properties, while his father Yeshi Jugney took care of the shopping complex owned by the family. Until a few years ago, Yeshi had worked as a teacher at the Tawang Monastery School. It was during this period that he had gradually set up their family's hospitality business on which he trained his entire focus after retiring from his job. The family now owned two hotels along with the shopping complex in Tawang. His wife Dolma was a homemaker.

Like most youngsters in Tawang, Tenzin spoke fluent Hindi and English and dressed like a software engineer even in that weather. His light, full-sleeved shirt and matching trousers, worn with a grey pullover, his wide smile, the thin-rimmed glasses that perched above the bridge of his finely shaped nose and his pleasant manners could have qualified him for a job in the service sector in any large Indian city.

'Why would an educated young man live in a godforsaken place like Tawang, which can barely manage four or five hours of electricity every day and lies a good fifteen hours away by road from the nearest railway station or airport?' I asked him, after exchanging pleasantries.

I felt he could have lived anywhere in the country.

'Oh, I tried living in the plains for a while,' he said in reply. 'But I wasn't very happy there and moved right back. Here in Tawang, I feel at home.'

It was a feeling shared by most people from the North East when they migrated to other parts of India, he explained. For the next hour or so, Tenzin tried to share his insights into the India he had seen during his time in the plains and explain why he felt at home in Tawang.

If Tenzin Dorjee had been born a hundred years ago in undivided Tibet, he would have become a monk or *lama* in keeping with Monpa tradition which decreed that the second son of every family from the tribe should take monastic vows and dedicate his life to spiritual practices. His father Yeshi was, however, among the few educated men in the community and understood the value of scholarship. He preferred, therefore, to send Tenzin off to the Tawang Public School for his primary and secondary education instead of to a monastery.

On completing his secondary-school education, Tenzin attended the Tibetan Children's Village School in Dharamsala for pursuing his higher-secondary education. On its completion, he was eager, like most teenagers from this part of the country, to leave Tawang and pursue higher studies in a larger, more cosmopolitan city. A little networking and push secured the young man a seat at Bengaluru's Garden City College, where he would study for a B.Com degree.

From the day he landed in Bengaluru, along with a few friends from Tawang, however, Tenzin was made to believe that he was different from the local students and from those who came from regions other than the North East. He was told that if he valued his safety, he would have to confine himself to the company of students of similar ethnicity. Within a few days of starting college, he was inducted into a group of students that included girls and boys from the North East, Bhutan and other South East Asian countries. They respected the veiled warning they had been given and kept their distance from Kannadigas, Tamils and those from other parts of India with ethnicity different from their own. And it was just as well that they had heeded the advice they were given on their arrival.

Whenever Tenzin went out to the market for some shopping or to a movie theatre with friends, local bullies would call out to him, taunting him as a 'chinki' for his distinctive features. Policemen would stop his motorcycle at random and demand a bribe to let him off, even if he was carrying all the necessary papers. Even finding accommodation was difficult, as most folks in Bengaluru refused to rent out their homes to youth from the North East.

'There was always this fear at the back of my mind that if I ever got involved in an argument or a fight, I would be isolated and attacked, with no one coming to my rescue,' Tenzin confided. 'So I rarely got into an argument, even preferring to put up with harassment or ill treatment, rather than protest. I got along well with quite a few of the Thai and Bhutanese guys there, rather than with Kannadigas or people from Chennai. Since we all had similar features, we stayed in the same neighbourhood and would help one another out.'

In fact, the perennial sense of apprehension which haunted Tenzin and his friends during their years in Bengaluru was so deep-rooted that he confessed to never having dared to look at a pretty girl if she was not from the North East.

'Forget about having a Kannadiga girlfriend, I was afraid to even speak to girls from Bengaluru,' he admitted. 'Some of them were really nice and friendly too, but I could sense that they also felt awkward about hanging out with us. Somehow, our cultures did not gel. Ironically, I was – and continue to be – more Indian than any of those guys back then. Despite my mother tongue being Monpa, I can speak, read and write Hindi more fluently than most Kannadigas or Malayalis. Yet, we were made to feel like outsiders and had to fear for our safety.'

Be it on the sports ground or at college cultural functions or any other event at the institution, Tenzin added, boys and girls from the North East were always in a separate group and mostly kept to themselves. Group clashes and violent assaults were also common between the locals and boys from the North East.

'I have even had unpleasant experiences while going out with my girlfriend to a movie or a night club,' he went on. 'People somehow feel that if you are from the North East, you can be bullied.'

As Tenzin narrated one incident after another, describing the experiences that had scarred him, I could not help but empathize with the young man, because much of what he related was reminiscent of many such moments from my own life. Despite looking as typically South Indian as a boy possibly could, I had been taunted and harassed in my teens. So, I suppose, are most people in any corner of the world who do not merge easily with the crowd – too fat or thin, tall or short, dark or pale, among other things. But nothing could be more humiliating for human beings than to be discriminated against as an entire race because of their distinctive appearance.

The three years that Tenzin had spent in Bengaluru killed his fascination with big Indian cities forever. After completing his studies, he returned to Tawang to help his father run the family business. Six years ago, he had married a local girl, Sangey Lhanu, and the couple now had a daughter Tenzin Yangte, who was four years old and ready to go to school.

'But I do miss Bengaluru,' he confessed. 'It's become a habit since my college days to stay up late and browse the internet, listen to music or just chat with friends. I had never stayed up late until I went to college, but now I am unable to fall asleep until midnight. And that is when I get in touch with so many of my college friends from across the country.'

* * *

Of all the border towns I have visited so far, no other place manifests an eternal sense of antiquity quite the same way as Tawang. Despite the hotels that have come up, the popularity of the small bars, the growth of retail outlets and the influx of tourists, the town and its residents seem content to live forever in a distant past. The most potent symbol of this timelessness is the Galden Namgey Lhatse (loosely translated, it means 'celestial paradise') or Tawang Monastery, founded in the year 1681. Legend has it that the town and even the district in which it is located derived their shared name from the monastery itself.

It is believed that Merak Lama Lodre Gyatso had obtained permission from the fifth Dalai Lama – his religious head in Lhasa, Tibet – to build a monastery in this region and travelled far and wide, exploring this mountainous area in quest of an appropriate site. When he was too exhausted to travel further, Gyatso had tethered his horse to a tree and entered a cave nearby to rest and pray. Emerging from the cave after his prayers, he had found that his horse was missing and gone in search of it. He found the mare resting in a lush green meadow on the summit of a hill overlooking the surrounding valley that was dotted with villages. It took no more than a glance for Gyatso to realize that he had found the ideal location for the monastery he intended to build. And the circumstances surrounding the site's discovery would finally inspire the name that the monastery shares today with the town it overlooks. Loosely translated from Tibetan, 'Tawang' means 'the place chosen by the horse' (*ta* stands for 'horse' and *wang* for 'chosen').

The institution, which is run by the Gelug school of Mahayana Buddhism (to which the present Dalai Lama and his spiritual predecessors belong), stands atop a hill about three kilometres from Tawang's Old Market area and is accessible by shared taxis. I visited the monastery, designed in the classic oriental style of Tibetan Buddhist architecture, on a weekday afternoon, when the sun was shining brightly and the air was crisp and cool. Entering the complex through the colourful, ornate gateway was like stepping into a Shaolin temple movie set. A rugged pathway laid with irregular stone slabs led up to the monastery's main building that housed the library and a few administrative blocks. To my left was a metal pipe with running water that jutted out of a concrete wall; visitors were expected to wash their feet here. Beyond it stood the community health centre. To my right, a high compound wall separated the monastery from the rest of the town.

The pathway led to a flight of stone stairs that ascended to the library. A comparatively modern structure, with plush interiors and weather-proofed walls, the library was divided into two sections: one that stocked English books on Buddhism and the other, Bodhi texts. The librarian Lama Jampa Tsundu, whom I had gone to meet, was not in his office. I was told that he was resting and would return after lunch.

I came down the stairs and walked past damp limestone walls that had weathered the effects of extreme cold and strong winds for centuries, before climbing more flights of stairs towards a large, level area where the monastery school building was located. In the open courtyard it overlooked, young boys, ranging from three-year-olds to those in their early teens, draped in long maroon robes known as *thache* in the Bodhi language, played with one another. Since this was their lunch break, young *lama*s carried aluminum vessels containing rice and soup to serve the children, who yelled cheerfully in play and chattered loudly in their native tongue in sharp contrast to the town's locals who mainly spoke Hindi and, only occasionally, Monpa.

As I paused on the open ground to snap pictures of the child monks, one of them, his nose streaming, approached and greeted me with a mischievous giggle and a 'Namaste'. When I turned to take more pictures of the background, the little monk snatched my camera pouch from under my armpit where I had tucked it and raced off towards his friends. As I chased after him playfully, he turned towards the residential quarters and climbed down the steep stairs at a run. A senior *lama* who was passing by then caught hold of the child, pried my pouch out of his hands and returned it to me. The little acolyte promptly apologized for his act and ran back to his friends.

It set me thinking about these little boys whose lives and destinies had already been decided for them. Although they were naturally lively and mischievous like other children their age the world over, they were being trained to lead the lives of ascetics and mendicants. Cheerfully noisy and impulsive, as was natural at their age, they seemed to have no clue about what their future held. Unlike Tenzin Dorjee's educated father, who had chosen to break with tradition and send his second son to a secular school that would prepare him for a life outside the monastery, the parents of these children, mainly from impoverished villages, had preferred to follow the centuries-old custom of giving up their second son to a monastic life. It was a commitment they, as members of a close-knit community, had felt honour-bound to make, a commitment that also went a long way in preserving their unique culture and lifestyle. Coming as I do from a society where a child gets to decide even the colour of his underwear, I could not help but feel a little sad for these children who had been denied the privilege of choice.

I asked the senior monk who had retrieved my pouch where

I could find the librarian Lama Jampa Tsundu whom I had come to meet. He directed me at once to his *sha* (a building where a *guru* and his disciples live and study) in the residential quarters.

Unlike the library and the school buildings, the residential blocks were so archaic that I wondered if they had ever been renovated since their construction in the seventeenth century. The outer walls were made of huge blocks of stone, arranged one over the other. They had either never been painted or if they had, time and neglect had worn away the last traces. The wood from which the doors and windows set into those walls had been made was rotting with age.

The door to Lama Jampa Tsundu's residence was made of solid hardwood and fitted with a metal bolt whose sadly faded sheen almost made it blend with the timber it clung to. Suspended beyond the door was a large bell tied to a rope that jangled loudly every time someone pushed open the door, alerting the *lama* to the presence of a visitor.

Stepping in, I discovered to my surprise that the monk's residence was far more well appointed than it had appeared from outside. The sun deck on the first floor, in particular, with its spectacular view of the blue-green mountains in the distance, seemed straight out of a multi-star hotel.

Having just finished his lunch, Lama Jampa Tsundu was going through the notebook of one of his students when I introduced myself. Following Tenzin's advice, I mentioned his father Yeshi Jugney as the person who had sent me to the monk to seek answers to my queries about the monastery and to find out how close its ties were with the locals. On hearing Yeshi's name, Lama Tsundu's initial doubts were dispelled and he offered me a chair to sit as we settled ourselves on the patio.

The *lama* considered the monastery the repository of Tibetan Buddhism and its centuries-old culture. For him, it was a reminder of the life their forefathers had lived and a pointer to the one they had envisioned for their progeny. Unlike the current heirs of other ancient kingdoms, the Tibetan people continued to revere their religious leaders and looked up to His Holiness the fourteenth Dalai Lama as the spiritual head of the entire community. And it was his wishes that were respected in all monasteries run by the Gelug sect.

'We follow the *gurukul* system here,' the *lama* explained. 'Every new entrant to the institution is chosen by one of the *gurus* and is taken under his wing. The *guru* is expected to teach his disciples the fundamentals of religion and the rituals involved in its practice. While the school here teaches English, Hindi, Maths and other subjects, apart from the Bodhi language and Buddhist philosophy, each *guru* is responsible for teaching his *shishya* the tantric aspects of the religion.'

At present, the Tawang monastery has seventy *gelong*s or *guru*s who lived in individual *sha*s and were responsible for 530 young acolytes. Despite the unforgiving climate, the monastery began its day at 4.30 a.m. with morning prayers and other rituals and continued its activities until five in the evening. In winter, with fewer daylight hours available, the activities wound up earlier, but the monks continued to read, pray and meditate until 11.30 p.m. Other than the young initiates, several local children also studied at the school run by the monastery, with the institution hiring staff from outside as well for teaching various subjects.

Going by the information I gleaned from Lama Jampa Tsundu, I came to understand how closely bound the Tawang Monastery was with the lives of the Monpas. The locals, 99 per cent of whom were Buddhists, looked up to the monastery as the institution that upheld their culture and tradition. Lama Jampa Tsundu, who was now 49 years old, had joined the monastery when he was just thirteen. As the second son of a Monpa family from Sheru village nearby, Jampa did not really have a choice. Like all devout Buddhists, his family believed that becoming a monk was the destiny preordained for him.

Having studied in a local school until then, Jampa joined the monastery under the guidance of his *gelong* Sherpa Lama, who came from the same village. Under the guidance of his *guru*, Lama Jampa Tsundu studied at the monastery for the next seven years and completed class VIII. As the Tawang Monastery offered lessons only up to that level, Jampa was then sent to the monastery at Sarnath for further studies in Buddhist philosophy and spent the next seven years of his life there. Returning to Tawang after his studies at Sarnath were over, Jampa had been at the monastery ever since, coaching and mentoring dozens of young *lama*s and guiding them on their spiritual journey.

I asked him if he had ever regretted becoming a monk.

'Not at all,' he replied. 'I enjoy my life as a *lama*. Besides, I do have the option of leaving the monastery whenever I wish to. There have been so many young students who joined the monastery and left it after studying here for seven or eight years. Some leave within a year or two, while there are many others who leave at a later stage. Nobody forces you to become a monk. You are free to leave at any time.'

However, he did concede that when an acolyte decided to leave the monastery, he had to pay a fine to the institution for breaking off midway.

'It is like any other school,' the monk explained. 'You have to pay the penalty for leaving midway. Moreover, one can leave the monastery at any age, just as one can join it and become a *lama* at any age. Even you can join the monastery and become a *lama*, provided a *guru* here accepts you as his disciple.'

Before he could finish his explanation, two little acolytes clad in traditional robes came running to him with their notebooks and handed them over for his inspection. I peeped into one of ruled notebooks and saw sentences neatly written in English.

Lama Jampa Tsundu informed me that he had nine *shishya*s in his care. While three of them had completed their graduation, two were studying in class V. The remaining four had just joined his *gurukul*. All these young boys, who came from neighbouring villages, looked up to His Holiness the Dalai Lama for spiritual enlightenment and to Lama Jampa Tsundu for guidance.

After meeting Lama Jampa Tsundu, I went to the monastery's museum at the far end of the complex. The institution's 300-year-old history had been preserved here in the form of utensils, weapons, religious artefacts, clothing in addition to many other relics from the past. Each specimen was neatly preserved and protected in a glass case with a descriptive label. The museum had put on display photographs of all the dignitaries who had visited Tawang and made it a point to stop over at this important monastery. I too clicked some pictures outside the main shrine to commemorate my visit, before returning to my hotel.

* * *

Situated in a remote spot and completely cut off from all vestiges of civilization is the nunnery run by the Gelug sect. A narrow road that winds its way out of Tawang past numerous tiny streams and army tents and eventually ascends steeply to the top of a rocky hill leads to this institution known as the Brahma Dung Chung Ani Gompa.

I arrived at the nunnery early the next morning, even before the penetrating rays of the sun had gathered enough strength to clear the mist. At that hour, about half a dozen women in thick maroon robes, their heads tonsured, were busy chopping wood with a rhythmic swing of their axes and stacking the pieces in a huge pile several feet taller than them. From a distance, I mistook the pretty *anis* (nuns) for *lamas*, as they looked no different from their male counterparts but for the additional layers of clothing they wore. Accustomed to visitors and pilgrims, the women went about their work, unmindful of my presence.

I was visiting the nunnery with a local youth Tashi Dorji who had agreed to be my guide for the day. I had been advised to take along a local person for two reasons: first, the nuns might feel awkward in the presence of a stranger; second, they, along with the women living in nearby villages, might not be able to communicate in either Hindi or English, thereby making my interactions with them quite difficult.

Tashi was 23 years old and, like most young men in Tawang, quite clueless about his future. His parents, both of whom were in government service, did not want their only son to leave Arunachal Pradesh and work elsewhere. So after graduating in English Literature from a college in Mysore three years ago, the tall, wiry man had returned home. He had been unemployed since. Naturally, when Tenzin introduced him to me and asked him to be my local guide, he was more than willing to accompany me on my outings in a hired Maruti Omni van, the most popular mode of transport in Tawang for a ride around town.

As Tashi and I now entered the nunnery's compound, two young nuns, who could not have been more than ten, blew conch shells, producing a mellow 'Om' sound that reverberated across the complex, announcing the end of morning prayers. Behind them, standing on a stone pathway that led to the main shrine, a few older *anis* were busy issuing instructions to their disciples in Monpa. Tashi now approached one of the nuns, introduced me to her and explained the purpose of my visit. The *anis*, who turned out to be far more welcoming than the *lamas* at the main monastery, invited us into a large, empty hall with red oxide flooring, where low wooden stools had been set up along the four walls. My guide and I made ourselves comfortable on the stools and waited for an appointment with the head of the institution. After a few minutes, a young *ani* came in with a giant teapot and poured us two large cups of butter tea.

'This is a different kind of tea – a local speciality. Try it,' Tashi urged.

I took a sip and was surprised by its richness. The tea had been prepared in the local way, using yak butter and salt, instead of sugar.

'It's good for the health and keeps the body warm during winter,' Tashi explained.

But I could not bring myself to take more than a few sips. As the hot beverage made its way down to my stomach, I felt the fat from the butter greasing and clogging my arteries.

While we were waiting for the abbess to finish her prayers, a petite young woman with a bright smile and a cute dimple on her chin peeped out of the doorway that led to the kitchen and spoke to Tashi in Monpa.

'She says the head priestess might be late in coming and that it would be better for us to return later,' Tashi said, interpreting her words for my benefit.

I asked him if I could speak to her, instead, and when he conveyed my request, the young girl looked at me and nodded with a broad smile that deepened the dimple on her chin.

Ani Pema refused to divulge her age. But she did tell us that she had joined the nunnery when she was fifteen and had been living here for the past thirteen years. Unlike Lama Jumpa, Pema did not believe that a life of renunciation had been preordained for her. Back home in a village known as Sherba, young Pema had witnessed the ordeal women went through in their efforts to make a living and keep the kitchen fires burning.

'It was a hard life,' she admitted to Tashi in Monpa. 'In

comparison, the *ani*s who visited our village looked well nourished and seemed to lead better lives. It was they who inspired me to become a nun.'

Having devoted thirteen years of her life to the study of Buddhist literature and philosophy, young Pema had been elevated to the status of a *guru* and lived with her disciples in one of the nunnery's 19 residential quarters. A total of 19 *guru*s and 31 disciples now lived in this nunnery that was reportedly almost as ancient as the main monastery and had been built soon after the latter became operational. Since no tradition existed, as it did in the case of young boys, of girls from Buddhist families having to take a nun's vows and devote themselves to a life of renunciation, all the young *ani*s at this nunnery had been inspired by senior nuns who came from the same village to choose this way of life.

Two years ago, Pema's niece Tuten Namo, who was just six years old at the time, had chosen to join the religious order as a novice. She had expressed the desire to follow in her aunt's footsteps and once Pema accepted her niece as her disciple, the family had sent her to the nunnery without demur.

Little Tuten now lived in Pema's *sha* and adhered to the nunnery's strict routine. This eight-year-old *ani*'s day began at 3.30 a.m., when she had to rise and complete her morning ablutions before joining her fellow *ani*s in the main shrine for the mandatory *tso* or daily prayer starting at 4 a.m. The session continued till 8 a.m., following which the group dispersed for a quick breakfast in their *sha*. By 9 a.m., Ani Tuten would be ready to attend her daily lessons at the religious school situated within the nunnery and remain there until noon, when they broke off for lunch. After the break, the students attended additional classes, while their seniors were engaged in the activities of the nunnery or involved in discussions related to religious or spiritual matters with their *guru*s. The *ani*s returned to their respective *sha*s in the evening to prepare for the next day's classes. This routine would continue through the year, except on holidays and on the rare occasions that the nuns went out to the villages to visit their families.

Pema confided that she went back to her village to visit her family just twice a year and only for a few days.

'Other than that, I do not go anywhere at all and prefer staying here,' she added. 'Unlike the villages, the nunnery is a very peaceful place and we find a lot of contentment here.'

I asked Pema if we could meet Tuten Namo and have a little chat with her, but the little *ani* had gone off to school by then.

After Tashi had drained his cup of butter tea, we took our leave. In the courtyard outside, the young nuns were still busy chopping wood and storing the pieces in a pile for the winter months. I took out my camera, preparing to shoot a few pictures, but the women protested. An older nun came running and addressed Tashi in Monpa.

My local guide interpreted her words for me. 'These women disapprove of people taking their photographs and are asking you to put your camera away,' he said.

When I obliged, the *ani*s returned to their tasks, laughing as they did so. I asked Tashi what they had found so amusing, but he simply dismissed the matter and refused to elaborate further. I guess those young women were having a little fun at the expense of the crazy man who had come all the way to their remote nunnery from south India.

On our way back to town, Tashi and I discussed how difficult life must be for women in the hill villages. Ani Pema had chosen the life of a nun just to escape the backbreaking labour that ordinary rural women in these parts were condemned to. Her case, Tashi acknowledged, was quite common here, as most members of a religious order – male or female – who had chosen a life of renunciation came from poor families and were denied a better option.

In fact, the situation was not very different for Tashi, despite his college education and his relatively comfortable middle-class background. He too remained uncertain about his future. Government jobs provided the only stable source of income in Tawang and surrounding areas. With no real private sector to speak of, other than the tourism industry, most youngsters in Tawang resorted to driving taxis and vans for a living. The town's remote location, which made it essential to ferry in almost everything from the plains, other than the meagre agricultural produce indigenous to the hills, had fed the huge demand for goods vehicles and their drivers. Avenues for temporary work also opened up for the local youth during the tourist season, when the town's retail outlets did brisk business with the influx of visitors from other states and countries.

'Otherwise, there are simply no jobs to be had in Tawang,' Tashi declared. 'Even finding out if there is a vacancy somewhere is difficult here, as the newspapers printed in Itanagar take three days to reach Tawang. Internet connections are erratic at best and with barely any power supply available to watch even the daily news on TV, we hardly ever get to know what is happening in the outside world. Living in Tawang is like being cut off from the rest of the world. How, then, do we find a job or start a profitable business?'

* * *

If there is anything more to Tawang beyond Monpas and monasteries, it is the imposing presence of the Indian Armed Forces. Tall, well-built soldiers in military fatigues could be found almost everywhere in town at any given time of the day, talking loudly into their mobile phones in their native tongues, oblivious to those around them. While the overwhelming presence of soldiers could unnerve residents of any other small town in India, the locals here seemed to have come to terms with the sight of camouflage suits and assault rifles in their midst. In a way, the bulk of business in Tawang depended on these soldiers who constituted an important customer base. In fact, observing the marked increase in the number of soldiers, army tents and camp sites in and around town over the past few years, some locals even wondered apprehensively if another war was lurking around the corner.

Unlike most of India's border areas, the prospect of war was an imminent reality in the minds of those living in this particular border town. Everyone over sixty had endured its repercussions first-hand. Despite the prominent presence of soldiers and the dozens of lumbering army trucks carrying ammunition and other supplies to the front, people here seemed to sense that the build-up of forces across the border was far more intensive. Sandwiched as this region was between two rising military powers, the possibility of another war breaking out between India and China, and if it did, the question of anyone here surviving its aftermath at all, continued to haunt every educated youngster living in Tawang. This situation also warranted that the average individual in Tawang be clear about his loyalties. The interesting revelation was that despite sharing history, culture and even physical features with people on the other side of the border, the average resident of Arunachal Pradesh could not have been more Indian.

I found it reflected in the spontaneous enthusiasm with which people in Tawang manifested their affinity with all things Indian. Despite Monpa being their mother tongue, people here seldom interacted in their own language and preferred to communicate in Hindi. When I first arrived in these parts, I had expected to find nothing but Chinese food on offer. I was, therefore, taken aback by the discovery that most local restaurants served parathas, rice and dal, which even the indigenous population seemed to prefer. In fact, during a conversation with Tenzin, I had brought up the topic, confessing my surprise at finding this distinctive element of 'Indianness' in the locals.

Visibly upset, he had retorted, 'If there is ever a war between the two countries, every man in our community will stay and fight to defend India, more so, in fact, than those from the mainland. We love India and I can claim with complete confidence that we are more Indian than the rest of you.'

I would never have doubted that. I would even suggest that these simple, decent people are needlessly burdening themselves with the wounds of India's 1962 war with China. It had, according to North East analysts, very little to do with the people of Arunachal Pradesh and was actually the fallout of a failed policy. It is common knowledge that the Chinese People's Liberation Army had marched into the country through the Bumla Pass, made its way past Tawang and carried on all the way to Bhalukpong and beyond, virtually unchallenged by the Indian armed forces. But the plot goes much deeper and senior citizens here can vouch for it.

Until 1954, the region now identified as the state of Arunachal Pradesh was known as the North East Frontier Tract. Renamed and reclassified as the North East Frontier Agency, it would become a Union Territory in 1972 and, 15 years later, India's 25th state. The administrative responsibility for the state remained under the Ministry of External Affairs until 1965 and it was only after the Chinese aggression of 1962 and its fallout that the Ministry of Home Affairs took over. That the Government of India did not even consider this region a homeland for a certain section of its population until 1965 is evidence enough of the Indian Army's lack of preparedness in countering a Chinese attack from this flank. Seasoned observers and experts on the region have pointed out in several scholarly works that the ambiguous status of the northeastern states originated from a policy adopted by the British Raj of empowering local kingdoms and chieftains in the North East, including Bhutan. This was to counter possible military offensives from the strong Burmese and Chinese armies across the fertile Gangetic Plain in which they had vested trade interests. The practice of maintaining a buffer zone between the Indian mainland and its neighbouring countries was perpetuated by the Indian government following Independence.

The administration's attitude to the state, however, could not in any way undermine the courage displayed by the Indian Army soldiers during the war of 1962. They battled it out until the very end, knowing full well that it was an exercise in futility. Tawang's striking War Memorial, constructed in the region's typical Buddhist style of architecture, is a tribute to the valour and patriotism of these soldiers, who fought bravely against a much more powerful enemy. The memorial records their tales of courage, detailing the various stages of the battle and the difficult conditions of the terrain on which it was fought – conditions to which most of the Indian Army recruits from the plains were quite unaccustomed. The memorial has also been engraved with the names of all the 2,420 Indian soldiers who lost their lives in the war, along with the names of the battalions they represented. One of them is Subedar Joginder Singh, whose platoon, in the frontline of combat, suffered heavy casualties from three waves of Chinese attacks. The story of his valour and sacrifice came to be known only after his death and the soldier was posthumously awarded the Param Vir Chakra, the highest honour of its kind. The citation for the award describes the details of his achievement:

*Subedar Joginder Singh was the commander of a platoon of the Sikh Regiment holding a defensive position at a ridge near Tongpen*

*La in NEFA. At 0530 hours on 23 October 1962, the Chinese opened a very heavy attack on the Bumla axis with the intention of breaking through to Towang. The leading battalion of the enemy attacked the ridge in three waves, each about 200 strong. Subedar Joginder Singh and his men mowed down the first wave, and the enemy was temporarily halted by the heavy losses it suffered. Within a few minutes, a second wave came over and was dealt with similarly. But the platoon had, by then, lost half its men.*

*Subedar Joginder Singh was wounded in the thigh but refused to be evacuated. Under his inspiring leadership the platoon stubbornly held its ground and would not withdraw.*

*Meanwhile the position was attacked for the third time. Subedar Joginder Singh himself manned a light machine-gun and shot down a number of the enemy. The Chinese however continued to advance despite heavy losses. When the situation became untenable Subedar Joginder Singh and the few men that were left in the position fixed bayonets and charged the advancing Chinese, bayoneting a number of them before he and his comrades were overpowered. Throughout this action, Subedar Joginder Singh displayed devotion to duty, inspiring leadership and bravery of the highest order.*

About 21 kilometres from the Sela Pass stands a memorial erected as a tribute to the courage of another soldier – Jaswant Singh Rawat, who single-handedly defended his post, killing many Chinese soldiers before he was finally brought down. The road between Tawang and Bhalukpong is littered with such tales of valour and sacrifice made by Indian soldiers, reminding every visitor of the perilous nature of the terrain they are travelling through. Even now, the army continues to suffer regular casualties mainly because of the rarefied air, the extreme cold and difficult living conditions. In fact, army personnel I interacted with claimed that at Sela and Bumla, winter temperatures dipped, sometimes, to several degrees below freezing point and that despite the necessary precautions, soldiers had died from the punishing climatic conditions and lack of oxygen.

* * *

Keen on an eyewitness account of the events that had led up to the 1962 war, I went in search of a senior citizen who had been present in Tawang at the time, unaware that my efforts would come to naught. I would discover, soon enough, that not too many people in this region lived to the age of sixty. Those who did were often in poor physical health or mentally unsound. The high altitude and low oxygen levels, the absence of quality health care and the addiction to alcohol in both men and women tended to adversely affect the longevity of the local population. Even in this day and age, most of the young men married long before they were twenty-five and would become grandfathers by the time they reached fifty, after which most of them devoted their lives almost entirely to drinking.

I was contemplating giving up my search, when Tashi suggested that we visit Sheru village, situated a few kilometres below Tawang against the backdrop of a picturesque valley. One of the oldest villages in this region, Sheru is home to around 500 families, mostly belonging to the Monpa community. As in other *bastis* in this region, the only occupation for men and women here is farming and the rearing of yaks and pigs. Of late, many of the younger men have been moving to Tawang, where they rent rooms and spend the week driving taxis or working in hotels.

When Tashi and I reached Sheru on a sunny afternoon, most of the homes in the *basti* were locked and, barring a few old women who sat outside their homes, running wooden combs through their thin strands of silver hair, there was hardly anyone about. Even the village head, we were told, had gone to Tawang on business and wouldn't return until late in the evening. So we decided to stop at a grocery store near the entrance to the village, where two old men sat on a bench, drinking beer. They were the only men we could find in Sheru.

On noticing us, one of the men, whose appearance suggested that he was from the plains, got up and walked away, leaving us with a short, plump, clean-shaven old man, neatly dressed in dark grey polyester trousers and a light blue checked shirt, with a faded brown jacket over it. The man had a huge paunch that looked as though it would burst through his shirt buttons.

'What would you like to know about Sheru village?' he asked, when we explained the purpose of our visit.

Behind the counter of the small grocery-cum-wine shop sat a young woman nursing her infant son. In my bid to avoid interacting with the old man who seemed drunk, I asked if her husband or any other male family member was around. She set out a couple of chairs near the old man for Tashi and me and replied that most of the men had gone off to work and would not be back until evening. With nothing else to do, I suggested to Tashi that we spend some time with the old man, until someone more sober and lucid turned up.

Soon, the old man launched into a long, rambling monologue, interspersing it with any number of irrelevant questions for which I had no answers. It seemed as if he simply could not stop talking. When I explained that I had come all the way to find someone who had been around when the Chinese invaded Arunachal, the man sprang up from his seat and declared that he was probably among the very few who were still living to tell the tale and wanted me to devote my full attention to what he had to say.

Like most men his age in this part of the country, Lama Khandu did not remember the exact year of his birth. At first, he recalled that it was in 1951 that his mother Pema had delivered her eleventh child by Lasang Gompu in their ancestral home in

Sheru. But it could well have been 1949, Khandu added, since nobody in those days ever bothered to get such births registered and certificates issued for the same or maintain other records relating to their progeny. Often, they did not even bother to keep track of the years that were passing by. It was the same case with their children. Khandu remembered being the eleventh child in the family, but had lost count of his siblings.

'Some of them lived and many died soon after they were born or while growing up,' he went on. 'When we grew up, there were seven of us. I remember that.'

Life in Sheru village had been quiet and peaceful as usual, until word got around in 1959 that their religious leader, the fourteenth Dalai Lama, had escaped from Tibet and taken refuge in India. Since that momentous event, there had always been apprehension and rumours about war with China. But Khandu's father would always dismiss such talk as mere conjecture and claim with assurance that such a thing would never happen.

One afternoon, when Lama Khandu was about eleven years old, the villagers received information that the Chinese had made incursions into Indian territory and were engaged in battle with the Indian Army.

'We were all asked to vacate our homes and escape to the plains for our safety,' Khandu recalled. 'At that time, my father and his elder brother were grazing our yaks up in the hills. I ran to them and conveyed the news we had received. But despite the urgency of the message, my father dismissed it and declared that we would not be leaving home. So I returned to our house and stayed with my sisters. Later that evening, I remember my mother running home to tell us that Tawang and its surrounding areas were on fire. Dozens of fire engines were racing back and forth, their blaring sirens rousing the somnolent villages. We watched army helicopters flying out of Tawang all day and ran to the spot from where we could see the flames and were told that the fires had been set by Indian soldiers [a common practice in wartime for retreating armies] fleeing from the invading Chinese army.'

As most villagers had already fled their homes by then, the few who remained decided to follow suit, leaving with the meagre possessions they could carry, as the Chinese army marched through Tawang and Dirang and all the way to the Assam border. The villagers ran to seek shelter in the bushes below and stayed hidden there for a couple of days. When Khandu's family ran out of food, he and one of his brothers accompanied their father back to the village so that they could kill the pigs there and take the meat back for consumption.

'We returned to the village to discover that the Chinese soldiers had already taken it over and set up camp on its outskirts,' the old man said, rising from his chair to point out the location to me. 'On spotting us, those soldiers waved in a friendly manner and said that we had nothing to fear. They assured us that they would not harm us and that we could return to our homes in the village and continue with our lives. They seemed friendly enough, but we thought it best to kill some pigs and carry the meat back to where our family had taken refuge.'

Since the villagers of Sheru believed that the Chinese were here to stay, they fled to Bhutan. They had been trekking for several days through thick jungles with scant supplies when soldiers of the Royal Army of Bhutan surrounded them. The villagers were taken in as refugees and detained in a makeshift camp at Tashigang in eastern Bhutan. Lama Khandu and his family were also taken to that camp and stayed there for nine days, after which they were transported in groups of 100 to another camp in Rangjung town, also in eastern Bhutan.

'Those were the darkest days of my life,' Khandu recalled. 'I was very young, but I still remember how we starved and how eagerly we waited even for that one meal a day. Our living conditions were so desperate that we often resorted to eating the flesh of dead cows and other animal carcasses that we found around our camps. The Bhutan Army ill treated and humiliated us.'

I could not help noticing that as the old man narrated what he described as the most important story of his life, the slur in his voice and the booze in his system had vanished. While reliving those days so many years later, the senior citizen was close to tears.

After being detained in Rangjung for a few days, the refugees, whose numbers had swollen by now, were taken to Yamla and then to Khaling, where they had to literally beg for survival, as the Bhutan government would provide them with very little by way of food or other basic necessities. Tired of being shifted from one camp to another, with no clue as to why they were being put through the ordeal, several of the refugees wanted to revolt, but could summon neither the strength nor the will power to do so. When the Arunachalis were shifted to Trongsa in central Bhutan, however, one of the camp's inmates, the only person in the group who could communicate in Hindi, got in touch with Indian government officials and informed them of their plight.

'At the camps in Bhutan, we had neither food nor clothing nor even a proper shelter and were forced to live like animals. The young women and children in the group felt particularly unsafe and vulnerable,' Lama Khandu recalled. 'After the Indian government came to know of our plight, however, we were rescued. We were first shifted to another camp in Giala and then brought back to Rangjung, where Indian officials gave us each a blanket, a plate, some rice and other basic necessities. Although we would lose a few of our people to hunger and disease, the majority survived, despite the treatment meted out to us by the Bhutanese government.'

Brought back to Tezpur by the Indian government, along with

the other refugees, Khandu and his family members covered the distance to Sheru on foot, taking nine days to reach the village. They were home at last, two months after they had left. By this time, the Chinese soldiers had all left. Khandu and his fellow villagers found their homes and property intact, with no traces of damage or desecration. As would be the case with many from this region, those few weeks of being shunted from one strange place to another, even before they had time to get their bearings, served as the turning point in Khandu's life.

On returning to the village, Khandu attended school in Kalimpong and Dharamsala, following which he joined the Special Service Bureau (SSB) in 1971, a military unit that would later come to be known as the Sashastra Seema Bal. Two years later, he married a local woman and fathered twelve children, seven of whom grew up to be adults. During his years with the SSB, Khandu would travel to other parts of India and learn a little bit of English and Hindi. He resigned from the SSB after 23 years of service and began teaching the Bodhi language to students at the village school. He still continued to do so and had just returned from the school after his classes for the day when we met him.

By the time, Lama Khandu finished retelling the story of his life, retaining its inherent drama in his narration, a small crowd, mostly comprising of women from the surrounding areas, had gathered around us. I came to know from them that the plump old man I had been talking to all this while and whom I had dismissed as just another drunk tribal actually enjoyed quite a reputation as a scholar and a wit in and around Tawang. Once or twice a month, he would even narrate stories with moral lessons on All India Radio as part of their Bodhi language broadcast, which was wildly popular among the locals.

'You can verify what I have told you with anyone in the Indian

Army or the Bhutan Army. Every word of it is true and I stand by it,' Lama Khandu said solemnly, as Tashi and I got up to leave.

I thanked the man for his time, paid for his beer and took a selfie with him before bidding him good-bye. Giving me a warm hug, he said that he was planning to visit south India soon and promised to look me up in Chennai.

* * *

Back in Tawang, I faced the prospect of another bitterly cold night. But as one night gave way to the next, things would turn out somewhat differently.

Following that first alcohol-less, joint-aching night in this hill town, when I had been forced to bury myself under several layers of bedclothes – a pair of comforters and a thick blanket – to keep my limbs from freezing, I resolved to ensure by noon the following day that I had a bottle of whiskey and some spicy snacks stocked in my room to eliminate unpleasant surprises after sundown, which usually took place around 4.45 p.m. in this season. Having done the needful and ensured that I would have access to a few drinks later in the night, I ventured out at around 4.30 p.m. and watched the town fold up like a water lily before darkness set in. But the rapidly plummeting temperature and the cold winds sweeping in from the mountains made it impossible for me to be outdoors for more than fifteen to twenty minutes at a stretch and I soon found myself rushing back to the warmth of my room by 6 p.m. and settling down for the evening in a t-shirt, dhoti and sweatshirt.

Within an hour or so, the cold was so intense that my knuckles began to hurt and I could not even move my fingers properly to form a fist. My sandals were of no use, as the chill from the icy floor tiles penetrated the soles. As usual, there was a power outage and the only source of light was a dim 40-watt bulb running on an inverter.

I opened the bottle of whiskey I had kept handy for just such a situation. By 9 p.m., I was four generous drinks down and still shivering. That was when I made my way to the dining area near the lounge to have my dinner, which consisted of chow mein and momos – served cold.

On my third night, I made a more aggressive plan to tackle the cold. By 4 p.m. (as the power supply was usually erratic after five), I filled a bucket with scalding hot water, the kind that would normally peel your skin off on contact, and had a bath. Then I put on a t-shirt, a sweater and a thick jacket, which I zipped up all the way to my throat, with matching denim jeans, woollen socks and shoes. And that was how I went to bed, diving under the two comforters and a blanket. Although I never stepped out of my room after six, I remained fully dressed to the last detail, making the cold, dark nights seem just about manageable.

On my last evening in Tawang, I could not resist the temptation to check out the only lounge bar in town that had closed down by the time I visited it on my first night. I was overtaken by curiosity at the prospect of meeting that brave soul who had had the guts – and the foolhardiness – to open a lounge bar in a town where no one ventured outdoors after sunset and there was hardly any power supply at night. Not wanting to take any chances this time, I was at the bar by 6 p.m., when the streets were emptying out and everyone was scurrying back to the shelter of their homes.

Unsurprisingly, I was the first and only customer for the evening. As the scheduled power cut was still an hour away, I could get a good look at the interiors, which were certainly far more well-appointed than I had been expecting. The owner Mr Kashyap, a tall, lean, balding young man who lived in New Delhi and came here once a month, had taken up position behind the counter, as his manager was away on leave. For a tiny bar in the middle of nowhere, his watering hole was well stocked, with a wide range of international liquor, as well as local brands, including my favourite bourbon.

Kashyap had been an avid biker and owned a 1977 Royal Enfield Bullet, on which he would often ride up to Tawang from Guwahati, where he lived at the time.

'Every time I came here,' Kashyap said, as we struck up a conversation, 'I would really yearn for a nice, warm bar, where I could enjoy a good drink and a satisfying meal with friends. Since no one was really keen on opening such a bar, I decided to do it myself.'

That was five years ago. Since then, Kashyap's bar-cum-lounge had come a long way. Inspired by his maiden venture, others had opened two more bar-cum-discos, but they had to be shut down within a couple of years for lack of business. Ever since, Kashyap had reigned supreme as the sole provider of night life in Tawang. Moreover, his bar continued to be the only licenced liquor outlet in the district, although booze was freely available even in small local shops.

'We used to get good support from the previous government, but of late, things have been quite rough,' Kashyap confided.

The night-life entrepreneur seemed to be facing problems and challenges that most other bar owners didn't. For instance, a few weeks ago, the generator at the bar had failed. In a town where a power cut was scheduled between seven and nine every evening and unscheduled outages were common for several hours after that, the inability to provide minimum illumination and heating could defeat the very purpose of running a bar and lounge.

'We called the manufacturer and they did send someone to pick up the generator set and take it to Tezpur for repairs,' Kashyap explained. 'But the service guy now tells me that he has to travel in a jeep for fourteen hours just to return my repaired genset, which is not a viable proposition for him. So he is waiting for more orders from this town which he can club together before visiting Tawang.'

Despite such setbacks, Kashyap said he had a decent business going here. When he declared that the bar had been open till 1 a.m. the previous night, I had to tell him in jest to stop kidding. Who, I asked, would even dare to go out at that hour, when the entire town was in freeze mode?

'Army officers,' came the prompt reply. 'I have a regular clientele of army officers who visit my lounge. As there is no other place in town to socialize, they come here often and spend a lot of time. Last night, a big group was here till one a.m. and we could not refuse to serve them, however late the hour.'

Apparently, Kashyap's outlet enjoyed quite a patronage. Most foreign tourists who needed a good place to eat and drink came to him. So did local youth who wanted to party hard, without having to travel to the plains.

'Business is not great, but I get by,' Kashyap conceded.

He only prayed that the locals would step out a little more after sunset than they were accustomed to doing and the power department would be more merciful towards businessmen like him.

By the time I finished my second drink, the power supply had been disrupted and Tawang was enveloped in darkness again. Before I could freeze in the cold, I quickly paid my bill and returned to my hotel room, winding up my day with more giant Patialas, until I passed out.

# 8

# MOREH

Two days before I landed up in Moreh, a nondescript trading town on the India–Myanmar border in Manipur, I was chatting with a journalist friend at his office in Imphal when I heard the word 'Mayang' for the first time. The senior scribe, who was on the phone with a friend, was trying to justify his Facebook post in which he had blamed the Mayangs for all the unrest in this northeastern state. I liked the sound of the word and was intrigued enough by it to find out what it meant.

'So who are these Mayangs?' I asked the journalist after he had hung up.

'People like you,' he replied bluntly. 'In fact, any outsider who comes to Manipur from another part of India is a Mayang.'

I was shocked to hear from a veteran journalist that Indians were considered outsiders in their own country, that too so many decades after Independence and especially at a time when the insurgency-prone state was going through a fresh wave of violence. Among all the border towns that I had visited, I had been most apprehensive about visiting Moreh, after all the horror stories I had heard from those familiar with the region. Kidnapping for ransom had become a lucrative business in Manipur and every one I spoke to acknowledged that the government had little control over the insurgents responsible for such abductions. I had been advised not to wander around freely, as I usually did in other places and to always have a trusted local contact accompany me. I was also asked to keep the local journalists' union posted about my travel plans in the state, in case something went wrong, as I was a Mayang from south India in a land where this breed was hated for apparently being the cause of all ills.

Probably sensing my discomfiture at his comment, the man took pains over the next couple of hours, while driving me across Imphal in his Mahindra Jeep on that cool, late-October evening, to elaborate on several related subjects: the six-decades-long insurgency that was devastating the state, the hatred the Manipuris felt for Mayangs and the alleged urgency of Imphal Valley residents to introduce an Inner Line Permit system – the most pressing issue in the state at the time of my visit.

I had arrived in Imphal that very afternoon and was yet to get a taste of Manipur and its complexities first-hand. All the information I had on this troubled state so far had been gleaned from newspaper reports, propaganda websites and friends. That alone was intimidating enough to keep me from venturing beyond my hotel room, until my journalist contact arrived to pick me up.

The hotel where I had put up was right in the city centre and from my room, I could see the main traffic junction. At least half a dozen police officials and Assam Rifles troopers, wielding light machine guns (LMGs), were conspicuous by their presence throughout the day. I had been told that there were at least a dozen underground organizations whose main source of income was kidnapping and extortion. Until then, 'underground' or 'underworld' had conjured up in my imagination an image of infamous mafia don Dawood Ibrahim and his cronies. Out here in Manipur, 'underground' meant all those groups and organizations that called for shutdowns, imposed curfews and basically decided when the state would work and when it would go on a mass holiday.

I had originally planned to visit Moreh after spending a night in Imphal and acquainting myself with local media persons, but on reaching the state capital, I came to know that the underground groups had called for a bandh on the following day, making travel impossible. I had no option but to spend another day in Imphal, holed up in my hotel room in fearful anticipation of violence. The truckloads of cops and paramilitary forces that roamed the streets of the city did their bit in creating an ambiance that seemed to justify such trepidation.

After normal movement of vehicles had gradually resumed later that evening, I walked to the Press Club that stood a few hundred metres from my hotel to plan my trip to Moreh. It was there that I would come to know that certain other insurgent groups had called for a 48-hour bandh, starting the next morning, to counter the apparent success of the one which had just ended. Once again, I was advised to remain in Imphal and defer my plans for visiting Moreh to a regular, strike-free working day, as travelling during a bandh would be quite unsafe. Somehow, I seemed to be the only one getting worked up over these successive bandhs. For everyone else in Manipur, the call for a bandh and spontaneous shutdowns appeared to be a way of life.

With another bandh being called, I was told that public vehicles might not operate in the hills and if they did, they could be stopped midway and attacked. If I had to travel on a bandh day, the only option open to me was to hire a private taxi. As I could not imagine spending two more days in Imphal confined to my hotel room, I decided to drop my initial plan of travelling to Moreh by public transport. I had noticed that several private taxis shuttled daily between Imphal and Moreh along Asian Highway 1 and considered hiring one of them and setting out for my destination, with a 'Press' sticker issued by the All Manipur Working Journalists' Union (AMWJU) affixed to its windscreen. I would also arrange for a local journalist to accompany me.

After making all the necessary arrangements at the Press Club, I returned to the hotel to retire for the night when the guy at the reception, a Bengali from Guwahati, surprised me by asking if I needed any booze.

'But Manipur is a dry state, right?' I countered.

Anticipating an endless succession of dry days in Manipur, I had purposefully gone on a binge before flying to Imphal and had not even considered asking the hotel staff for booze on my first night there.

'But you can get anything you want, sir,' the receptionist replied. '*Thoda* extra *hota hai*.'

I paid him enough money for two beers and went to my room. About ten minutes later, a room-service boy arrived with my dinner and two bottles of chilled beer.

* * *

The frisson-inducing prospect of driving through the hills on a day observed as a bandh by the hill insurgent groups and the general excitement of travelling all the way to the Myanmar border through rural Manipur were enough to make me leap out of bed by sunrise, which is around 4.30 a.m. here at this time of the year. My liaison and local guide Biseswar, an Imphal-based journo from the Meitei community, was expected to arrive at 6.30 a.m. with the car in which we were to travel, but I was ready an hour earlier and could not wait to leave.

With time hanging heavy on my hands, I stepped out of the hotel in search of an ATM to stock up on cash and was surprised to discover that none of the ATM machines in the Thangal Bazaar area could be operated late in the evening and were kept locked up until morning. Unlike other state capitals, Imphal completely shut down after dark, waking up only around eight in the morning. Until then, getting something as simple as a cup of tea or a pack of cigarettes could demand quite a bit of effort, for the only people visible on the roads at that hour were policemen armed with rifles, paramilitary troopers wielding LMGs and sanitary workers carrying brooms.

After unsuccessfully scouting around for an open ATM and a tea shop, I returned to my hotel, only to find that despite the bandh call, at least half a dozen Maruti Omni vans had left for Moreh with passengers and provisions. But it was too late now to cancel the private car that had been booked for the trip.

Biseswar and his friend arrived with the car an hour later. We rushed to the Press Club, printed AMWJU stickers and pasted them on the front and rear windshields and had hit Asian Highway 1 a few minutes before nine.

Contrary to what I had been anticipating, the first half of the 110 kilometre journey turned out to be smooth. Despite the bandh call, several private vehicles were visible on the highway and the taxi service between Moreh and Imphal seemed to have resumed fully as well. The only jarring note for someone from outside the state was the overwhelming presence of machine-gun-wielding Assam Rifles personnel, with a soldier posted every fifty metres along the highway. They were even present in the little village bazaars we passed on the way, but the locals seemed unperturbed, as most residents of this state had not seen a demilitarized, insurgency-free Manipur in their lifetime.

The seeds of insurgency were sown on the very day that Manipur became a part of the Indian Union on 15 October 1949, after Maharaja Budhachandra Singh had signed a Treaty of Accession, merging the kingdom with India. At the time of the merger, Manipur already enjoyed a democratic form of government that had been established under the Manipur Constitution Act, 1947, with an elected legislature and the Maharaja as the Executive Head. With the signing of the 1949 treaty, the Legislative Assembly was dissolved forthwith and Manipur became a part of India. Even today, many locals express outrage over the fact that despite having a democratic government in place, the Maharaja had gone ahead and signed a merger treaty without consulting the people or their elected representatives. Those who were opposed to the merger with India questioned its legitimacy and broke away, forming insurgent groups which would engage in a long armed struggle to establish an independent state.

One of the first separatist factions, known as the United National Liberation Front (UNLF), was founded in November 1964 to wage war against India. A few years later, more insurgent organizations, such as the People's Liberation Army of Manipur, often referred to as the People's Liberation Army (PLA), the People's Revolutionary Party of Kangleipak (PREPAK) and the Kangleipak Communist Party (KCP), came into being and joined the war. Following the spurt in insurgency, Manipur was declared a disturbed area by the Indian government which imposed the Armed Forces (Special Powers) Act, 1958, on the state of Manipur in September 1980. This would aggravate the festering resentment among the people and give rise to more insurgent groups.

The same period witnessed the rise of Naga nationalism in the neighbouring state of Nagaland, its fallout evident in the dominance of the National Socialist Council of Nagaland (NSCN) in the tribal areas of Manipur. Clashes between the Isak-Muivah and Khaplang factions of NSCN further aggravated tensions, as other tribals, including the Kukis, began creating their own guerrilla groups in a bid to defend their interests against alleged Naga violations. More ethnic groups, such as the Paite, the Vaiphei, the Pangals and the Hmars followed suit, establishing militant outfits of their own. Manipur thus earned the infamy it has not been able to shake off till date of being the insurgency capital of India.

But I was yet to see any evidence of it.

After driving for about an hour, we reached Pallel, the last village before the road climbed up into the hills. Here, we would halt briefly at a modest roadside eatery for a breakfast of puris and *sabzi* with sweet curd, apparently a popular dish in this part of the country, before resuming our journey. Home to the Kukis, the hills overlooking the village were allegedly infested with members of the militia. Due to the increased security concerns in these areas, Assam Rifles troopers, as well as police and commando forces, had set up a number of security check posts, where all vehicles were thoroughly scanned for contraband before being allowed to proceed further.

We reached the first of these check posts soon after crossing Pallel village. A long queue of cars, Omni vans and sundry other transport vehicles had lined up before the check-point. My local guide Biseswar stepped out of the car and approached an army Major. He informed him about having already spoken to the Defence PRO for special permission to allow our vehicle to pass through these check posts without being subjected to the mandatory screening. The obliging officer waved us through after noting down our names and the car's registration number.

By the time we reached the next security check post, the military personnel manning it had already received our names and our vehicle number, along with the message that we had special permission to pass through without being screened. When the guards saw our vehicle approach, they simply waved us through and we waved back at them in friendly acknowledgement as we passed.

We continued on our way through the hills, until a roadblock set up to stall traffic for safety reasons, following a landslide, forced us to an unscheduled halt. While waiting for the road to be cleared of debris, I learnt that since the big earthquake which had devastated Nepal earlier this year, tectonic movements in the earth's crust had triggered frequent landslides in these hills. Two earth movers were clearing away the rubble that blocked the road and about twenty minutes later, we were able to resume our journey. We drove past at least half a dozen more Assam Rifles check posts and an equal number of villages, before descending towards the scenic Kabaw Valley in Myanmar.

The first palpable sign of having reached the gateway to tropical South East Asia was the dramatic change in weather and vegetation. The rise in temperature was quite apparent and the humidity was so intense, it seemed to force the fluid and salts out of my body through the pores of my skin in the form of perspiration, just as it would have back home in Chennai. The lush green shrubs lining the road on either side had given way to solid teakwood trees, most of them less than five years old. Further down Asian Highway 1 were dozens of tiny shops set up in bunker-like structures and restaurants built almost entirely of wood and supported on stilts, standing approximately one to two feet above ground level. They sold everything from groceries and cigarettes to liquor from Myanmar. Even the people here looked different from the ones I had seen in Imphal. They had smaller frames and a pale yellow complexion. The women were slender, with well-defined noses and cheeks smeared with *thanakha*, a tree-bark paste that was the local equivalent of sunscreen lotion. While most of the men went about bare-chested, the women wore colourful blouses with loose pajama-style pants. One look around was enough to tell me that we were in a tropical town, more suited for a vacation. But that was just a façade for the benefit of unsuspecting tourists by the residents of this colourfully diverse town.

Although it spans hardly three-square kilometres of land, Moreh is home to virtually all the major communities found in the country, including Tamils, Punjabis, Bengalis and Nepalis, not to mention the Meiteis and several other hill tribes who have settled here in phases over the past several decades. While the residents of Moreh take pride in their diversity and in the harmony in which different communities co-exist. Violent clashes have broken out regularly between them in the past and have also been resolved quite amicably. Exactly two months before my visit, for example, Moreh was almost razed to the ground, not for the first time, following violent clashes between the Kukis and the Meitei community over an Inner Line Permit issue. Shops were burnt down, people were forced to flee their homes and trade came to a halt, at least for a few days. This had been preceded over the years by similar clashes between the Kukis and the Nagas, the Tamils and the hill tribes, costing dozens of lives. Locals jokingly attribute the simmering tension between the communities to the hot weather that prevails here throughout the year.

On reaching Moreh, we parked our car outside a small restaurant set up in a wooden cabin with hundreds of Burmese beer bottles lined up on the counter. Our local contact was waiting there and led us into the restaurant and ordered authentic Manipuri food (or so I was made to believe). It consisted of boiled rice with vegetables and chillies, chicken gravy, fried fish and two mugs of beer.

While sipping the chilled brew, I checked with Bises if we were still in Manipur.

'It's a dry state, right?' I asked.

Bises indicated a building across the road that faced the restaurant.

'That's the local police station,' was his answer. 'Here in Moreh, no problem at all.'

With that, he gulped down a mouthful of chilled Burmese beer.

I told him that I had not faced a problem getting booze even in Imphal, for that matter, and resumed my meal.

* * *

After lunch, I set out to meet the office bearers of the Tamil Sangam, one of Moreh's oldest institutions, while my liaison man Bises and his friend Dimjit went across the border to Tamu to do some shopping. I was dropped off near the office of the Tamil Sangam, where Kajah, the media coordinator of the Sangam, was waiting to receive me and accompany me to the home of the Sangam's secretary Subramani.

The Tamil Sangam had been active since the mid-1960s when Moreh was little more than a handful of shops and teakwood cabins. Located in the congested Morning Bazaar area, very close to the Indo–Myanmar Friendship Gate, the Sangam had been set up by some of this border town's first Tamil settlers. Their objective was to preserve their own culture, even as they engaged in charitable work that would benefit the locals.

Secretary of the Sangam, K. Balasubramani, was 41 years old and lived alone in a modest old house built almost entirely of sliced teakwood logs. Like most other Tamils here of his age, he had been born and raised in Moreh. An active member of the 400-strong Tamil Sangam, Subramani could speak Manipuri, Burmese, Tamil, Hindi and even local tribal languages fluently and took great pride in calling himself a resident of Moreh.

When we visited him that afternoon, Subramani was supervising carpentry work at his home, in between exchanging Burmese currency for Indian rupees for clients who had approached him for the purpose. Until two years ago, Mani's wife and children were living with him in Moreh, but had now moved to Red Hills, a Chennai suburb. With his daughters growing up, Mani was worried about their lack of connect with their roots in Tamil Nadu.

'I preferred to send them off to Chennai so that they could stay in close touch with our culture,' Mani explained. 'Out here in Moreh, children are more fluent in the local languages and do not even know how to speak Tamil properly.'

He had admitted both his children to a private school in Chennai and had sent his wife along to take care of them. Mani flew down to Chennai five or six times a year to visit his family, but preferred to live in Moreh and take care of the family business.

Among the earliest Tamil settlers in Moreh were Mani's parents who had arrived here in 1965. His ancestors from his mother's side had been living in Myanmar (then known as Burma) for several generations. While Mani did not have the precise details about his mother's family, he had been told that his great-grandparents were among the earliest Tamil migrants to Myanmar when the country was under British rule and many civil servants were hired from south India and sent to Rangoon (now Yangon) to help the country's colonial masters with the task of governance. Other than government servants, several families from central Tamil Nadu had migrated to Burma during the early 1800s to establish successful businesses in the country with the blessings of the British. When these families flourished, they brought in more families of helpers, servants and other workers from India to work in their homes and businesses. Soon, the Tamils had become a major, thriving community in Burma.

The situation, however, changed dramatically in 1962, when General Ne Win seized power through a military coup and ordered the expulsion of all non-indigenous people from the country that had been their home for generations. At the time, Subramani's grandfather had a well-established business in Takita near Rangoon. He had married his daughter to a youth from Chidambaram in Tamil Nadu who moved to Takita to help his father-in-law with his business. But in keeping with the new Burmese government's diktat, Subramani's father, who was not a Burmese citizen, had to leave Burma, while his grandfather who had been born in that country and served its government in the past was allowed to remain in Takita.

Moving to Tamil Nadu, Mani's parents tried setting up several businesses during the next few years, but none really took off. Deciding to return to Burma, they came all the way to Moreh, where they were prevented from crossing the border. Not keen on going back to Tamil Nadu, Subramani's father set up a small trading business in this border town and built a home in a new neighbourhood called Prem Nagar, where he raised his family. Subramani and his siblings were born here and studied in local schools. In the mid-1960s, there were just fifteen Tamil families in Moreh, mostly migrants from Burma who had nowhere else to go. These people soon re-established their ties with friends and family in and around Rangoon and sought their help in setting up businesses in Moreh.

Over the years, cross-border trade – both legal and clandestine – thrived in Moreh and its Tamil settlers began to prosper. They invited more relatives from Tamil Nadu to help them with their expanding businesses and the new migrants brought in more families from back home. Over the next three decades, the number of Tamil families grew to around 3,000, making them one of the largest communities in the border town. During that period, Tamil was taught in schools, Tamil movies were screened in Moreh's movie theatres and a south Indian-style temple was also built for the benefit of the community.

Reminiscing about his childhood, Mani declared that those were the best days of his life in Moreh.

'There were so many Punjabi, Nepali and Bengalis families here, in addition to the Manipuri and tribal ones,' he reflected. 'We all went to school together and spoke each other's language. In Moreh, we participated in every single festival celebrated by the different communities. For Pongal [the harvest festival in Tamil Nadu], we organized grand celebrations stretching over several days. They were even more extravagant than the ones back home and Manipuris, Nepalis and other members of the community took active part in the festivities. Similarly, we celebrated Durga Puja and other Manipuri festivals with pomp. Living in Moreh was the truest experience of a mini India. That was why our colony was called Prem Nagar.'

As the Tamil population was more numerous than any other community in Moreh during the 1980s and 1990s and represented a significant segment of the votes. It was this community's members who decided on the candidate most suitable for the post of the local MLA and MP.

'But all that simply vanished after violent clashes broke out between the different communities in the early nineties,' he sighed.

Among the most bitter conflicts that have taken place in Moreh till date, the one between the Kukis and the Tamils is the most likely to linger in local memory for the number of lives that were sacrificed and the extent of the losses that businessmen suffered.

'That incident reversed the trend of small traders coming over from Tamil Nadu to settle in Moreh,' Subramani went on. 'As a fallout of that clash, several small traders were forced to return to Tamil Nadu so that they could live and work in peace. Since then, there has been a steady decline in the Tamil population in this border town.'

The Tamil Sangam, which used to have over 3,000 family memberships at one time, has seen its numbers dwindle to around 400. Even among the 400 families that are on record, many, like Subramani's, are fragmented, with only the male members remaining in Moreh, while the rest live in Tamil Nadu. Though Subramani outwardly claimed that his intention in sending his family back home was to ensure that his children established a firm bond with their roots and utilized the state's excellent educational opportunities, the actual reason – which he communicated to me in a hushed voice and in Tamil to prevent members of other communities from overhearing him and grasping his meaning – was different: Tamils like him no longer felt safe in Moreh.

'This is a border town and there are already so many different ethnic groups fighting for power,' Mani went on. 'Our life is rooted here and we don't have a choice but to stay on. However, we do want our children to stay away from all that is going on.'

If this trend continued, I asked him, would there be any Tamils left in Moreh two or three generations hence?

'It is certainly becoming difficult for us to continue with our lives here,' he replied. 'We still control a majority of the trade locally, but whether we can live here in peace is doubtful. It is quite possible that the Tamils in Moreh will become history in the not-too-distant future.'

While that possibility could not be laughed off, the institutions the Tamils had built, the south Indian temple where they worshipped, the local restaurants that served idlis and dosas and Tamil culture, which had become part and parcel of Moreh, might be hard to erase from the multi-faceted identity of this remote northeastern town.

Before we parted, Mani invited me to have breakfast with him at the south Indian eatery next morning and offered to take me along to the local Sri Angala Parameswari Temple, the second largest south Indian temple in the entire North East region.

* * *

About a decade ago, when a proposal was put forth for setting up an integrated check post in Moreh to facilitate the growing bilateral trade between India and Myanmar, businessmen in this shantytown were enthused. Finally, a dream that had first seen the light of day 25 years ago with the Indian government's 'Look

East' policy was showing signs of being realized – or so they assumed. Since the time of its inception, this border town had been envisioned as a commercial hub and a gateway to South East Asia. Sharing a border with the bustling town of Tamu in Myanmar, Moreh had the geographical advantage of being the hot seat of trade with not just Myanmar, but the entire South East Asian market.

To understand the town's trading potential and get a grasp of the business that takes place through this gateway, I went to the Nepali Basti on the other side of Asian Highway 1 to meet Surinder Singh Pateja, Secretary of the Chamber of Commerce, Moreh, at his spare motor parts store on Thali Road. The stoutly built, turbaned sardar with a flowing grey beard invited me into his shop and sat me down on a stool for a chat, while attending to the occasional customer who dropped in.

Born in what was then Burma to a Burmese Sikh mother and a Pakistani father, Surinder, now 66 years old, had gone to school in the country of his birth until class IV. While most Sikh families moved to Delhi and other parts of India after Partition, Surinder's father had decided to relocate to Yangon (then Rangoon) and had subsequently established a successful business there. In 1962, when Surinder was about twelve years old, the family, driven by the apprehension that the political situation in their adopted country had become too unstable, moved to Delhi, where they lived for the next ten years. They discovered, however, that doing business in India was not the same as it had been in Burma.

'The Burmese are soft-natured and easy to do business with, but in Delhi, we found that we could not cope,' he now recalled.

It was during this period that the political situation in Burma took a turn for the worse, particularly where resident Indians were concerned. In 1964, the country's new leader General U Ne Win nationalized all the businesses, thereby divesting hitherto wealthy Indians of their property and money. As the country had deliberately isolated itself from the rest of the world, export and import came to a halt, cutting off its citizens' access to even essential goods like salt, tinned fish, cycle spare parts and clothes, among other items.

'It was around this time that goods started moving from here and making their way across the border,' Surinder Singh remembered. 'Because of the long and porous border, it was easy to smuggle rations and other essentials to Tamu, where there was a ready customer base. And thus trade resumed between the two countries, but it was completely illicit. It was also around this time that some of our relatives suggested that we move to Moreh, where we could begin doing business with the Burmese again, since we were already familiar with their ways.'

In 1969, Surinder's elder brother Malik Singh arrived from Delhi and set up a spare motor parts store in Moreh. Soon, the rest of the family joined him. While there was not much business, the family made enough money to get by and remained in the border town. Apart from their outlet, about 50 to 100 other shops dealing in all kinds of goods also came up close to the border and soon, business recorded a rapid growth in volume. The only customers were Burmese citizens who crossed the border and purchased goods from the market or sent for them.

Meanwhile, the colony of Prem Nagar was coming up. As the name suggests, Prem Nagar was created to promote harmonious living among diverse communities that included Tamils, Punjabis, Bengalis, Marwaris and people from different parts of India. The new colony was supposed to set an example of peaceful co-existence for the rest of the country.

'Some people, though – I can only describe them as anti-social elements – seemed to resist the idea and made attempts to sabotage the growth of Prem Nagar,' Surinder went on. 'So the season of fires began. The first fire that razed Prem Nagar to the ground took place in 1972 when I had just arrived in Moreh after completing my graduation in Delhi. Since then, there were regular fire-related mishaps, when the entire colony was burned to the ground and we would painstakingly rebuild our homes and lives. This went on till 1979.'

When the fires became a recurring menace, the residents of Prem Nagar addressed their grievances to the chief minister of Manipur, who urged them to vacate that locality and allocated land for them in hilly areas for resettlement. But many of the traders refused to relocate to the hills, as they felt it would adversely affect their business. Instead, they moved to the Nepali Basti and other neighbourhoods close to the border. Thus, the main market in Moreh moved from its original location to its new one, while Prem Nagar disappeared from the town's map.

As there were no legal avenues for trade to be conducted between the two countries, all the businessmen in Moreh, including Surinder and his friends, were branded as smugglers.

'But the state government was asked to turn a blind eye to our activities and thus, business went on as usual,' Surinder explained.

In 1994, the then Union Minister P. Chidambaram signed a trade agreement with his Burmese counterpart, resuming barter trade between the two countries that covered forty different goods. This move was welcomed by all the South East Asian countries which sent delegates to Moreh and Tamu in Myanmar to cover the prestigious event. This was followed by the announcement that an Integrated Check Post would be set up at the Moreh–Tamu border early in the new millennium to facilitate the anticipated surge in trade volumes. But local businessmen like Surinder remained sceptical of the growth projections.

'Now, as the Secretary of the Chamber of Commerce, I can affirm that no check post is going to be set up even in the next five years and any improvement in the situation is unlikely,' Surinder asserted. 'Look at us. In terms of overall growth, India's North East has not taken a step forward since Independence, while the rest of the country has moved ahead.

'Back in the early seventies, when we arrived here, the place was full of anti-social elements and insurgents, but life was good. We could go to Imphal and return any time of the day or night without hassle. We would sit outside our homes and chat until as late as ten or even eleven o'clock at night without any fear. Then gradually, things began to change.

'The demand for an independent Greater Nagaland grew more strident and along with it, the Nationalist Socialist Council of Nagaland (NSCN) began to consolidate its power. The hills of Manipur also came into their sphere of control. And so began the NSCN's rule in Moreh. They collected taxes from us regularly and gave us protection in return. The Government of India was well aware of the situation, but could do nothing to change it. The NSCN's rule continued for more than a decade. Despite their terror tactics, the positive thing about the NSCN was that if they gave you their word, they stood by it, no matter what.

'During the early nineties, the Kukis began to move to the hills of Manipur in large numbers and along with the increase in numbers, armed groups started wresting control of the region from the Nagas. In 1993, an all-out battle broke out between the Kukis and the Nagas, resulting in much bloodshed in Ukhrul district. Following this development, the Indian government relocated a number of Kukis to these hills. And thus began the Kuki Raj in Moreh. Soon, several splinter groups like the Kuki National Organizaton (KNO), the Kuki National Army (KNA) and half a dozen other militant outfits also entered the fray.

'Things have come to such a pass that today, we pay taxes to at least a dozen different organizations, including the NSCN, to ensure our protection. Yet, neither the Indian Army nor the Indian government makes any effort to offer us protection from these insurgent groups. On the contrary, they accuse us of encouraging militancy in this region by paying taxes to these groups without pausing to consider that it is their failure to provide us with even a semblance of official security that has forced us into buying the goodwill of the insurgents. The sad part is that these government forces have also joined the bandwagon: they collect private taxes to allow goods to pass. Now from whom do we seek redress for such wrongs?

'If a pencil costs ₹10 in Delhi, the same pencil will cost at least ₹15 in Moreh, as the local shopkeeper has to cover all the additional taxes he must pay to various parties. In such a situation, how can we hope to compete in business with those living outside the state? The cost of transporting a product from Imphal to Myanmar is higher than it would be if we shipped the same product from Kolkata or any other port to Myanmar via Singapore. Such is the situation we live in. In fact, so great are the uncertainties and risks involved, that nobody can ever be sure of travelling to Imphal and returning home safely, despite the presence of a dozen security posts along the way. And these people call that road Asian Highway 1! What a joke! If the Indian government is keen on facilitating trade with South East Asia through land routes, it will have to tackle the North East and its insurgencies on a war footing. It is already too late. And if it continues to drag its heels over this issue, it will cost the government dearly.

'Look around you – you will find evidence of all that I have said,' Surinder went on. 'Do you see any young Mayang in Moreh? My children are not here. Neither are Subramani's. Nobody who has smart, educated children would wish them to stay on in Moreh. This place is unhealthy for tranquil young minds. Besides, there are so many opportunities elsewhere.'

When I reminded him of the perils he could invite by making such a statement in public, the senior sardar said, 'Oh, don't worry about it. I am willing to say this to anyone who will listen. It's just that nobody comes and asks.'

Later, he would serve me a soft drink and direct me to Nepali Basti, one of the oldest residential neighbourhoods in Moreh.

* * *

The sun rises and sets in Moreh earlier than anywhere else in India. By 4 p.m., Indian Standard Time (IST), the Indo–Myanmar Friendship Gate had closed and in the next half-hour, the temperature began to drop and dusk set in. Across the border in Tamu, the time was already 5.20 p.m., as there is a fifty-minute time difference between IST and Myanmar Standard Time (MST). All vehicles that had ventured out to the neighbouring country from either side of the border were now involved in a mad rush to return home along Asian Highway 1, racing past each other to cross the border before dark. I called up my journo friends Bises and Dimjit, who had driven me here from Imphal, to find out where they were. It so transpired that they were still in Tamu and almost done with their shopping. Bises, along with his friend, promised to be back soon at the Trade Centre where we had booked our rooms.

With some extra time in hand before I was due back at the Trade Centre, Kajah, who had accompanied me around Moreh since we met near Subramani's home, suggested that we meet some more local communities before heading back. Right across the street from Surinder's shop was a provision store run by Durgaprasad Acharya in the Nepali Basti. Durgrapasad and Kajah were good friends who had grown up together in Moreh in more peaceful times. Despite belonging to different communities that had nothing in common, their families were very close and celebrated festivals and family occasions together.

Reminiscing about their life in Prem Nagar, Durgrapasad said that growing up in Moreh was an experience unlike any other. His closest friends were Tamils, Punjabis and people from different parts of India in whose homes he had eaten, played and slept with the same ease and freedom that they had enjoyed in his home. Holding Kajah by the hand, he said that they had celebrated all Tamil festivals. In turn, the Tamils and other community members would join them in their festivities. Durgaprasad even remembered watching Tamil movie idol Sivaji Ganesan's films in Moreh's movie theatres.

'Those were the good old days,' he sighed. 'Now all the theatres have closed down. But still, we are far more cosmopolitan than people living anywhere else in the North East. Inter-community marriages are so common here, with Nepalis marrying Tamils, Punjabis and Kukis, that most parents do not object to their children marrying someone from a different community, as long as that person is from Moreh.'

The Nepali community in town is among the oldest and moved here way back in 1949, after devastating floods caused by the Brahmaputra River swept away their native villages in Assam. A total of eighteen Nepali families, whose members had lost their homes and livelihood to the floods, were offered land in Moreh to re-establish their lives. Most people we spoke to in the *basti* had not even been born at that time, but knew about the hardships their parents and grandparents had faced when they were asked to move to Moreh and resettle here.

When the first Nepali settlers arrived, they discovered an area that had neither a clearly demarcated border nor any trace of a market. It was, in fact, a thick jungle, infested with wild elephants and filled with scrap from the battle of Imphal that had taken place between the British and Japanese armed forces during the Second World War. During the battle, the 20th Indian Infantry Division of the British Army, which was stationed at Tamu, clashed with the approaching Japanese forces. So much scrap had piled up in the forest that the Nepalis made a living simply by collecting it and selling it to merchants in Imphal.

With the money they would earn selling scrap, the Nepalis, who were traditional cow herders, bought cows and sold their milk to the Assam Rifles personnel in Moreh, as well as to customers across the border in Tamu. Over time, the families made it their home. The second generation of Nepalis gradually shifted their focus to other trades and played an active role in setting up the bazaar. Over the years, however, as insurgency peaked in the hills above Moreh, the cow-herding families were forced to turn to other ways of earning a living, as there was no certainty that the cattle they let out to graze in the jungles every day would return home safely. The Nepali community in Moreh is now involved exclusively in trading.

As the sun set in the hills behind us, Kajah and I headed for Muslim Nagar, located almost on the international boundary line behind Nepali Basti. Muslim Nagar is home to the local Muslim community which consists of around 350 families of Manipuri Muslims engaged mostly in casual labour. A minority community, they work as porters at the international-border gate or as woodcutters in the forests. Members of this community migrated from different parts of Manipur and arrived in Moreh relatively later than others in the late 1960s and early 1970s, following the expansion of Moreh Bazaar and the increasing demand for daily labour.

As we walked down the congested, potholed streets of this locality, it became obvious to me that it was among the most neglected in town. It was not as if the other roads I had seen in Moreh so far were well-maintained. They were no more than expanded dirt tracks full of bumps and hollows, but the ones in

Muslim Nagar were far worse. Autorickshaws and motorcycles kicked up swirls of dust and dry soil as they sped by and smeared entire neighourhoods with dirt. At the end of the *basti* was the international boundary line, where scantily clad children played in small mud pools right next to the barbed-wire fencing on which work seemed to have been abandoned.

* * *

'This is the international border and behind that fence is Myanmar,' Kajah announced. 'They stopped erecting the fence midway, as there is some dispute, yet to be resolved, over ownership of the land beyond that point. Both India and Myanmar claim it as their territory.'

The children who had been playing in the mud pool now ran to the other side of the fence and began flinging sticks at one another. Every now and then, scooters and motorcycles would ride through these dirt roads whose tracks had formed naturally over years of use. They would move across the international border, making their way from Muslim Nagar into Burmese territory without any screening or verification whatsoever.

It struck me suddenly that none of the two-wheelers plying in Moreh had any number plates and asked Kajah about it.

'Did you see those people going to Tamu on their motorcycles?' he asked. 'Vehicles shuttle between Tamu and Moreh all the time and it is illegal to drive Indian vehicles in Tamu without a permit. But who has the time to get a permit for every single visit to Tamu, which is virtually at our doorstep? So we just take these back roads and enter Burmese territory, finish our work and return home. That's why we don't use number plates here. The local police on both sides of the border are well aware of it.'

Standing near that open border, I could relate to what Surinder Singh had said about things beginning to move across to Myanmar. If it was so easy to travel to the other side in broad daylight and return safely without any checking, I could imagine the kind of trafficking that was likely to take place after dark along a border that was notorious for all kinds of smuggling, including that of narcotics and arms. As Surinder had stated earlier, it was just a matter of demand and supply. For all the restrictions imposed by countries and their regimes on the movement of goods, locals out to make a quick buck did not really give a damn. They just fulfilled their needs from the nearest available source, whichever country that might be. If it was considered illegal, so be it. After all, what was deemed legal or illegal was subjective and bound to change with time.

On our way back to the Trade Centre, Kajah and I discussed the pathetic condition of the roads in Moreh and the lackadaisical attitude of the civic body officials who fuelled communal politics and swindled the funds allocated for the town's development. By now, the lights had been turned on in the roadside shops and the streets were emptying. With the border gate and the bazaar closing for the day, most of the people would return to their homes and prefer to stay put, as groups of Assam Rifles personnel and local police returned to their positions for the night. When I reached the Trade Centre, Biseswar and Dimjit had already returned from Tamu and were sitting in their room with a bottle of whiskey with the choicest of pork dishes and fried fish to go with it. They greeted me and invited me to join them.

By 9 p.m., we had run out of liquor and decided to go out for dinner. By then, most of the eateries and other shops in Moreh had already downed their shutters. We headed to one of the remaining few restaurants that was still open and ordered a simple meal of rice and dal, along with two bottles of beer, that we shared between us. On our way back, we stopped by at a cigarette and paan shop run by a pretty Kuki woman. While we were waiting for the sweet paan we had ordered, Biseswar and Dimjit, who were completely sozzled, started flirting with the woman and I also joined them in my broken Hindi. When she realized that we wouldn't stop blabbering, the well-endowed woman simply laughed at us and shooed us away. With a lit cigarette in one hand and a mouthful of paan, we laughed, yelled and staggered our way back to the Trade Centre, just as three drunks would have done anywhere else in the world. On the way, groups of Assam Rifles soldiers who were standing sentinel at street corners cheered us on. I shook hands with some of them and took several out-of-focus selfies, before stumbling back to my room. It was difficult to imagine that barely a month ago, this very town had been ransacked and razed to the ground in one of the worst communal riots between the Meiteis and the tribals.

* * *

At a quarter to seven the next morning, I left the Trade Centre to meet 90-year-old Babudon Morangthn, one of Moreh's oldest residents. Babudon belonged to the Meitei community and lived with his son and daughter-in-law in their concrete home on the bank of a clear stream very close to the town's police station.

The tall, lean man was clad in nothing but a blue *lungi* and had thick, straight hair that was only slightly greyer than mine. He received us courteously and invited us into his living room, where he spread out a coir mat on the floor and sat down. He explained that he was more comfortable stretching out his legs and offered us chairs to sit on. He spoke in a loud, gruff voice that did not falter even once during our long conversation that morning.

'I'm growing a little deaf in one ear and I also had to undergo cataract surgery recently,' he told us. 'What to do? I just have to live with it.'

A native of Kakching in Thoubal district, Babudon did not

remember the exact year of his move to Moreh, as it was a long time ago. He did recall, however, that he was around 21 years old when he moved to Tamu from the interiors of Burma. He had gone there as part of a group of Manipuri traders seeking work in the other country. It was 1948 and Burma had just gained independence from colonial rule.

'Earlier, no border had existed between the two countries which shared the same laws and dealt in the same currency under British rule,' Babudon explained to me. 'But subsequently, we came to know that independent Burma had introduced its own laws, along with a currency that was different from ours.'

Following the formation of an Indian government after Independence, the first chief minister of Manipur visited Tamu and advised businessmen from his state to move to Moreh, as Tamu was now a part of independent Burma.

However, the suggested move to Moreh – no more than a dense jungle at the time, infested with wild animals and quite unfit for human habitation – was not considered feasible by Babudon and his fellow Manipuri businessmen. The chief minister's advice went unheeded and the traders remained in Tamu and continued selling goods at the market, which included everything from clothes and candles to cookware imported from China, Thailand and other South East Asian countries.

'Then one day, a conman from China arrived at the market and bought up almost everything there was for sale, promising to pay us for the goods within a few days,' Babudon went on. 'We realized we had been duped when he vanished without a trace. We approached the Tamu Police for help, but they turned us down, suggesting that as Indian citizens, we should register our complaint in our own country. We had no choice but to take our grievances to Manipur's chief minister, who now informed us bluntly that if we continued to live in Tamu, he could do nothing to redress the injustices done to us and that it would be best if we moved to Moreh and set up a village.'

Following that incident of fraud and the Tamu Police's refusal to help the Manipuri settlers, the state government of Manipur arranged for some of Moreh's forested areas to be cleared, allocated plots of land and helped them set up a village. The homes that came up in the village were built around five kilometers from the border, beyond the range of bullets from the Burmese armed forces rifles. One after the other, the Manipuri businessmen gradually shut down their shops in Tamu and set them up again in Moreh. Thus, a fledgling bazaar grew on the Indian side of the border, where most of the goods sold were imported from China.

Babudon recalled that when they initially settled in Moreh, the hills surrounding the area were completely uninhabited and inhospitable.

'Over the years, however, business picked up and the bazaar spread, growing bigger and bigger, and Moreh acquired the status of a township in 1980,' he added. 'By then, many Mayangs from Yangon [formerly Rangoon] and the rest of India had arrived and settled here, giving business a boost.'

As one of Moreh's oldest residents, Babudon had witnessed or been aware of almost every major event, including the clashes between the different communities in the area, the visits of dignitaries and the proposals for development over the years. I asked him if he was happy with the way Moreh had turned out six decades later and if this was what its original founders had looked forward to.

Babudon's response was to recall the promises made by the then chief minister of Manipur.

'When the chief minister was informed of the problems we were facing in Tamu and the complete indifference of the local police to our plight, he had advised us to move to Moreh and set up a bazaar, assuring us that this market and the town surrounding it would become a very important destination in the coming years, as the place would develop into an international-border town. His promise is yet to be fulfilled even after so many years, but I still nurture hopes of Moreh becoming an international city in the future.'

All through our conversation, Bises and his friend insisted that Babudon try and recall if Kukis or members of other tribal communities had been present in Moreh or in its surrounding areas when they originally moved in. When the nonagenarian emphatically stated that not a single tribal had been living in Moreh or in the surrounding hills at the time, my companions were keen that I should make a special note of it. In fact, during my interchanges with Babudon, I came to know that even those referred to as Moreh's original Manipuri settlers had actually arrived here from different parts of what was then Burma, after the British handed over the administration of India and Burma to the respective countries. With this knowledge in my grasp, Moreh acquired in my mind the distinctive status of a town without any native residents.

While I was still engaged in conversation with Babudon, I got a call from Subramani, reminding me that he was waiting to take me to the only south Indian temple in Moreh before breakfast. After apologizing to the town's oldest settler for not joining him for the morning meal, Bises and I rushed to Mani's home which was located a few hundred metres from the Sri Angala Parameswari temple down Temple Road.

The sprawling temple complex spread across a few acres of land right on the international border. The temple itself was built in the classic Tamil architecture style, its towers and deities almost replicas of the ones that could be seen back in Tamil Nadu. As we took off our slippers and washed our feet at the entrance before going in, Subramani informed me that he visited the temple every morning to offer his prayers to the main deity Angala Parameswari, before going to work. Interestingly, it was not just Tamilians like him who did so, but also people from different communities and faiths, including the Meiteis, the Kukis and the Nepalis.

The Angala Parameswari Temple was built to stand as a symbol of communal harmony. That purpose has, in a certain way, been fulfilled, for this may well be the only Amman temple in the country with one shrine dedicated to the Buddha and another to the Burmese Tamil deity Poochi Thatha who, I would learn, had been a Burmese Tamil so devoted to the welfare of the Tamil community in Myanmar that after his death, people had built a shrine to him.

The Tamil Sangam that managed the temple's affairs had also brought over a Tamil priest from Yangon to perform the puja so that the rituals involved were strictly observed, with no deviation from the way they were followed in that Burmese city.

While walking around the temple, Subramani told me that the Tamil Sangam took great pride in maintaining the place and was planning to further increase the height of the temple tower.

'Who knows?' he mused, as we approached the rear entrance of the temple complex, beyond which lay Burmese territory. 'A few years later, this may well be the only proof that Tamilians once lived and thrived in this town. We want to preserve the temple in such a way that it will endure, regardless of what becomes of the local Tamil population.'

Stepping out of the temple complex, Subramani announced that we were officially in Myanmar. Standing before us was a smaller temple, now abandoned. Much older than the main temple, it was in a dilapidated condition. Even the shrine's main deity was missing.

'Since this small temple stands on land that Myanmar claims as its own, we built a larger one in what we know as our territory,' Mani explained. 'Now that too is being disputed. The Sri Angala Parameswari Temple draws devotees not only from the entire Mayang community, but also from among the tribals and the Meiteis. I have even known Burmese Buddhists to cross the open border and come to pray in our temple.'

* * *

After the temple visit, Mani took us along to a traditional south Indian restaurant for a sumptuous breakfast of idlis and dosas with coconut chutney and sambar. Over the years, idli and sambar have become common fare in this region. I even spotted a few Manipuris dipping soft white idlis in a pool of sambar until they were soaked in the lentil soup, before popping them into their open mouths. Next to the restaurant was a barber shop, also run by a Tamil. Beyond it stood a shop selling utensils. This too was owned by a Mayang. I learnt that in the early years, when Moreh was developing as a township, this was the very neighbourhood that had been known as Prem Nagar. With most of the Mayangs having moved elsewhere, driven away by the recurrent fires of the past, the few Tamil families that still held on to their homes and the properties that had been converted into business outlets over the years were the only reminders of this failed experiment.

Having criss-crossed the little town, visiting one *basti* after another, I was now left with the task of interacting with members of just one other major community which also called Moreh home. Unlike the others, the Kukis were a great deal more reluctant to speak with outsiders. This could have been due to their lack of education and their miserable living conditions which isolated them further from the mainstream. Kajah suggested that I meet the office bearers of the Hill Tribal Council, an umbrella organization of various tribal units that operate in the hills.

Joseph Ginkhosei, vice president of the Hill Tribal Council (HTC), was waiting, along with another senior member of the council, to receive us when we reached the office building of the Hill Tribal Council at 9.15 a.m. The HTC represents the interests of tribals (mostly Kukis) in and around Moreh and is the umbrella organization that brings together several smaller units such as the Kuki Students' Organization. Among the most prominent tribes in this part of the North East, the Kukis are spread across a wide terrain, including parts of Manipur and Nagaland, some areas of Mizoram and even Myanmar.

Painted on the wall of the HTC office's main hall was a large map marking Kuki-inhabited territories as 'Kukiland'. This area spread across Manipur and its surrounding states, including significant territory in Myanmar, with small pockets marked in different colours to represent the Meitei and other communities. While the Meiteis considered the Kuki tribes as migrants from Myanmar, who were waging a guerrilla war both against the Indian state and other tribal groups, the Kukis claimed that their tribe had historically been at the receiving end of many injustices in every state where they had a presence.

The Kuki uprising of the 1970s and 1980s, largely attributed to the suffering faced by the community at the hands of the Nagas and the Meiteis, had been documented in the HTC's Silver Jubilee souvenir that was handed to me as soon as I arrived at their office.

Joseph Ginkhosei was a smart, soft-spoken, middle-aged man who had arrived in Moreh as a schoolteacher. Moved by the plight of his people, he had subsequently become actively involved in their welfare. Since then, he had been a key member of the HTC and had worked with all community leaders to ensure that peace and harmony prevailed in Moreh.

I asked him about the Kuki community and its background.

He pointed at the HTC souvenir and said, 'You will get most

of the information about our community and the Hill Tribal Council from this. I don't think I have anything further to add.'

Joseph had moved to Moreh in his twenties, after he landed a job here as a teacher. Originally from Tengnoupal, he completed his higher studies in Imphal and Shillong and was now settled in Moreh with his family. Of his seven offspring – a son and six daughters – three were now in Bengaluru, pursuing higher studies, while the remaining four, school-going children, lived with him in Moreh.

'Living in Moreh is a unique experience,' he began, 'as nowhere else in India can we find so many communities co-existing in relative harmony for so many years, that too in such close proximity with one another. We have representatives from every major community here and have faced many violent conflicts in the past, but we have managed to move on. The HTC works very closely with all the other community organizations in Moreh and together, we strive to take the peace process forward. Every now and then, we fail, but we gather together again and continue the process.'

The Kukis are among the most recent migrants to Moreh. Joseph said that members of this community began moving to Moreh during the 1970s and 1980s, when this place was a small village and illicit trade thrived between Moreh and Tamu.

'Living here was easy and several tribals who moved here got jobs as porters and carriers for the larger business communities from the mainland, like the Tamils and the Punjabis,' Joseph explained. 'A couple of trips between Tamu and Moreh could fetch the tribals enough money to make a decent living and life was good. Hence, many families from the community moved here within a short period of time to escape poverty in the hills.'

But the scenario changed in the 1990s after the free-trade agreement between India and Myanmar came into effect, eliminating the need for such carriers in a big way. The transition from village life to an urban settlement was difficult for the tribals, who were the least educated of the settlers and among the lowest on the social ladder. When they lost their jobs as porters and carriers, many took to making charcoal from wood or mining sand and rocks from the river banks, activities which were neither economically sound nor healthy for the environment. Unemployment and poverty were the natural fallout of this transition and the HTC played an important role in helping its members cope with the challenges of urban living, which was a new concept for them.

In any city, where great economic disparity exists between its various communities, simmering tensions between its members are but natural. Moreh was no exception to the rule. Since the Kukis were native to the region and had significant numbers on both sides of the border, the other communities blamed the Burmese Kukis for all the problems on the Indian side and claimed that they were operating with vested interests.

When I asked Joseph about the most recent clashes in Moreh, he replied, 'They were not caused by residents of Moreh. Outsiders streamed in from other places and tried to organize a protest here. Otherwise, there would not have been any violence at all. It is a sad reality of our lives that when we people from the North East go to any other city in India, we stay together as a close-knit group, but out here, we fight bitterly among ourselves. Although we look alike and share a similar culture, our history is filled with bloodshed.'

Since he seemed to be the sanest person I had spoken to over the last few days, I asked him about the term 'Mayang' that had been irking me for a long time. Laughing a little over my query, Joseph remarked that it was just a casual reference.

'Personally, I feel we should be Indians first, then Manipuris – and then Kuki or Meitei or whatever,' he said.

'You have three children living in Bengaluru. Do you think they have a right to settle in that city and become Bengalureans – if that is what they prefer?' I asked him.

'Yes,' he replied, 'they should be able to do that. Similarly, any resident from another state should be free to come and live in Manipur. As I said earlier, we are Indians first.' He paused for a moment, before adding, 'But that's just my personal opinion.'

* * *

Having visited almost every other *basti* and community hall in Moreh, I finally left for the international border which I had been itching to visit since I had arrived. While one can simply walk to the Burmese town of Tamu through the Indo–Myanmar Friendship Gate by flashing a valid identity card at the guards, driving to the same town requires a permit. The permit can be obtained in Moreh and is valid for a six-hour period. Bises and Dimjit had arranged for the required permit while I was busy interacting with Joseph Ginkhosei and were ready with it before noon. Therefore, we chose not to pass through the Friendship Gate to cross the border and preferred, instead, to take a winding road that diverged from the gate and led to a bridge painted half-yellow and half-silver. The yellow side of the bridge was in Myanmar and Dimjit, who was driving, announced our arrival in the neighbouring country by swerving the car so abruptly to the right side of the road that the tyres screeched in protest.

'In Myanmar, we have to drive on the right side of the road,' he explained.

A little ahead of the bridge stood the first Burmese check post, where my two companions presented the permit for inspection and were issued a visiting pass for six hours. Propping up the pass behind the front windshield, we drove towards Tamu.

As had been my experience with all the other border towns

I had visited so far, the other side seemed greener and more prosperous. The roads on the Burmese side were neatly laid and wide enough for at least three or four cars to drive abreast. Lined along the curbs were rows of tall teak trees and beyond those trees lay dense tropical vegetation which I had not come across in Moreh. About a kilometre into Burmese territory, we spotted cute wooden cabins standing at least four or five feet above the ground, supported on stilts made from sturdy logs of teakwood. In fact, every home we saw here stood at least a couple of feet above ground level. The walls of these thatched roof houses were fashioned from wooden planks. Plying on the road were pushcart vendors who had attached to their motorcycles wheeled carts laden with their goods – fruits, ice creams and other perishables – which they sold to customers along the way. Large, colourful fabric umbrellas had been unfurled and set up over these goods to protect them from the scorching sun. The traffic was noticeably sparse and we hardly came across an automobile on the road, for most of the locals here seemed to prefer high-power motorcycles, to which they had attached pushcarts and wagons, and rode them at top speed.

A few blocks ahead, we spotted a Dagon Beer Station and halted. Bises informed me that liquor was dirt cheap in Myanmar and suggested that I check out the local brew. We walked into the rustic open bar and sat down at a table for three. The plump Burmese woman at the beer station did not, however, understand Manipuri or any other Indian language. Neither Bises nor his friend were familiar with her language. Resorting, finally, to sign language, we ordered three mugs of chilled beer and savoured it, almost incredulous at the thought that it had cost a mere ₹40 a mug. I was told that a canister full of beer was available for as little as ₹500.

Having downed the beer, the three of us drove to the popular

Namphalong Market, located right at the border near the Indo–Myanmar Friendship Gate on the Burmese side. It was as famous for the sheer range of the products on offer as for their throwaway prices.

'You can get everything here, from *ganja* and heroin to an automatic rifle,' Bises volunteered, as we drove into the parking lot.

The Friendship Gate was about a hundred metres from the parking lot and the road leading to it was lined with shops that sold mostly vegetables, spices, flowers and other household items. In addition, there were a few electronics and mobile-phone outlets. A majority of the salespersons were pretty Burmese women with delicate features and finely sculpted noses who had *thanakha* paste smeared on their cheeks and wore wide-brimmed hats made of thatched leaves to shield them against the blistering sun. Their poise reminded me of Burmese politician and the country's first State Counsellor Aung San Suu Kyi, whose posters were plastered all over Tamu.

Bises and I approached the International Gate on foot. Here, the pedestrian traffic split into two distinct queues for Indian and Burmese nationals. We joined the queue marked for Indians and walked back through the gate into Moreh.

The difference in road conditions and infrastructure was glaring as we entered Indian territory. The shops on this side, all made of bamboo, stood cheek by jowl and appeared on the verge of collapse. Just inside the gate on the Indian side were at least two dozen pushcarts, lined up one after another and piled with plastic chairs, huge sacks and cardboard boxes packed with coconuts and vegetable oil cans and a variety of other goods. Porters, dozens and dozens of them, carried these sacks and cardboard boxes on their backs or heads from the Namphalong Market on the Burmese side and loaded them on to these waiting pushcarts on the Indian side. When one of the carts was fully loaded, another porter would take charge, pulling it away towards the Moreh town bus stand.

In the ten minutes I spent at the gate, watching these porters carry goods to the pushcarts which were pulled away as soon as they were loaded, at least a hundred sacks and boxes must have been transported to the Moreh bus stand. I was told that this activity went on non-stop from 7 a.m. to 4 p.m., seven days a week. It was only after spending a little time at the International Gate that I obtained an idea of the volume of trade that was taking place across this border every day, that too solely with the help of porters moving on foot.

I stopped one of these men and asked him where he was headed. The cart puller, a Bihari settled in Moreh for ten years now, answered that he was taking goods to the town bus stand, from where they would be transported to different parts of the country. He charged ₹100 for pulling a cart to the parking lot and helping to load goods on to trucks and other vehicles. Hundreds of porters from across the country made a decent income by working a few hours every day at this border.

After a while, we returned to Tamu by crossing over to the other side through the Indo–Myanmar Friendship Gate. On this occasion, I was asked to produce a valid identity card for inspection. We walked past several pavement stalls towards the Namphalong Market about which I had heard so much. Its most striking feature turned out to be the difference in price between the goods – even branded ones – sold here and those available in the larger Indian cities. I discovered that the prices of even electronics goods like TVs, DVD players and home-theatre systems were significantly lower than in Chennai or Kolkata. Liquor was sold in every shop, including electronics showrooms, and at prices that would make any tippler delirious with joy.

After window shopping along the main road, we forayed

into one of the many lanes, also lined with shops. It was only then that it struck me how vast the range of goods available at this international market was. Clothes, woollens, watches, water cans, artificial flowers, hair clips, cosmetics, firecrackers, motors and even fire extinguishers were sold here. As we made our way from one lane into another, I could not conceal my astonishment at the phenomenally low prices at which the products were offered. Digital watches sold in India for no less than ₹250 a piece were available here for ₹200 a dozen! Hair clips, toy guns, walkie-talkies – all were being sold by the dozen at shockingly low prices. Moreover, if you were purchasing them in bulk, you were allowed to bargain even further. We stopped by a shop selling watches and asked the young Nepali girl, who spoke fluent Hindi and seemed to be in charge, how they could afford to sell their goods at such prices.

'All these goods come from the border at wholesale rates,' she explained. 'This is a wholesale market.'

'Which border do you mean?' I asked.

'Oh, different border areas, including those of China, Thailand and other Asian countries,' she replied.

The goods, she elaborated, arrived daily from all over South East Asia and China in the Burmese city of Mandalay, from where they were transported to Tamu. The young girl added that business had been a little slow for the past few days, as the road between Mandalay and Tamu was damaged and undergoing repairs.

Lured by the attractive prices and the wide range of goods, I could not resist the temptation of shopping at the market despite my shoestring budget.

Observing my enthusiasm over the dazzling array of diverse weapons – huge daggers, Samurai swords and air guns – on public display in one of the outlets, Biseswar quipped, 'For the real guns, you need to know the right people.'

After scouring the Namphalong Market and purchasing all that we could load into a car, including heaps of dried fish, the three of us were famished and made a beeline for the food court located right behind the main market. Here, Indian, Chinese and Burmese dishes were served straight off the stove with beer or any other liquor of one's choice. We ordered three plates of chicken fried rice and it came with unlimited refills of soup and dried fish.

Having stuffed ourselves to the gills, we drove to downtown Tamu, about three kilometres from the border, and picked up more booze at literally throwaway prices from a grocery store, before heading back to India. As we drove along the picturesque Indo–Myanmar Friendship Road, I noticed more shops by the roadside doing business, while young men stood around in groups and played cards and board games under the shade of large, colourful umbrellas. Through the window of the car, Myanmar seemed like a really fun place to be in and I felt sad at having to leave so soon.

We returned to the Trade Centre in Moreh at 2.30 p.m. Bises reminded me that we would have to leave Moreh by three, if we were to get past the Assam Rifles check post by 4 p.m.

'Vehicles are not allowed to ply this route after dark without a special pass,' he explained.

Accordingly, we packed all our luggage and left Moreh by 3 p.m. On our way back, my thoughts drifted to the time I had been sceptical and apprehensive about visiting this border town. As it turned out, the trip to Moreh was among the more pleasant journeys I had made. Never had I felt insecure or under threat during the entire trip. It was probably nothing but a stroke of good fortune and a matter of timing that I was returning home without a scratch. I can only describe what I have experienced and to me Moreh will always remain a warm, cosmopolitan and international town.

We reached the Assam Rifles check post at Khudengthabi well before dark, but were stuck in a long queue, as the soldiers at the post almost tore apart the cars, vans and jeeps that had lined up in their search for contraband items. I had stepped out of the car and was standing by a steep slope on the roadside, facing a green valley, when a sudden commotion broke out. It transpired that the soldiers had found a loaded, unlicenced single-shot rifle in a Maruti van and confiscated it. The routine checking resumed in a few minutes and we were soon cleared to proceed to Imphal.

A few kilometres downhill, as the sun began to disappear behind the hills to our right, I noticed a slim, middle-aged man with a thick walrus moustache, like that of forest brigand Veerappan, casually walking along the curb with a rusted rifle slung from his shoulder. I gestured towards the man and asked Bises what was going on.

'Oh, this is quite common here,' he replied. 'He must be a hunter looking for some dinner.'

# 9

# The Indo-Bangladesh Border Trail

The most pertinent among the various preoccupations that haunted me ahead of my long journey through a difficult-to-define Indo–Bangladesh border was my lack of clarity over where I should go. India and Bangladesh share a 4,096 kilometre-long border, the fifth longest land border in the world, out of which 2,217 kilometres lie in West Bengal. The border also passes through Assam, Tripura, Mizoram and Meghalaya, cutting across uninhabitable hilly terrain, passing through rivers and slicing villages into separate segments. Its only concrete manifestation is a giant fence constructed by the Indian government, wherever possible.

Searching for an Indian or Bangladeshi identity seemed a futile pursuit in a land where people think of themselves exclusively as Bengalis and do so with pride. For most of those living along this international border, the boundary line separating the two countries is merely a technical hindrance that they choose to ignore. However, it is a chronic headache for members of the security establishment in both countries, who describe these borderlands as havens for traffickers and smugglers and a base for countless other illegal and anti-national activities.

Considering the enormous and confusing task ahead of me, I decided to take the border trail right through the fertile Gangetic plain from North 24 Parganas district in the southern part of West Bengal to Mashaldanga, a Bangladeshi enclave in India, with Cooch Behar district skirting its northern boundary.

My first stop was Taki, the picturesque tourist destination on the banks of the Ichamati River. While the watercourse is a prime tourist attraction during the day, this stretch of the riverine boundary is notorious for its nocturnal smuggling-related activities through which humans, cattle and all kinds of contraband change nationalities. My intention in visiting Taki was to explore a few layers of that darkness.

* * *

The promenade along the banks of the Ichamati in Taki springs to life in the evenings. Bright lights illuminate the neat line-up of palm trees along the walkway, while melodious Bangla film music wafts out of a speaker system installed in the clock tower, luring visitors – mostly young lovers and large families. The first cuddled cozily together on the corner benches and the second gathered around cement benches with backrests, munching on puffed rice and gossiping as they gazed at the river flowing past. On weekends, the pier invites more footfalls in the form of tourists from Kolkata, who stay at the guest houses surrounding the promenade. For these vacationers, Taki is an ideal weekend getaway, just a two-hour drive from their city, and they all congregate at the promenade after sunset, as there is little else to do.

Beyond the river, the promenade and the guest houses, Taki is a neat little town in the Basirhat subdivision of North 24 Parganas district. One of the oldest municipalities in West Bengal, it was formed in 1869. For a small riverside town, Taki has a surprisingly large number of educational institutions and an impressive public library. The streets are clean and the homes are spread out, with brick compound walls separating one from the other. Behind these walls lie paved pathways lined with ornamental potted plants and crotons that provide shade and cover to concrete homes. According to the municipality's records, around 38,000 people live in Taki. Its narrow bylanes are among the few spots in the world where one can still hear music composer Salil Chowdhury's Bengali classic '*Amay proshno koray neel dhrubo taara*' streaming out from ancient speakers early in the morning when one steps out to have tea.

I reached Taki on a weekday afternoon when the sun was blazing down on the Ichamati River with such intensity that most residents of the town had preferred to stay indoors, enjoying a languid lunch, followed by a siesta. The seat of the open van rickshaw I had hired – basically a rectangular slab of wood placed on four wheels pulled by a cycle – was so hot that I could barely rest my thighs on it without feeling my skin being singed. The rickshaw dropped me off at a guest house on the banks of the Ichamati and I checked into a luxurious room that offered a view of the river and the green thickets on the other bank which lay in Bangladesh.

Unable to resist the temptation of looking at a neighbouring country from up close, I rushed to the pier, braving the heat and humidity. Here I bumped into boatman Barun Das, who was leaning on a parapet leading to the pier and smoking a beedi. The middle-aged man in a lungi folded halfway so that it hung to his knees, approached me as soon as I reached the pier and offered me his services.

'For ₹1,000, I can take you for an hour's ride along the river to a nearby island,' he announced. 'For two thousand, we can go up to the mini Sundarbans, cross the international border and have a look at Bangladeshi fishing boats and villages.'

I was interested in neither of the rides and told Barun that all I wanted was to cross the border and meet Bangladeshi fishermen in their territory.

'That's not possible,' he declared, pointing at a Border Security Force (BSF) watch tower to his right.

Positioned on top of the tower were two burly BSF guards armed with self-loading rifles (SLR).

'If they see us crossing the border, they will shoot us down,' he elaborated.

I told him that I was well aware that this stretch of the Ichamati River was a hotbed for smuggling activities and that thousands of humans, cows and all kinds of goods were clandestinely transported across the river on a daily basis, without attracting any attention.

'Not possible. It used to happen in the past, but not any more,' Barun retorted and walked off.

On his way, he waved at the BSF guards posted on the watch tower. They returned the gesture with a half-wave, as if to acknowledge their approval of his conduct.

* * *

Barun's son Debasish, who turned 23 recently, worked part-time with the Taki municipality and was in charge of keeping the lights on and the music system playing at the promenade all through the evening. The songs aired through the huge speakers were chosen according to his mood on a particular day. A graduate of Taki Government College, Debasish was paid ₹2,000 a month for taking care of the clock tower and filling in vacant positions when permanent employees went on leave. To make ends meet, he helped his father with the boat rides during the day.

In the evening, after turning the lights on and plugging his USB pen drive, loaded with Bangla songs, into the music system, Debasish, who liked wearing shorts and colourful printed shirts when on duty at the promenade, approached tourists to persuade them to book boat rides in advance for the next morning. He made the same pitch for the shorter and longer rides, but did promise that the longer one came with a perk – a free peek into a foreign nation without the aid of either passport or visa.

The stretch of the Ichamati River that flows through West

Bengal's North 24 Parganas district is among the few water bodies in the country to be recognized officially as an international boundary. At a certain location between the two banks of the river that flows over a flat plain lies the Zero Point separating India and Bangladesh. Although local fishermen, the BSF and even the Border Guards Bangladesh (BGB) claim to know the exact location of this line of demarcation, no one here is really sure.

The ambiguity surrounding Zero Point worked in favour of Barun and Debasish, who charged extra money for the transnational boat trip.

'You can go within ten feet of the Bangladesh border and click pictures of their boats and fishing villages. If the BSF offshore-patrol vehicle is not in the vicinity, we can even shake hands with Bangladeshis,' Debasish apparently told prospective clients at the boardwalk. 'Besides, you can get a feel of the Sundarbans without having to travel far.'

All evening, father and son would look for prospective clients to take on boat rides. While the rates had been fixed by the municipality, the income generated was split, with half the money going to the local-body coffers.

Unaware that his father had already tried selling me the rides, Debasish too made an offer for a ride early next morning, when the river would swell with the opening of the sluice gates in some distant reservoir. Not wanting to disappoint the earnest young man, I kept the conversation alive by agreeing to take the longer ride next morning, the one offering a look at 'foreign' territory. Our conversation touched upon a variety of topics, but when he came to know that I had written a book, Debasish confided that he too wrote poetry. He pulled out a folded sheet of paper from his shirt pocket, which contained his latest creation – an ode to a lost love – and read it out loud in chaste Bengali. After that, I felt we gelled better.

Like his father Barun, Debasish was also born and raised on the banks of the Ichamati. While the older man had never been to school, working on tourist boats from the age of eight, he had ensured that Debasish and his other children received a sound education. Debasish was even allowed to continue his studies until he had graduated from college in the hope that the next generation, at least, would land better jobs and bring the family much-needed prosperity. For his part, Debasish had passed out of the Taki Government College with a BA Honours in Bangla.

'When I came out of college, my dream was to get a government job,' Debasish told me that evening. 'So I applied for all the vacancies I chanced upon for government posts, but did not get so much as an interview call from anyone. I even went for recruitment in the Police. Citing my short stature, the West Bengal Police rejected my application.'

After several such futile attempts, the young man began to help his father on boat rides, while working part-time at the Taki municipality. His dream now was to become a teacher in one of the local government schools. He declared that he had always admired the teaching profession and wanted to encourage other youngsters to get ahead in life. But this too was very likely to remain just a dream. Teaching vacancies were hard to come by and there were so many applicants for a single vacancy that Debasish felt it would be difficult to land a job anywhere in West Bengal without some political and financial backing.

'Our state government has repeatedly failed us,' he lamented, beginning to wind up for the day.

At exactly 9 p.m. every evening, Debasish turned off the music system. The lights would go out shortly afterwards. On good days, he would have one or two boat trips lined up for the following morning before he returned to the base of the clock tower to unplug the USB device playing his favourite songs. After the music had died down and the lights were turned off, the boardwalk and the shops surrounding it would become deserted. The eateries and other outlets elsewhere in town would also pull down their shutters, as locals and tourists retired for the night. Debasish too would return home to his wife, the high-school sweetheart he had married just a year ago.

Just before he left the promenade that night and headed home, I asked him if he would take me across the border by hoodwinking the BSF guys.

'But what do you want to find out?' he asked.

I replied that I had come to Taki to experience life in a border town as he saw it. 'You all know what happens here. Now I too want to find out,' I told him.

'Well, you've just heard about what happens in Taki,' he said. 'My father was illiterate and made a living operating a tourist boat. I, his son, have an Honours degree in Bangla and yet, I too survive by operating the same tourist boat with my father. This is Taki. Here, it doesn't matter whether you're educated or illiterate. If you are honest and not connected with the right people, you will remain poor. I also have the choice of becoming rich and there are, in fact, so many people who amass money, thanks to this river. But then, I would have to become like them and I don't particularly want to.'

Debasish's disappointment with Taki and life in general had made him sound brusque to the point of rudeness when he uttered those words. But being an enterprising guy, he soon changed the topic and focussed on the opportunity that lay before him.

'So many things happen on this river in one night. Let's find out tomorrow,' he suggested.

* * *

After parting from Debasish, I walked along a narrow, winding road that ran close to the river bank and reached Sodepur, which is situated less than a kilometre from the promenade. A few hundred families live in this border village and make a living by catching fish. Spotting a stranger walking towards their village late on a moonlit night, a crowd, mostly of women, immediately gathered around me. When I explained that I was a journalist and had come to spend the night in their village, they directed me to the house of an old fisherman, Puran Mundol, who was preparing his country boat, along with members of his family, for the nightlong fishing trip. Depending on the season, Puran and his crew, operating in teams of four and six, would venture out on the river in their boats well after sundown, flying the Indian tricolour high enough to be visible to the border-security guards. After the boats had moved out far enough to reach a certain depth in the river, the fishermen would lay out their nets and, on good days, return with a good catch several hours later.

'So what is it that you want to know about our lives?' Puran asked me bluntly, when I went to his hut.

'I would like to witness whatever happens on the river at night,' I told him. 'I hear that so many things take place here after dark.'

'This is an international border and many things happen along it. As long as we mind our own business and don't invite any trouble from the BSF, there is no problem,' he declared, taking out a beedi from behind his ear and lighting it.

Puran's family had been living in Sodepur for the last 60 years after his ancestors moved here from somewhere near Dhaka (then Dacca) soon after Partition. Settled along this shore since then, the family now owned a boat, in addition to some land and an artificial pond where they bred fish. The way Puran saw it, there was nothing unusual about their lives, apart from the fact that he had to carry an Indian flag when he went out fishing and turn a blind eye to what was happening around him.

Every fisherman here knew that hundreds, if not thousands,

of cows from across the country were brought to these border villages to be smuggled to Bangladesh every day. The cows were herded across by smugglers who swam along with the animals until they reached the other shore safely. Besides cows, gold and other items were also being smuggled out. Villagers like Puran, who had been witnessing this for years, were sympathetic towards the BSF guards and claimed that their hands were tied.

'Senior officers might be taking bribes and allowing the operation. What can these jawans do?' asked his nephew Karthik Mundol, just as lean and bony as his uncle, but younger, and standing so close that I felt uneasy. 'The cows come all the way from Uttar Pradesh, Maharashatra and other parts of India. If they can travel all the way to Taki and Sodepur without being detected, what is the point in blaming the poor BSF alone?'

By now, a crowd had gathered around me and the fishermen who had been hesitant to interact with me initially, were now chatting quite freely. According to them, while human trafficking and smuggling of gold and narcotics had been taking place along this border for years, cow smuggling had gained notoriety over the past decade or so.

'Everyone here knows about it. Sometimes, when large-scale smuggling is planned for a particular evening, the guards send us a signal, warning us not to venture out. We wait till it is "all clear", before resuming our fishing activities,' volunteered an elderly woman, who even yelled out the name of the person she believed was controlling the riverside smuggling. 'Every now and then, some cows and herders get shot or arrested, but not much is made of these incidents.'

Soon, the number of people around me had swelled dramatically and some were openly mentioning the names of alleged smugglers. Noticing the commotion, two BSF guards who were passing by on a bicycle stopped to enquire what was going on. Finding me there, the men advised me to return to the guest house at once. I obliged and hitched a ride back to Taki with them.

* * *

For the residents of Sodepur, Taki and other neighbourhoods on this side of the Ichamati, smuggling of people and goods across the river is a reality they face every day. It is also a source of income for many among them. While each of them had a theory about the origin of these smuggling activities and the identity of the gangster who controlled the operations, few in the region had explored this menace thoroughly or encountered it first hand, unlike Dilip Banerjee. The ex-chairman of the Taki municipality had held the post for eighteen long years until he was toppled by a rival Trinamool Congress leader a few years ago. Dilip was also among the few persons here to have first-hand data and information about this important town.

When I went to meet him on a balmy evening at his medical shop on Kalinath Munshi Sarani, the 71-year-old veteran communist leader was seated on a rickety old wooden chair, resting his hands on an equally ancient wooden table and reading a magazine. In his younger days, Banerjee could hardly spare the time to sit in his shop as he was caught up in local politics. After his party lost control over the municipal administration, however, Banerjee was able to spend a few hours in the morning and evening at his pharmacy, selling medicines to a few loyal customers. Born and raised in Taki and having completed his graduation from the Government College here, Banerjee knew more about the history of the town and its politics than most.

Dilip Banerjee was born into an influential Brahmin family in Taki just a few years before the country gained its independence when the town was part of an undivided Bengal whose borders lay far beyond the Ichamati River. Even in those days, this scenic riverside town was known for its educational institutions and its progressive zamindars, who introduced several social reforms for the benefit of their subjects. The town itself, now almost 300 years old, was established by wealthy zamindars who had originally owned all the land. They lived in large, ostentatious palaces and were addressed as 'raja' (king) by their subjects. While most zamindars who ruled during that era were primarily interested in amassing wealth and waging wars either against the British or among themselves, those belonging to Taki set great store by education and believed in the importance of social reforms. One of the first zamindars to have taken a step in this direction was Babu Kalinath Munshi. A disciple of Babu Ram Mohan Rai, Munshi spearheaded the movement towards the abolition of the heinous tradition of *sati*, whereby widows were forcibly burnt alive on the funeral pyres of their deceased husbands. In fact, Babu Kalinath Munshi was the first signatory in the memorandum prepared by the local zamindars in this connection and was known to have little regard for the country's British rulers. He even built the road from Barasat to Taki for the government on the condition that it would be called Taki Road. This action did people living in the area a great service, for in those days, there was no connectivity between Calcutta (now Kolkata) and Taki and in the absence of a road, the general public had to travel several kilometres through dense jungle, exposing themselves to the risk of being attacked and looted by dacoits.

Over 140 years ago, Taki had been declared a municipality by the British government, for in those times, it was among the most developed and sophisticated municipalities in undivided Bengal. The government-run school here was built by Sir A.K. Rai who, apart from his philanthropic activities, also held the post of Solicitor General in the British-ruled government. Students from faraway places, even villages that now lie in the interiors of

Bangladesh, would come all the way to Taki to attend this school, as it was the only centre for miles around that had the authority to conduct the matriculation exams. In those days, the Ichamati was a narrow watercourse that one could actually cross on foot by using the little bridges and stone pathways spanning it. Banerjee still remembered stories of students crossing the river and coming to Taki to sit for their board examinations at the school here.

The veteran Marxist had also attended Taki's Government School and his first initiation into politics took place when he joined the Students Federation of India (SFI) at the age of sixteen. So actively involved was the young Brahmin lad in campus politics, while in high school and college, that he was elected General Secretary of the college students' union for three successive terms. It was also a time when the Communist Party was strengthening its hold in West Bengal and the surrounding region, which was still recovering from the trauma of being severed brutally in two during Partition and searching for an identity of its own.

'In those days, politicians were bound by ethics and principles and the eminent leaders we were blessed with were individuals we could admire and emulate,' observed Banerjee. He was so firm in his beliefs and dedicated to the Party that he did not even attend the funeral of his parents because the rituals involved conflicted with his chosen ideology. 'There was fierce competition between the politicians, but their activities never degenerated into *goondagiri* [hooliganism].'

But by the time Dilip fought his first local-body elections, East Bengal had undergone one more transformation and had been reborn as Bangladesh, with the Ichamati River serving as the political line of demarcation between the two countries.

Over the years, with the changing fortunes of the two Bengals, the politics of the land gradually acquired a different complexion.

With the rise in unemployment, poverty and the lack of industrial growth in Bangladesh, on the one hand, and the increasing need for money and muscle power in West Bengal, on the other, the Ichamati River and its muddy grey waters became an El Dorado for those living around it.

'Today, politics in Taki revolves around the river. Whoever controls the river, controls the area's politics and the outcome of elections in this region,' Banerjee said in conclusion, winding up his long chat. 'And since those who now enter politics are no longer the kind known for their integrity or principles, guns and goons control this land. This is Taki's plight now.'

Dilip Banerjee was not one to give up so easily, however. He declared that although he and his comrades were now on the back foot, having lost to the Trinamool Congress during the most recent municipality elections, they would come back to power in the next term. The irony was that the Marxists too would have to pledge their rights over the river, if they sought to fight their way back to power.

* * *

On my last day in Taki, I remarked to my local contact Siraj, a young Muslim who aspired to be a policeman, that while there was so much talk about human trafficking, cow smuggling and other clandestine activities across the Ichamati, I was yet to see any sign of them.

Siraj lived with his wife, son, parents and brother's family in their ancestral home about six kilometres from Taki. Despite being born and raised in one of West Bengal's poorest neighbourhoods, the enterprising youth had managed to complete his graduation with an Honours degree in English Literature. The 26-year-old was not only the sole graduate in his family, but also in the whole of Talpukur. Due to the elite status he enjoyed in the village as an educated man, he had earned the good will of his neighbours and was quite popular. I sensed that with a little prodding, Siraj would be able to provide me with ample evidence for all the rumours that had reached my ears so far.

'I cannot prove it in a big town like Taki,' Siraj said, in response to my probing. 'Come to my village and I will show you ample proof.'

Before the heat could dampen my spirits, I sat pillion on Siraj's Splendour motorcycle. We travelled all the way to Talpukur along a winding tar road flanked by rice and jute fields, vegetable gardens and reservoirs brimming with muddy water. Like the several identical-looking villages that we passed on our way, Talpukur was a nondescript settlement, with a busy bazaar stretching along the main road that consisted of about a dozen shops selling everything from meat and clothes to grocery supplies and even *rosogollas*. A couple of pushcart vendors selling fruit and puri/*kachodi* fought for space with tempo vans parked there for transporting goods, choking the main road.

Beyond the bazaar, the tar topping on the road simply wore away and the width of the thoroughfare narrowed considerably. As we parked the bike and made our way through the village on foot, the dirt road narrowed down still further to a kind of pedestrian path flanked on either side by reservoirs filled with dirty water. The soil was greyish black and the land almost barren but for a few mango, guava and other fruit trees battling for space with the fish ponds. Ahead of me, I could see little huts with mud walls and thatched roofs. Playing with soiled toys outside these dwellings were bare-bodied little children.

Within a few minutes, we had reached a tea shop.

'This belongs to my younger brother,' Siraj stated and ordered two cups of tea for us.

As we drank the brew, I peeped inside the hut, whose entrance was shielded by a curtain, and found dozens of able-bodied young men sitting in groups, smoking beedis, playing cards and carrom. I asked Siraj about these men who could sit around playing cards on a weekday at 11 a.m.

'They are all from our village and its surrounding areas,' he said.

These young men were from poor Bengali families that did not own land and depended on casual labour for survival. As there were hardly any jobs available in the village or in the nearby towns, except for the rare road-building work or other construction activity taken up by the panchayat, men from Talpukur and its surrounding areas would travel across the country seeking work. With very little education to their credit, they were employed as construction workers or casual labourers in Mumbai, Delhi, Bengaluru and even in Chennai and Coimbatore, where they would live for several months a year. When they returned home after earning a substantial sum, the men would remain in their villages for three to six months at a stretch, before returning to work in some other city. When they spent time in the village, they had nothing to do and invariably ended up in this tea shop-cum-recreation centre or bar.

'This is life in a Bangla village,' Siraj sighed.

When we passed by a tiny shop that sold candies, homemade sweets, cigarettes and other cheap articles, he motioned for me to stop.

'The owner of this shop is from Bangladesh and has married a woman from our village,' Siraj informed me, before hurrying into the place. 'He will tell you all about the human-trafficking racket.'

A few minutes later, a lean, dark, bearded man, dressed in a long grey kurta and pajama, emerged from the shop with Siraj. He introduced himself as Shahjahan and set down the couple of chairs he was carrying under a nearby mango tree. After we had settled down, he volunteered the information that he was from Barsila village in Bangladesh's Khulna district and had come to India when he was just sixteen years old.

Back in 1985, Shahjahan's mother had paid 300 takas (the Bangladeshi currency) to an agent to take him across the border. But Shahjahan did not cross the Ichamati River. He was trafficked, instead, through the land border near Zero Point a little further down from Taki.

He was taken, along with a few other men, to Taki and put in a bus to Malatipur, a village near Bashirhat in North 24 Parganas district, where his sister and her husband lived. Shahjahan would live with his sister's family for the next ten years, helping out with their chores and doing odd jobs. During this period, he learnt tube-well-boring work and got a gig as a casual labourer to do boring work for the Oil and Natural Gas Corporation (ONGC). Impressed with his work, his contractor found him jobs in Maharashtra, Andhra Pradesh, Tamil Nadu and in several other Indian states. This went on until 1998, when the young man had saved enough money to marry.

Shahjahan's family, who were looking for a suitable Indian bride, found a match for him at Talpukur. After the wedding, he settled down with his wife's family and visited his mother back in Bangladesh twice a year. Over the past few years, Shahjahan had built a small home in the village. His wife had given birth to four children. He still went out for contract work, but did not stay away from his family for long.

'I sit in my shop when I don't have jobs to do outside,' he explained. 'When I am out working, my wife runs it.'

As he regularly visited his parental home and the trafficking agent he knew was also from Barsila, Shahjahan did not need to pay any money to the boatmen these days.

'They are good friends and allow me on board free of charge.

Normally, they charge anywhere between ₹500 and ₹2,000, depending on the situation at the border,' he confided.

Men and women who intend to go to Bangladesh would sit in the fishing boats late at night, with the Indian flag flying and approach as close to the Bangladeshi border as possible. A boatman from the other side would then arrive at that point and transfer the passengers to his boat. In half an hour or so, the entire activity would be complete.

Over the years, Shahjahan had transformed himself into a full-fledged Indian. He had a voter identity card, a ration card and an Aadhar card. He had voted in several Parliamentary and Assembly elections in the past and claimed to be a communist. On the occasions that he travelled back to Barsila, Shahjahan was careful to not to carry any of his Indian identity documents. He claimed to have a separate set of Bangladeshi identity documents that he carried with him when he was visiting the other side of the border.

'If I am intercepted there, I will show them my Bangladeshi identity card. If someone asks me for identity proof in India, I will produce my Indian card,' Shahjahan declared, proudly flaunting both cards for my benefit.

I asked him if he considered himself an Indian or a Bangladeshi.

'*Ami* Bangali,' was the simple reply.

* * *

Barely a hundred metres from Shahjahan's shop stood the home of Moina Beebi, where she lived with her husband Shamsu Ahmed and their children Sareena and Sadipur. Moina was born in Bangladesh's Paruli village on the banks of the Ichamati and lived there till the age of 22, helping her mother with her daily chores. An aunt who lived in Talpukur village had urged Moina's mother to send the young woman over to her village so that she could find a suitable groom for her.

'Bangladeshi women consider themselves lucky if they can marry an Indian citizen, as there are virtually no employment opportunities on the other side of the river,' Moina explained. 'If I marry a man in India, he will be able to work and take care of me and my family.'

A few days later, Moina's mother paid a boatman 500 takas for ferrying her, late one night, to a point midway across the Ichamati River. There were twelve others in the boat. Under the cover of darkness, the young woman, along with the others, switched over to a boat with the Indian national flag flying and landed on the outskirts of Taki, where her aunt and uncle were waiting to receive her. While living with them in Talpukur, Moina would visit the village fair and meet Mohammed Shamsuddin, who was young and handsome at that time. It was love at first sight. Soon, their respective families were approached, negotiations took place and the marriage was solemnized in Talpukur. Since then, Moina was known as the bride of Talpukur.

Now in her middle age, Moina still regularly kept in touch with her mother and visited her once every three months by getting on to an Indian fishing boat and transferring later to one bearing the Bangladeshi national flag.

'Most families here have relatives on the other side of the river,' Moina said. 'How can we not visit them? What right does the BSF or the Indian government have to prevent us from visiting our parents and siblings on the other side?'

I asked her if she had ever considered getting a passport for herself and using the officially sanctioned route to Bangladesh, as visitors from West Bengal were given free access to the neighbouring country.

'All that is too much work,' Moina said dismissively. 'We have to produce identity cards and pay money to get a passport. I want to get my son a passport so that I can send him to Dubai. Why would I spend money to get a passport simply to visit my village just across the river?'

After bidding Moina and her family good-bye, we continued to explore the place on foot. I soon realized that there were several people like Shahjahan and Moina in poor fishing villages in this part of West Bengal with roots in the neighbouring country. These people had arranged for identity documents to be issued by both countries and did not seem to consider travelling across the river to Bangladesh without legally authorized documents an offence. For these villagers, who were among the poorest in the country, paying ₹500 or the equivalent amount in Bangladeshi takas to a fisherman to visit their families across the border in a matter of hours was infinitely preferable to waiting for long hours, even days, to cross the border through the proper channels. They merely looked upon their chosen mode of travel as a means of saving time.

The intelligence and law-enforcement agencies perceived a security threat in this large-scale migration, particularly in the context of the rapid spread of radical Islam in the neighbouring country. But locals like Siraj felt that almost all those who were being trafficked from Bangladesh did so out of sheer poverty brought on by the lack of employment in their own country. They felt no threat from these migrants and dismissed such reports as false and misleading.

* * *

Later that afternoon, we returned to Taki and struck a deal with Barun for a ride along the Ichamati at a much lower fare. The senior Das anchored the boat, while Debasish threw water out of the vessel with a plastic bucket. In less than ten minutes, we were cruising barely 10 feet from Bangladeshi territory, waving to their fishermen and to those camping along the bank on the other side of the river. A little distance away, I noticed a bunch of crows feeding on a floating carcass and asked Debasish to steer the boat closer. As we neared the spot, the stench of rotting flesh overwhelmed us.

'It's a dead cow,' Debasis announced. 'So many cows like this one die during the smuggling operation. The animals are flogged and forced to swim across the river. Some of them are unable to do so and die midstream. Their carcasses are left to rot in the river.'

I clicked some pictures of the floating carcass and we continued on our way.

As we moved away from the carcass and towards Bangladesh, Debasish remarked, 'Didn't I tell you that you should come back in the morning just to see the river expose everything that goes on at night? Now do you understand what I mean?'

## COOCH BEHAR

I do not remember exactly when or where I had read about an Indian farmer from Cooch Behar district in West Bengal, whose house was divided by the international boundary in such a way that his living quarters were in India, while his toilet lay in Bangladesh. But that farmer and Cooch Behar had been on my list of 'people and places to visit', since this book was conceived.

Having no clue about this farmer, other than the fact that he lived in Cooch Behar and had to cross over to a neighbouring country's terrain to take a dump every morning, I arrived in Cooch Behar town, hoping to meet the man. As usual, my first knock was on the doors of local journalists who apparently had no clue about the existence of such a person. I asked local activists and even the BSF officials posted in Cooch Behar about him, but they too were of no help.

While none could throw light on the farmer's whereabouts, the responses did throw up insights that gave me a ringside view of life along one of the most intriguing international boundaries anywhere in the world. I came to know about farmers who had to cross the international border to work on their farmlands, about women who had barely escaped being shot at while trying to defecate in their fields and even about children who had been mistaken for cattle smugglers and killed by BSF guards.

Cooch Behar district is situated in north Bengal, with Jalpaiguri and Alipurduar districts to its south. It shares a border with Assam in the east. Bangladesh lies to its south. Of the 549.45 kilometre-long border that Cooch Behar shares with Bangladesh, more than 300 kilometres are fenced in. The rest of the stretch, covering 250-odd kilometres, is an open, porous border guarded by a heavy deployment of BSF personnel, with at least eight battalions posted in the district. The riverine parts of this stretch of the border, such as the international border in Taki on the Ichamati River are much more vulnerable than the land border. The construction of barbed wire fencing along the land border is still in progress. Work on it has been delayed in several areas because of geographical complications; in certain areas along the border, due to constraints imposed by local topographical conditions, the fencing has had to be erected not at Zero Point, but at a distance varying between 150 metres and 600 metres from the designated Zero-Point line, leaving isolated territories in what is considered no man's land. These lands, usually fertile agricultural tracts that stretch across the district's southern end, are the most difficult to define with precise boundaries, especially in certain pockets such as Dighaltari, where only a road separates India from Bangladesh.

* * *

Having had no success in tracking down the man whose house supposedly sat squarely on the international border between India and Bangladesh, I hired a local cab from Dinhata, situated about 28 kilometres from Cooch Behar town, and asked the driver Shafiq, a Dinhata resident, to take me to Dighaltari village near Nazirhat in the southeastern part of the district, where a road divides India from Bangladesh.

Dighaltari, located around 30 kilometres from Dinhata, lay at the end of a narrow, potholed country road whose condition worsened as we passed Nazirhat. The latter is, perhaps, the last reasonably populated town in this area, with schools, a hospital, a couple of chemist's shops and a marketplace. Beyond this lie vast farmlands separated from one another by little clusters of tenements made of corrugated iron.

For the next ten minutes, we drove past verdant jute and paddy fields brimming with water, thanks to regular nocturnal showers. On their way home to prepare lunch, groups of men and women paused here and caught tiny fish by spreading out the loose ends of their dhotis and saris in the accumulated water. The catch would certainly enhance their midday meal.

Shortly afterwards, we crossed our first BSF check post, manned by a sub-inspector and a jawan. They did not order us to halt as we approached, but stared at us curiously, as if we were entering a high-security prison. Shafiq waved at them, pointed with his right hand at the potholed road ahead and drove on. The next check post was about two kilometres further on, a makeshift hut with a thatched roof made of dry palm leaves that stood beside an uneven, gravel road. Inside the hut sat two BSF personnel wielding SLR guns. The senior officer, Sub-Inspector Pappu Singh, approached our car and asked Shafiq to wind down his window glass.

'We are going to Dighaltari,' my driver announced to the officer in Hindi and turned back to indicate my presence. 'This man is a writer,' he added, 'and he would like to meet and interview the residents of Dighaltari to know more about their lives. We will return after the interviews are over.'

The police officer asked to see our identity cards and walked back to his hut for the mandatory inspection. Shafiq and I stepped out of the car and went to the check post to hand over our identity cards to him.

Pappu Singh, who hailed from Chandigarh, looked at my voter identity card and said, 'Chennaiiiii… You have come a very long way indeed.'

I nodded and explained once again that I wanted to visit border villages and talk to the people living there.

Singh pointed at the paddy field to my left and said, 'Look, that signboard is the border.'

I turned and gazed in the direction of his pointed finger. Barely 30 feet from where we stood was a rusted, fading board, almost buried in the stagnant water. I asked him if the signboard was the Zero Point between the two countries.

'It is,' he replied. 'The other side of that board is Bangladesh. This side is India.'

I realized that we were in Dighaltari and the road on which I was standing was the same one that the local journalist had mentioned.

'So what do you want to find out from these villagers?' Pappu Singh enquired. 'Do you want to find out how bad and ruthless the BSF officers are? Let me tell you that the only important activity in these villages is cow smuggling. And it is not as if just one or two people are involved in it; the entire village is hand in glove and each one makes a good income out of it. People always find it convenient to blame the BSF guards. What can we do? Can't you see for yourself? It is an open border and only two of us are assigned to guard a one-kilometre stretch.

'On rainy nights, it is pitch dark and foggy,' Singh continued. 'If I were to sweep the light from my torch this side and walk, a dozen cows would cross the border behind my back. And if we happen to catch anyone red-handed or seize the animals they are smuggling, a hundred villagers on the Bangladeshi side of the border and another hundred on the Indian side will come and hurl stones at us in protest, blaming the BSF for its alleged atrocities. Nobody ever bothers to find out how so many cows manage to arrive in these remote border villages every day. If the cows can travel all the way from Uttar Pradesh and Haryana to this place without being intercepted, would it be that difficult for them to cross this open border? But we have to take all the blame when they do.'

Singh watched me scribbling in my notepad and paused in his monologue. Then he urged me to go ahead and write down whatever he had shared with me. 'If you write about this, my bosses will either yell at me or I will be transferred. But someone has to tell the truth.'

Meanwhile, Shafiq had filled in the In/Out register maintained by the BSF and also handed over his driver's licence card to Singh's deputy for inspection. He was told that the card would be returned to him on our way back. This practice, I learnt, was not only mandatory for visitors, but even for locals. Anyone intending to pass this check post, even if it were simply to go to his workplace in Nazirhat or return home to Dighaltari and other border villages, had to fill in the register and submit to frisking by the BSF. The villagers were also expected to have whatever they were carrying with them ready for inspection when they went out or returned home.

As we walked back to the car, I turned again to look at the international border – a series of decaying granite posts splitting a waterlogged paddy field in two.

'But this is not the last border village,' Shafiq informed me. 'There is another village called C.G. Jora or Chhoto Gorul Jora, about five kilometres from this place. It is the last Indian village at the point where the BSF has erected fencing along the border. Let's go there.'

We resumed our bumpy ride along the gravelled road. The BSF posts now stood closer to one another, but were unmanned. Even when guards were present, they did not bother to flag us down for a check. All through the journey, Shafiq had been a useful source of information, narrating interesting anecdotes and providing me with other trivia that I would otherwise have missed out on. He was turning out to be one of those drivers who knew something about everything. He could identify local flora, provide information on the crime rate in different neighbourhoods and even listed out the problems faced both by BSF guards and the locals in these border areas.

Considering the extent of his knowledge and the intensity of his urge to express an opinion on everything, I asked Shafiq about the rampant cow-smuggling activities that everyone who lived along the West Bengal–Bangladesh border was concerned about. Since my visit to Taki, I had been really curious about the reason behind so many cows being smuggled to Bangladesh from India. After all, with both countries having similar topography and vegetation, it was very likely that there would be cows on the other side of the border as well. If so, where was the need for such rampant smuggling of these bovines? I put the question that had been hovering in my mind to Shafiq.

'It is the most profitable business in West Bengal,' he replied. 'A cow that costs ₹5,000 here could fetch up to five times that price once it crosses the border. And handlers could earn anywhere between two thousand and ₹5,000 for smuggling out a single cow. That is why this business is so rampant here. As the BSF officer said, every villager in these border areas has a role to play in cow smuggling and makes a lot of money.'

He added that while there were enough cows in Bangladesh to satiate the local need for beef, the cows that were smuggled out from India were primarily intended for the Middle East market.

'The cows that are smuggled out from here are not slaughtered,' Shafiq went on. 'They are killed slowly in boiling water and their hide is peeled off. Then the meat is sliced and packaged as various products, such as beef sausages, ground beef and even steak slices, before being exported. Beef exports represent the biggest industry in Bangladesh. Healthy cows, bred under the right conditions, can fetch up to ₹100,000 each.'

A little research confirmed the driver's feedback. According to a Reuters report, at least two million heads of cattle were smuggled into Bangladesh from India every year. Annually, this trade was worth at least US $600 million. The smuggled cows were auctioned by Bangladeshi traders to facilitate the sale of cattle to slaughter houses, beef-processing units, tanneries and bone-crushing factories, which contributed approximately 3 per cent to the country's $190 billion economy. Most of the beef flesh and beef products were marked for export and sent to the Middle East; Singapore, Malaysia and other countries in the Far East.

'All the beef consumed in the Arab countries and in South East Asia are processed from Indian cows,' Shafiq volunteered, while driving past deserted check posts and green fields.

Driving on for another three or four kilometres, we halted near a petty shop, where four clean-shaven young men, neatly dressed in t-shirt and jeans, were standing together and chatting. Their bikes were parked at some distance from the shop.

Shafiq turned his head towards me and then pointed at those boys.

'Do you see? The villagers here are not as poor as those are in other parts of West Bengal. This just confirms what the BSF officer said: Everyone here is involved in the smuggling racket and makes some profit out of it.'

A little beyond the petty shop on the same dirt road stood a government primary school. Beyond it lay Chhoto Gorul Jora, the last Indian village in this part of Cooch Behar. Around 500 people lived in this picturesque village located a few dozen metres from a tall, barbed-wire fence. Thought the land beyond the fence was still a part of Indian territory, it was of little concern to either the BSF or any other Indian agency. Village pradhan and panchayat board member Nizmi Beebi lived at the far end of the village in her modest home, which was just a shelter put together from a few sheets of corrugated metal. The doors and windows were all made of pieces of these cheap, weather-resistant sheets with parallel ridges and furrows. A poster of the Trinamool Congress was pasted on the front door of her home.

When we arrived at her place, Nizmi was cooking lunch for her husband, who was out in the fields. Her son, a class III student, was at the government primary school. Nizmi's husband, who had been active in the Party and took an interest in village affairs, could not contest the local-body elections, as their ward was a reserved one. He had, therefore, convinced his young, literate wife to contest and had got her elected as the village head. She, however, had remained the docile housewife. It would need a lot of persuasion for her to come out and talk to us about life in a border village. When she did consent, however, her neighbours Sameena, Rizzat Mia and Mimi Beebi also joined in.

'What is different about life in a border village...,' Nizmi mused. 'Nothing much, actually. It is just like any other village in West Bengal. We wake up, prepare meals and go out to work. Then we return home in the evening, eat dinner and sleep, just like other villagers do, except that the BSF always keeps an eye on our movements.'

Having spent so many years under such surveillance, Nizmi had got so used to the daily pattern of her life that she could initially recall nothing unusual that was worth remarking on.

'Of course, our lives are strictly regimented,' she added. 'Every time we leave our village, we have to make an entry in the register at the BSF check post and explain the purpose of our trip. When we return, the guards go through our belongings quite thoroughly to ensure that we have brought back nothing in excess of what we actually need. We cannot, for example, buy large quantities of sugar, rice or other essentials when we are out, as the BSF won't allow us to bring the stuff home. Any item we buy should be just enough to satisfy our immediate needs. Nothing more.'

The others nodded in agreement.

'Though we are allowed to go out of our homes after dark, it is not considered safe, as there is a risk of the BSF shooting us down on the mistaken assumption that we are smugglers,' Nizmi went on. 'So we ensure that our family members reach home by six p.m. and do not venture out again after dark. If any of us falls ill at night, the only way we can be taken to the nearest hospital in Nazirhat, eight kilometres away, is in BSF vehicles, as private ambulances are not allowed in this area at night. We do not mind all that, as it is for our own safety.

'The most annoying part, however, is that most of us have farmland on the other side of the barbed-wire fence and cannot visit it whenever we need to. The BSF opens the gate no more than thrice a day and it is only during those breaks that we can go to tend to our land or return home from it. For the rest of the day, the gates remain shut.

'The BSF has given us specific windows of time to go and work on our land. If I am not back at the gate by four p.m., I have to stay back in the fields or spend the night in one of the homes on the other side, until the gate opens again at ten, the following morning. Even in the case of an emergency – a fire breaking out on our farm after dark or thieves trespassing on our property – we cannot run out of our homes to put out the fire or chase the intruders away. Stray cattle from elsewhere graze on our fields and destroy our crops before our very eyes, but we can do nothing about it, as the BSF won't open the gate for us after four in the afternoon.

'In such a situation, how can we possibly carry on with our farming and produce a good harvest?' Nizmi lamented. 'Most of us are unable to even make a living through farming due to the tight security imposed on us by the BSF. This is the most unfortunate aspect of our lives.'

The other three nodded again in agreement. As Nizmi continued to talk, narrating one incident after another, more and more anecdotes of their arduous life poured out. She recalled an occasion when one of the children could not return home in time and had even tried jumping over the fence on finding the gate locked and then described another on which her brother Fareed, who lived on the other side of the fence, had fallen seriously ill one night. Nizmi could not go over to tend to him, but had to wait till morning to do so. It occurred to me that these long-suffering villagers had become so inured to the restrictions that had made life a sort of prison for them that they did not even think of complaining, until they had been persuaded to recapitulate their past experiences and revive the bitter memories buried deep in their minds. It was only during such moments that they wished they had been born elsewhere and not in a region that had a barbed-wire fence running through it, with armed guards monitoring their every move.

But all these were relatively new developments. I was told that these restrictions had been put in place only over the last ten years after the barbed-wire fencing was erected. Prior to this period, the area was free game. As of now, the BSF officials had set up six gates along the stretch of fencing in C.G. Jora, each entry point guarded by a pair of armed security personnel. The gates were opened at 10 a.m. and closed an hour later, then opened again at noon. They remained ajar until 1 p.m. Later in the afternoon, the gates would be opened at 4 p.m. and closed an hour later.

After meeting Nizmi and her neighbours, Shafiq and I decided to cross the fence and meet some of the families on the other side. On the other side of Gate No. 6, about a hundred metres away, lived thirteen families, in addition to that of Mehboob Hassan's. The latter lived with his wife Fathima, two daughters Samona Parveen and Saplar Parveen and son Munna in a house erected on his agricultural land, which grazed the official boundary line between the two countries. Technically, the area was regarded as no man's land, as it lay beyond India's official border fencing and was not a part of Bangladeshi territory either. Residents of these areas had to produce documentary proof of their Indian identity whenever they crossed the barbed-wire fence to the mainland, but could travel freely in Bangladesh, which was, in a manner of speaking, their backyard.

When we walked through Gate No. 6 and arrived at Mehboob's home, the 43-year-old farmer was sitting on a plastic chair in the shade of a mango tree near a large, muddy pool of water and playing with his five-year-old son Munna .

Mehboob was among the few Indian citizens who had more Bangladeshis than his own compatriots as neighbours and friends. If he had to buy groceries or other basic commodities, the nearest shop or bazaar was in Bangladesh and accessible all through the day, unlike the market in Nazirhat, which he could visit only when the border gates were opened at the specified times thrice a day.

'I always carry both currencies with me so that I can use the relevant one, depending on where I am,' Mehboob confided, taking out a few Bangladeshi taka notes from his shirt pocket to show me.

Unlike the concerns of the remaining 1.2 billion-odd people who were his fellow Indians, Mehboob's were related to simple things that we often took for granted. The most recent cause of his vexation had been his inability to get his youngest daughter a bicycle. Saplar Parveen, who studied in class VIII at the government school in Nazirhat, had to travel eight kilometres to attend school every day. To ease her burden, the teenager had been pleading with her father for the past one year to buy her a bicycle. Despite having the means, Mehboob had been unable to fulfil Saplar's wishes, as his application for a permit had not yet been approved.

'It's been eight months since I submitted all the necessary documents to the BSF head office for the permit I will need to buy Saplar a cycle,' Mehbood declared. 'I am yet to get a response. Whenever I ask the BSF people about it, they reply that they are still looking into the matter. I don't understand what is so complicated about issuing me that permit.'

And it was not just bicycles that needed clearance from the BSF officials. Villagers living here also needed a permit for buying motorcycles, cattle and other livestock and even certain kinds of farm equipment.

Children from this area seemed to be the hardest hit. After completing their schooling up to class V, they were required to go to the high school in Nazirhat to continue their studies. As the border gates did not open before 10 a.m., these children were almost always late for school and had to skip the first period. On days when they were held up in school because of a special class or some extra assignment, the children ran the risk of not being able to make it through the gates by 5 p.m. In such circumstances, they were forced to spend the night at the home of neighbours on the other side of the fence.

'Now we can, on rare occasions, allow our boys to spend the night in the homes of our neighbours across the fence, but it would be unthinkable for us to let our girls do so,' said Fareed, Mehboob's next-door neighbour, who had emerged from his home to find out who we were. 'Therefore, we have no option but to put an end to their schooling after they complete class V.'

Since not many people visited these areas and the villagers were unaccustomed to seeing strangers in their midst, a small crowd soon gathered around Shafiq and I, and more tales of woe were shared with us. Mehboob, our host, offered me a plate of betel leaves, areca nut and slaked lime paste, a combo that these folks folded and prepared into paan, which they would chew all day.

'The situation isn't always so bad. Some BSF officers are kind enough to allow the children to pass even after the gates have been shut,' Mehboob added, 'but there is no guarantee that the officer on duty will always be as obliging, especially if he is in a bad mood.'

When Mehboob was looking for a groom for his eldest daughter Alpana – now married and living with her husband and in-laws – a few years ago, none of the families in the neighbouring villages had come forward with a proposal. This situation was the outcome of the severe grilling to which the BSF guards at the gate tended to subject unfamiliar visitors so that they felt humiliated and went away.

'Even when we tell the guards ahead of a visit that we are expecting guests, the latter are not spared the intimidating interrogation,' Mehboob lamented.

Fortunately for him, an older brother of his who lived in Cooch Behar had used his political connections to intercede on his behalf, personally meeting the BSF Inspector General and wangling an assurance from him that his niece's prospective groom and the latter's family members would not be harassed at the border gate when they came visiting.

'That is how I got my Alpana married,' Mehboob sighed. 'But every farmer here does not have a well-connected brother in Cooch Behar.'

While money itself was hard to come by in these lands where farming was the only legal occupation for most residents, there was not much use for wealth, if it could be acquired at all, for trying to maintain the desired lifestyle would have been impossible in an area where every purchase, even an electronic or electrical one, was subjected to screening at the gates before it was allowed to be taken home. Fearing the scrutiny, most villagers in these borderlands tried to keep their lives as simple and austere as possible.

After chatting with Mehboob and his neighbours, I asked him to take me to Zero Point, just so that I could take a selfie and send it back home. Mehboob led me through his backyard to a row of tall eucalyptus trees. Standing near one of the trees, he stated, 'These trees mark India's official border with its neighbour.' Then he moved one step back and said, 'Now I am in Bangladesh.'

I joined Mehboob in Bangladesh and Shafiq took a picture of the two of us standing together.

Mehboob then hugged one of his eucalyptus trees and said, 'This farm and these trees are mine. But if I have to cut down one of my trees, I will have to go to Bangladesh and inform the border guards of both countries of my intentions and get their approval.'

* * *

On our way back from C.G. Jora, Shafiq and I hardly spoke to each other. I suppose it was because he too was shocked and saddened by the conversations we had had with the villagers. To lighten the mood, I told my driver about my futile attempts to trace a man whose strange story I had heard before arriving here, a man whose living room apparently lay in India, while his toilet was located in Bangladesh.

Shafiq's immediate response was to exclaim loudly that he knew exactly where that home was located.

'The farmer you are talking about lives in Jari Dharla on the other side of the Dharla River. Some 600 families living there are completely cut off from the mainland by the river. They are living in India, but are Bangladeshis, for all intents and purposes, as they go to the other side to fulfil their every need. My brother visits Dharla regularly and happens to know the man you mentioned. But recently, this man had his home rebuilt in an area that is squarely in Indian territory.'

I patted Shafiq on the shoulder and declared that he had just identified my next destination.

We returned to Dinhata, then proceeded to the Gitaldaha BSF check post further west, which was the point where one could board a raft and cross over to the other side of the Dharla River.

When we reached the outpost at Gitaldaha, a raft had just arrived from Jari Dharla, carrying about two dozen villagers. I was told that it would leave in another thirty minutes. Shafiq suggested that we board the raft right away and wait there for the other passengers. If we delayed, the vessel could get crowded.

Just as we were about to board, however, a BSF constable caught hold of my hand and restrained me, asking me to meet his superior, who was sitting inside the check post with a register open in front of him. I handed the BSF officer my identity card and told him about the purpose of my visit.

'But you cannot go there,' he said. 'We have strict orders to ensure that only locals living on the other side are allowed to go.'

'But it is still Indian territory, right?' I protested. 'And I am an Indian citizen. Why can't I go?'

'Well, you can, but you'll need permission from my commandant's office in Cooch Behar. If he allows you to go, you can,' said the officer. 'You want to know about the border villages and the life of people living there, right? Then why don't you interview people living in Gitaldaha? Why would you need to go all the way to Jari Dharla?'

Then he paused and examined my identity card again. He tidied himself up, adjusted his shirt and threw back his shoulders.

'Or you could interview me, you know,' he offered. 'I can tell you everything you'd want to know about Jari Dharla and the people living there.'

I thanked him for his kindness and left.

## RUMMAGING FOR AN IDENTITY IN NO MAN'S LAND

If you thought the lives of lakhs of Indians and Bangladeshis who live along the international border was miserable, consider the following: until recently, there were at least 51,000 people living in India and Bangladesh who wished they could call these border badlands home. These people are inhabitants of little pockets of land called '*chhit mahals*' or enclaves – in other words, one country's territory located within the borders of another. At the time of writing this book, India had 106 enclaves inside Bangladesh, while there were 92 Bangladeshi enclaves in India, whose residents were, for all practical purposes, stateless and devoid of an identity.

Even before I reached Cooch Behar, I had been well apprised that if there was one person who could take me in and out of these enclaves safely, it had to be Diptiman Sengupta, convenor of the Bharat Bangladesh Enclave Exchange Coordination Committee (BBEECC). Diptiman's father and former Dinhata MLA, the late Deepak Sengupta, had set up the BBEECC to fight for the rights of these enclave residents. The committee opened offices on both sides of the border and had a fixed agenda to press India and Bangladesh towards the implementation of the Indira Gandhi–

Sheikh Mujib Land Boundary agreement of 1974, which had been ratified by the Bangladesh government, but not by India. Deepak Sengupta had spearheaded the fight for the enclave-exchange agreement until his death in 2009, after which his son Diptiman took over.

I met Diptiman at his family home in Dinhata on the day the prime ministers of both countries had jointly announced the exchange of these enclaves in Dhaka, bringing the two-decades-old struggle by the enclave residents and the BBEECC to a fruitful conclusion. On that rainy morning, Diptiman's house was already abuzz with supporters and a number of enclave residents moving restlessly around the fruit trees and bonsai plants in his neglected garden. Bearded, bespectacled and dressed in a white vest and matching cotton pajamas, the 44-year-old activist was smoking one Gold Flake cigarette after another and speaking loudly on his mobile phone.

'Dada, it's a very busy day for me,' Diptiman said to me, interrupting his conversation over the phone. 'I won't be able to sit and chat with you until ten tonight. Is there anything else I can do? Are you planning to visit some place?'

I explained that I had hoped to have a talk with him before setting out to the enclaves and would wait till 10 p.m., if that's what it took. At around 9.45 p.m., I called Diptiman. His mobile was busy. A little after ten, he called back to say that he was still tied up and could only meet me the following morning. He wanted me to be at his home between 8.30 and 9 a.m.

'We can squeeze in a few minutes,' he promised.

When I reached his large old house with its corrugated iron roof at 8.30 the following morning, Diptiman was briskly pacing up and down the long corridor in his familiar white sleeveless vest and matching cotton pajamas, smoking incessantly and talking fervently on his mobile phone.

'I have been really busy,' he told me. 'We can fit in a short conversation and then you're welcome to accompany us to a Bangladeshi enclave. You can see it all first-hand. Today is a very important day for the people who live there.'

We sat down on the cane chairs set out in the portico and Diptiman spoke about the BBEECC and their long struggle against an inept system.

'This long, bloody fight has actually been a struggle for identity,' he explained. 'You must come along with us and see for yourself how the situation is. These people have nothing – no laws, no educational facilities, not even birth certificates. They are living like animals for no fault of their own. It's so unfair!'

When Diptiman's father had taken the first step towards creating a movement against this historic injustice, he was very clear that it should be an apolitical movement with no hidden agenda. True to that vision, his son had remained apolitical and his movement had earned him friends and foes both in the Left block and in the ruling Trinamool Congress party.

The BBEECC had been fighting against a powerful lobby which had vested interests in ensuring that the enclaves remained exactly the way they were. These little lawless territories had continued to be a favourite hunting ground for traffickers, smugglers and a whole industry of fake-document creators who would collect large sums of money from the enclave dwellers to prepare falsified identity documents and certificates for them.

Diptiman informed me that since these enclave dwellers were not mentioned in any census register, they did not constitute a vote bank that could be counted on at election time. They had no political relevance whatsoever. Consequently, neither the Left Front government nor the ruling Trinamool Congress had bothered to address their needs or grievances.

'So we decided to beat them at their own game and pushed

the enclave residents into getting voter identity cards by hook or by crook,' Diptiman continued. 'Those who lived in other cities easily managed to obtain address proofs and acquired voter identity cards. When we had sufficient numbers, we made one of the enclave dwellers contest in the 2011 Assembly elections from the Dinhata constituency. The candidate Mahima Khatun, an Indian lady married to the resident of a Bangladeshi enclave in India, garnered three thousand five hundred votes in the election. For the first time, politicians in West Bengal were forced to take note of the political clout wielded by people from the enclaves.'

While the Dinhata constituency had 3,500 voters from the enclaves, the Cooch Behar parliamentary constituency, which includes at least twenty-odd enclaves, easily accounted for 20,000 votes. Ahead of the 2014 Lok Sabha elections, A.C. Nielson had come out with a constituency-wise prediction for West Bengal, in which it claimed that the Cooch Behar seat would swing the way enclave voters cast their ballot. Although not significant enough to win a seat, the 20,000 enclave voters could change the game for Cooch Behar, the report stated. Sensing this trend, West Bengal Chief Minister Mamata Banerjee had rushed to Cooch Behar and announced in a public meeting that if elected, her party would ensure that the enclave residents had their way.

'It was the first time that a major politician had taken up the cause of the enclaves,' Diptiman declared. 'We welcomed the move and said we wanted nothing more than the implementation of the 1974 Bill, as it covered all the issues that these folks wanted addressed.'

With the usual detractors and powerful lobbies taking a back seat, the rest of the journey for the BBEECC had been a smooth one.

Even as Diptiman talked about the chain of events that had led to the historic swapping of enclaves, local journalists and supporters of the cause trickled in, one after another, to congratulate him. Soon, sweets were being distributed and the atmosphere became festive. Sometime during this melee, as I was coaxed into consuming *rosogollas* by one activist after another, Diptiman walked off, leaving my interview incomplete.

I put aside my digital recorder and started chatting with the local journalists outside Diptiman's home. More sweets were thrust into my mouth, my hand was clasped innumerable times and given a violent shake and I found myself enfolded in many warm hugs.

At around 10 a.m., I saw Diptiman in a black helmet straddling the driver's seat of a Bajaj M80 scooter.

'Dada, come and sit behind me,' he called out to me. 'We are going to the Mashaldanga, a Bangladeshi enclave in India. You can meet its residents and those of the surrounding enclaves there.'

I sat pillion behind Diptiman and he took off on the 20 kilometre journey to Mashaldanga along potholed, worn-out roads, flanked by at least twenty other bikers, including local journalists and members of the BBEECC. Riding past jute fields and vegetable plantations, Diptiman kept receiving one phone call after another. As he answered those calls, I could hear him hurling abuses at the top of his voice. All along the way, he smoked. With a lit cigarette in his right hand and a mobile phone sandwiched between his left ear and the flap of his helmet, he drove past numerous villages. Along the way, groups of people recognized him as we passed and waved out to him.

I could not help but wonder if I would safely reach my destination. Here I was, sitting pillion on a scooter driven by an activist-leader who manoeuvred the vehicle with one hand, his entire attention focussed on the telephone conversations he was carrying on with important people who were obviously not too pleased with him. For a fleeting moment, I wondered if I had done the sensible thing by agreeing to accompany Diptiman. After all, this was north Bengal; if someone wanted to settle scores with him by hurling a petrol bomb in his direction or pointing a loaded a gun at him, this was a prime opportunity for doing so. If the activist had quick reflexes and ducked in response, I would end up being the target. Or he might simply lose control of the scooter while navigating a pothole and we would both end up in a ditch with broken bones.

With these thoughts playing in my mind, I did the best I could under the circumstances: I held the seat's backrest as tightly as possible and kept a sharp eye out for a possible ambush, as Diptiman manoeuvred his M80 like an expert with one hand, the other holding a lit cigarette all the way.

* * *

When Diptiman turned his scooter off the tar road and onto a mud road leading to Mashaldanga, a blast of music and loud slogans welcomed us.

Hundreds of residents of the *chhit mahal*, including women and children, had gathered in an open space and were bursting crackers, greeting one another and distributing sweets in celebration of the historic announcement that enclaves would be exchanged between the two neighbouring countries. TV journalists who had arrived about the same time as us immediately sprang into action and started taking video bytes from the residents. Diptiman and the other office bearers of the BBEECC lit a lamp and spoke to the crowds about their struggle and related how the final victory had come about. Every now and then, someone from the crowd would cheer Diptiman, his father Deepak Sengupta and the movement itself. I found myself a quiet corner from where I could enjoy the spectacle. The piece of land on which I stood was yet another lush expanse of farmland with neither demarcation lines nor BSF check post nor even a signboard setting it apart from rest of the landscape. What was clear, though, was that this land had belonged to another country and the villagers living here were not yet Indian citizens.

Away from the partying crowds, clusters of men and women stood in the shade of tall trees and watched the celebrations with apparent scepticism. One of them was Anwar Hussain, who lived in Madhya Mashaldanga with his wife and two children.

Anwar was 34 years old and had six siblings – four brothers and two sisters. All the members of his family lived in the same village, tilling their ancestral land and selling the produce for a pittance. Even as most of his neighbours were celebrating their '*azadi*', as they called it, uncertainty was writ large on Anwar's round face with its week-old stubble; he watched the cheering crowds with apprehension. His life, so far, had been nothing short of an ordeal, mostly because he did not have an identity or a nationality. While India considered Anwar a Bangladeshi citizen and refused to grant him the recognition he needed, the Bangladesh government withheld from him every one of the privileges to which its own citizens were entitled. And all because this man was living on a plot of land that was surrounded by Indian territory. For all practical purposes, he was out of reach and not the responsibility of the Bangladesh government.

Unlike most other youth in Mashaldanga who had not received a formal education, Anwar was a graduate and had obtained his BA degree from a college in Uttarakhand after enrolling for the course with forged identity documents. Thanks to his college exposure, he spoke fluent Hindi, unlike the other young men here who only spoke Bengali. Observing the disconsolate, puzzled look on Anwar's face, I asked him why he was not participating in the celebrations.

'Are you not happy about becoming an Indian?' I asked him.

After some hesitation and much coaxing, he said without much enthusiasm, 'Let's see how things turn out. I have only seen empty promises and false hopes so far. Many such celebrations have taken place in the past, but nothing ever changes here.'

Initially reluctant to pour out his woes, Anwar slowly unveiled the details of the tragedy that life in an enclave had turned out to be. The charade usually began right from the moment of a person's birth. A child born in a *chhit mahal* had to tell a lie the moment he or she completed three years of age and needed to go to school. It involved passing off strangers as his or her parents at the time of admission. Since only Indian citizens could admit their children in the government school at Nazirhat, about 2.5 kilometres from their village, Anwar's parents had been forced to pay a large sum of money to get Indian citizens living in neighbouring villages to masquerade as the boy's parents to get him admitted at the local school. Moreover, a regular sum had to be paid to these fake parents all through the boy's education for keeping their role-playing intact. In some cases, an affidavit was prepared, declaring the children of enclave residents to be the foster children of Indian citizens, merely for the sake of their education. This was a lucrative proposition indeed for the adoptive parents.

Despite being citizens of that country, Anwar's parents had not been able to admit him in a Bangladeshi school. Without official papers to prove his identity, his father could not risk crossing the border for fear that the Indian BSF might declare him an illegal immigrant and arrest him.

'Technically, we are locked in. Without an identity card, I can neither move around freely in India nor in Bangladesh,' Anwar sighed.

Getting access to quality education was just one of the many problems that he and his family faced. Whenever a family member fell ill or became pregnant and needed to go to a hospital for a check-up or the delivery, the nightmare recurred. Indian hospitals do not treat Bangladeshis. Yet again, the Bangladeshi had to enlist the help of an Indian citizen who would agree to take care of the necessary paper work and produce documents – for a price – to get the concerned family member admitted in the Nazirhat government-run clinic, the health centre closest to their village.

'For the last 30 years, we have received nothing from either country. No roads, no schools, no hospitals and no voting rights either,' Anwar declared bitterly. 'Even if there is a dispute between two people or two families, no policeman or government official will come here to settle it. There is no law in this land. The parties involved in the argument will end up assaulting one another until they either cool down or one of them dies. Even if someone commits a murder here, he or she is neither arrested nor legally tried for the crime, as neither the Indian authorities nor the Bangladeshi police ever come here to intervene. Village elders usually decide on the punishment to be meted out to the culprit. Otherwise, it is up to the victim's family to avenge the crime and make the murderer pay a price for it.'

Noticing my shocked expression, he went on to add that a few years ago, riots had broken out between Muslim and Hindu families (who were a minority here). More than twenty-five homes were razed to the ground.

'Still nobody came to investigate. We were left to settle the problem on our own. Village elders intervened and mediated to resolve the issue, but the concerned parties were not willing to listen to them, until someone died.'

Over the years, as the BBEECC became increasingly powerful and the West Bengal government had begun to express more concern about the plight of the enclave dwellers, giving them access to hospitals and schools. Yet, the historic blunder and the resulting lack of accountability had led to a thriving illegal racket that continued to rake in crores of rupees from these poor and hardworking enclave residents on both sides of the border.

As Anwar was speaking, a crowd had gathered around us. Encouraged, other people also stepped forward to share their woes openly. Since I could only understand the Hindi speakers, I approached these men and women. Banu Sheikh, who was 24, had learnt Hindi while working in Delhi, where he had spent a few years. Unlike other men here, Banu looked suave and sophisticated. He was clean-shaven, with a good physique. He also owned land that he had inherited from his parents. Yet, he was unable to find a girl to wed, as nobody in his community wanted to get their daughters married off to an enclave resident.

'This is not merely my personal situation,' Banu clarified. 'No father will ever send his daughter to Mashaldanga, as we do not have any legal status. In addition, those parents who have daughters living in our villages are also much keener on suitable grooms with Indian citizenship, as this would automatically entitle their daughters and their grandchildren to avail of superior education facilities and health care. Unless someone in the extended family agrees to give us their daughter's hand in marriage, it is almost impossible for men like me to find a wife.'

The problems didn't end there. Residents of enclaves could not legally buy or sell property, even if they had the means, because they had no access to a registrar's office in Bangladesh. Until ten years ago, according to Banu, they had managed to do so by arranging for a registrar to come over from Bangladesh and prepare the necessary documents, but that practice had come to an end after the relationship between the two countries soured. In Banu's village, if a person had to buy or sell land, he created the required documents and simply handed them over to the other party in the presence of village elders. The same process was applied in solemnizing a marriage or even ending it through divorce.

By now, more men and women had gathered around me and were recounting similar horror stories, the experience, of living without a nationality or a country to call their own. While the men in these enclaves at least had the option of moving out to the larger cities for education or work, life for the women had remained unchanged since Independence. For them, their urban counterpart would have seemed foreign, even surreal.

Fathima, who turned 40 recently, was among those rare enclave women who had seen the outside world. Her husband, working as a casual labourer in New Delhi, had taken her along with him to the city, where they had spent 15 years in a slum in one of the older localities. Despite living there for so many years, Fathima could not recall the exact address of the place where she had lived. She spoke a little Hindi, but did not know how to read or write in any language.

Fathima, who had been in her early twenties when she moved to Delhi, had left her two children Kudeja and Ali Hussain with her parents in Mashaldanga. Her husband Imran, who had obtained a ration card with his Delhi address marked on it, had also managed to get Fathima's name added to the card. While he was busy working on construction sites, she remained a homemaker and took care of the house. As the couple lived in one of Old Delhi's Bengali neighbourhoods, nobody really came to know that they were not Indians.

Three years ago, a policeman had visited their home while she was alone and informed her that Imran had died in a road accident. He had apparently been driving a two-wheeler when a metal rod fell off the lorry in front of him and pierced his body. When Fathima went to the morgue to collect his body and bring it back to her village, the local police discovered that their documents were forged and the address given by her was not an authentic one.

'So I could not bring back my husband's body and had to bury him in Delhi,' she lamented. 'After his death, I had to return to the village alone.'

Since then, Fathima had remained in Mashaldanga, doing farm work within the village. She said that people in the mainland constantly abused her and other women like her, despite taking money from them on every pretext.

'Even now, if I fall ill and have to get admitted in a hospital, I have to persuade an Indian man to masquerade as my husband and he is obviously not going to do me this favour for free.'

Fathima's two children were now attending a madrassa in Nazirhat under assumed identities and their mother hoped that with the successful swapping of enclaves, they would not have to endure the humiliation and sorrow that she had gone through. If the promises made by the two governments were not empty ones, her children could go to a hospital without enlisting the help of substitute parents. Their progeny would have birth certificates and voting rights and they could get employment anywhere in India or travel abroad with a valid passport.

* * *

As I spoke to more people, I managed to unearth a plethora of stories similar to those of Anwar and Fathima. The despondency in their lives numbed me.

Even before I could collect my thoughts and make jottings on my notepad, a huge crowd had gathered at the meeting venue. It set off now towards Nazirhat, raising slogans in praise of Diptiman Sengupta and his father Deepak, the Indian and Bangladeshi prime ministers, West Bengal Chief Minister Mamata Banerjee and the historic exchange of enclaves. As it moved from one village to another in the sweltering heat, more people from other enclaves joined the procession. The young men in it tossed fireworks into the fields, sprayed coloured powder on one another, danced and generally seemed to go wild. It was probably how people had celebrated back in 1947, when the rest of India got its *azadi*. I walked alongside for a while to capture the mood of the celebrations, until the heat had sapped my spirit and I found myself falling behind.

* * *

It was raining heavily that night when Diptiman visited my room at around ten to complete the interview we had started the very same morning. Even before we could resume our discussion, however, he received a call from Mashaldanga. I took out my voice recorder and notepad and waited.

When the call ended, Diptiman seemed tense. Without sparing me a glance, he dialled another phone number and spoke rapidly. From the words he used and his tone, I sensed that he was talking to a cop. Then he called senior BSF officials and spoke for a long time. More frantic calls kept coming in. Diptiman rose from his chair and started pacing the balcony attached to my room. His voice grew louder and more abusive. At around 10.20 p.m., he announced that something very urgent had come up and he would have to leave immediately. Despite the rain, he ran out of my hotel into the darkness, leaving behind one of his mobile phones in his hurry to attend to whatever had spurred him to action.

When I visited him at home late the following morning to return his phone, Diptiman confided that he had not slept all night.

'Those who were dead against this exchange of enclaves set fire to a few homes in Mashaldanga last night,' he said. 'I had to intervene at once or the damage would have been far more extensive.'

I asked him if it was something serious. The activist dismissed it as a trivial incident and one he had anticipated.

'We have put an end to a thriving multi-crore racket. It's only to be expected that the beneficiaries will be upset,' he said in conclusion.

# 10

# Campbell Bay

The Pawan Hans helicopter to Campbell Bay in Great Nicobar, the last civilian settlement in the Nicobar group of islands, departs from Port Blair every morning at 7.15 with six or seven passengers. But getting a ticket to fly to this remote island lying off India's southeastern coast is as rare a possibility as spotting, say, a naked Jarawa – a member of one of the indigenous tribes – in Port Blair; for the three lucky passengers (the rest fly to Car Nicobar) who get to make the trip are shortlisted only on the eve of their departure by the Department of General Administration of the Andaman and Nicobar Islands.

I had applied for a ticket early on a Tuesday morning for the following day's flight to Campbell Bay. After flashing my Press Card at several senior government officials and following up with earnest entreaties, I had managed to get my name included in the list.

'But just because your name is on the list put up outside the Secretariat is no guarantee that you'll get to travel. You're in the Andamans; here, nothing is certain,' declared my contact at the Secretariat, who had helped me wangle the ticket. 'You can't be sure you'll be travelling, until you actually board the helicopter. By the time the list is forwarded by the Secretariat to the Civil Aviation department office in the airport complex, your name could have been taken off it, for all you know.'

As though to endorse that statement, the concerned official at the Civil Aviation department office near the Port Blair airport helipad, where I would head later that evening, refused to accept payment and confirm the ticket I had in hand, even after I had showed him a scanned copy of the passenger list with my name on it. Instead, he asked me to show up at the office early the following morning.

'Six sharp and only cash payment. No card,' he said brusquely.

A casual perusal of the list put up by the Department of General Administration offered an idea of the ordeal people had to go through on any given day to reach Campbell Bay, Car Nicobar and other remote islands in the Andaman and Nicobar archipelago. Of the two other passengers selected to travel to Campbell Bay that morning, one was Rajesh Khanna, 44, an executive engineer with the BSNL, whose stated purpose of visit was to 'check the OFC work', while the other was Dr Johnson, Medical Officer from the Health Department 'on duty'. Obviously, I was the odd man out. The stated purpose of my visit was baldly marked as 'visit'. Among the passengers who travelled with us up to Car Nicobar, located midway between Port Blair and Campbell Bay, was a certain 'Shri Nahore', the purpose of his visit defined as 'returning home after treatment', and a 19-year-old woman, whose reason for being on the Pawan Hans flight that morning was: 'Father very serious'. After browsing that list, I felt a little ashamed for having used influence to get on the flight; there were so many others who were more deserving, going by the urgent reasons they had cited to be on it.

The next morning, I presented myself at the Civil Aviation office fifteen minutes ahead of the stipulated time. To my surprise two other persons, a young man and woman, had arrived before me. I had met them both at the Secretariat the previous evening, when I was there to check if my name featured on the list of passengers for Campbell Bay. They had gone there for the same purpose and left disappointed that their names were not on the list. I remembered them asking me how I had managed to get mine included. Noticing the two waiting outside the helicopter terminal ahead of me, I approached them and asked if they had managed to get tickets.

'No, we've been wait-listed again,' the man replied. 'But we both have to join duty and have been applying for a ticket every morning for the past three days; we have been wait-listed on every single occasion. We've turned up again today to see if we can try and board the flight, in case there is a last-minute cancellation.'

Apart from the daily helicopter service, there is a weekly ferry service from Port Blair to Campbell Bay when weather conditions are favourable. I had initially considered travelling by ship, as it was a far less expensive option and the ferry halted at most other islands along the way. So on reaching Port Blair, I had rushed to the harbour to check the ferry-service schedule, only to discover that I had missed the ship for the week which had sailed that very morning. I had then met a senior official of the Directorate of Shipping Services to explore other options for reaching Campbell Bay.

'Getting a ticket on a ship to Campbell Bay is like winning a lottery,' the man had remarked. 'Anyway, why not wait for a week before you go there? Then you'll have a better grasp of how truly isolated the islands are and can write about them with more authority.'

I was actually considering that possibility, until his response to my next question, which concerned the schedule for the return trip from Campbell Bay, made me change my mind.

'Oh, of that I have no clue,' he said. 'The dates have not been released as yet. Under normal circumstances, there should be another one in a week, but you never know. If the ship has to undergo repairs or if the weather is unfavourable, the next service could be delayed by yet another week or more. I don't have the data for it yet. I've known people to be stranded in Campbell Bay for weeks, as they waited for the next ship to arrive.'

Following that exchange, I did not think twice about flying to my destination, although the heli ride would cost me at least five times more than travelling by ship would have.

By around 6.15 a.m., more people – passengers and others – had gathered outside the civil aviation office where the helicopter terminal was located, but no official had arrived yet. At 6.30 a.m., the staff member, who had suggested that I return the following morning with cash, arrived and went straight to the office desk from where he dispensed his duties. Even before he could settle down, a crowd had gathered around him, imploring him to reserve a seat for them in the 'copter. I pushed my way through and informed the man that on his advice, I had come with the cash to purchase my ticket.

He took out a receipt book, filled out my name, then turned to me and asked, 'ID proof?'

I handed him my voter identity card.

He glanced at the document and said in a not-too-polite manner, 'What am I supposed to do with this? I need a photo copy of your identity card.'

'But you never mentioned that yesterday,' I countered, surprised.

'I had clearly told you that I would need ID proof for issuing tickets,' he insisted. 'Originals will not do.'

I tried to reason with him, pointing out that it was highly unlikely that I would find a photocopier shop open at 6.30 in the morning.

'That's not my headache,' he shot back. 'If you can't produce a Xerox copy of your ID card, I can't issue you a ticket. So please get it and come back soon. I don't have all the time in the world.'

I ran out with my backpack and, fortunately, chanced upon a friendly autorickshaw driver. He drove me across town to a photocopier shop that he knew would be open at that hour. We were back at the civil aviation office just before 7 a.m. By then, the number of people swarming around the ticket-issuing official had increased. I pushed my way in again and handed the man two photocopies, just in case. He gave me a look, sighed, filled out a receipt and accepted the cash for the ticket. I was speechless with relief.

With the ticket safely in my wallet, I rushed to the baggage-weighing counter, where a clerk was weighing the passenger as well his luggage and noting it all down on the back of the ticket. When his eyes fell on my backpack, the clerk immediately put his foot down. It was too big and heavy, he said flatly. We went ahead and checked its weight – a little over 10 kilograms.

'That's not allowed,' the clerk said. 'Only five kg is permitted. Your baggage weighs twice as much.'

With that, he sent me right back to the guy issuing the tickets.

The ticketing official checked the weight mentioned on the back of the ticket.

'Oh, sorry,' he said. 'You can't take that backpack along with you. You can either travel without your luggage or go back today and return tomorrow with a lighter bag. There are so many people waiting to get on that flight. How can I allow someone to carry excess baggage? I'm sorry.'

The man asked me to wait outside his office.

By now, I was so furious with the whole set-up that all I wanted to do was grab the ticketing official by his shirt collar and give him a mouthful. After all, I was a 'Press' guy and this was not supposed to happen to people like me. I could feel my blood pressure surging and decided that the sensible thing to do would be to simply wait till the helicopter had left and then give the whole bunch of them a piece of my mind and wake up all my contacts at the Secretariat. There was a ship going to Campbell Bay next week, anyway. Perhaps, I would find a place on it?

After all the other passengers had checked in and just minutes before the 'copter was due to take off, the ticketing official called me in.

'You're lucky,' he announced with a smile. 'Today, there is not much freight. So you can pay for the extra baggage and board.'

I smiled back as politely as I could, paid the cash and boarded the Pawan Hans. Within minutes, the ageing helicopter had lifted off the ground, nose down, tail up, in the typical way of helicopters, and into a cloudless sky. I was on my way to Campbell Bay.

* * *

Like any other island in the archipelago, Great Nicobar was a captivating sight, even from several hundred feet above ground level: emerald green waves lapping gently against a sandy white coast, hills and mounds rich with vegetation and tall trees covered in dense foliage, their sturdy trunks and thick barks supporting dozens of vines and other creepers. A long, cemented airstrip, adjacent to a shallow bay, was the only evidence of civilization on that vast expanse of island visible to me through the glass windowpanes of the helicopter as it made a jerky, successful landing at Campbell Bay. The three of us (the other two passengers had disembarked on Car Nicobar) had barely jumped out on to the tarmac and were making our way towards a group of people waving to us from a distance when the helicopter took off again.

My fellow passengers were met by their local contacts and left the airstrip within minutes. I headed towards a small office building and paused in front of it, trying to figure out the exit route, as there were no signs indicating entry or exit points. At that moment, a young man approached and asked for my name. He explained that anticipating the difficulties I might face in Campbell Bay, my contact in Port Blair had sent him to escort me to the Andaman and Nicobar Public Works Department (APWD) guest house. It was apparently the only decent accommodation available on the island for a visitor – be it the Lieutenant Governor of the Andaman and Nicobar Islands or an ordinary citizen like me.

After checking into a neat, air-conditioned room, my first task in Campbell Bay was to rush to the shipping-services office to book my return ticket on the next ship to Port Blair; I had been warned that if reaching Campbell Bay was an ordeal, leaving the place would be twice as difficult. Since the APWD guest house was just a kilometre from the jetty area, where tickets could be purchased in advance, I decided to set out on foot right away.

My first impression of Campbell Bay was that it was a cute, little tropical paradise. The roads were wide and neatly laid out, with hardly any traffic, except for the rare autorickshaw or the even rarer government-run bus. Tall trees planted on either side of the road provided a thick canopy of branches and foliage that completely shielded the road from the rays of the sun and kept the thoroughfare comfortably cool. The only buildings I could see near the APWD guest house were spacious government bungalows, reserved for district-administration officials, and modest residential quarters for other island-administration staff. There was hardly anyone about and even the mounds of garbage I had grown accustomed to seeing in other parts of the country were conspicuous by their absence. The lush green surroundings, the tropical weather and the beautifully serene beaches were so inviting, it was a miracle that the tourism industry had missed out on promoting this virgin destination so far.

I put on a cap to ward off the heat and started walking towards the jetty through Zero Point – Campbell Bay's town centre. Having covered nearly half a kilometre along a shady stretch, I took a right turn at Zero Point and entered Jetty Road, which went all the way to the island jetty. Walking down this road turned out to be quite an ordeal. There was not a single tree along this stretch and the scorching rays of the afternoon sun seemed to singe my flesh. After twenty minutes of this torture under a blazing sun, I reached a government-building complex, where the shipping-services office was located.

Although there were many offices in the government complex, their front doors were securely padlocked from outside. Although it was only 11.30 a.m. and lunch break was still an hour away, no official was in sight. I had been waiting for about half an hour outside the shipping-services office when I was told by a social welfare department employee, who had just arrived on a bicycle, that the booking clerk had gone to the bank to deposit some money and would not be back before 2 p.m. I returned to my guest house and promptly turned up at the office again at two. The front door was still locked.

About half an hour later, sometime after lunch was supposed to be officially over, a government staffer working for another department appeared, his dark face lavishly dusted with talcum powder. He informed me that the booking clerk was on his way and should be there by 3.15 p.m., give or take a few minutes.

'He usually closes by four. But don't worry. There are enough tickets, as this is not peak season. You should be able to get a ticket,' he said helpfully.

At exactly 3.15 p.m., another lean, frail man arrived at the complex on a bicycle and parked it outside the shipping-services ticket counter. Before he could open the counter and get ready to work, three other men approached the counter and formed a little queue. Since I was the first person in the queue, I was able to buy a cabin-class ticket on the ship *MV Campbell Bay*, scheduled to depart a week later for Port Blair. Relieved at the ease with which I had been able to buy the return ticket, I approached the jetty, where I had noticed a few shops, to buy a soft drink and quench my thirst. The sun was still relentless and the humidity was so high that I was completely soaked in sweat and felt totally dehydrated.

The first shop where I asked for a soda was a little shack that sold grocery items and vegetables. The shopkeeper said that they did not stock drinks, because they did not have a refrigerator, and asked me to enquire at the tea shop nearby. The tea-shop owner too did not stock drinks of any kind, not even bottled water, and suggested that I try a particular bakery in the Jetty Bazaar. When I reached the bazaar, a chain of shops in a rectangular complex, the bakery in question turned out to be one of the only two outlets still open that afternoon. However, the man behind the counter said that he had no soft drinks or soda in stock, as the ship had not yet arrived with the weekly supplies.

'Here, all shops run out of provisions and can only be restocked when the next ship arrives,' he explained, offering me cold, homemade *lassi* – the only drink available. 'I may even run out of this drink soon, if the next ship is late in coming. It is expected to arrive this week, but who knows? It may. It may not. Sometimes, we have to carry on without any stocks for as long as a month. This is life in Campbell Bay.'

Since the tall, lean, dark-skinned man with a grey moustache and a slight hunch looked as though he could be from my part of the country, I asked him if he was a Tamil.

'Of course,' he replied, beaming. 'I am originally from Ramnad district.'

Now 50 years old, Kathiresan had first set foot on the island three decades ago to help with the thriving business his brother had set up near the jetty after settling in Campbell Bay ten years earlier. This remote part of the country was now home for them both.

'Two of my elder brothers had been living here, but one of

them died and the other went into depression,' he elaborated. 'So our father asked me to join my brother here and help with the business. At the time, I had been working in a cotton mill back home and earning a decent salary.'

In those days, flights between Port Blair and Madras (now Chennai) were irregular and unaffordable. So Kathiresan had taken a train to Madras from his native place and spent several days there, waiting for the ship to Port Blair. Once he boarded the ship, it had taken him four days, as was usual then, to reach Port Blair where he had to wait another week to board the inter-island ferry to Campbell Bay.

'It took me an entire month to reach here from Ramnad,' he said.

The Great Nicobar Island and Campbell Bay, in particular, was in the grip of a malaria epidemic at the time. People were succumbing to the disease every other day and more and more were falling ill. They did not even have clean drinking water or proper health-care facilities, but still, the brothers managed to carry on with their lives.

In time, Kathiresan opened his own establishment – a paan shop – at the jetty. His business grew over the years, encouraging him to upgrade his little paan shop to a full-fledged bakery. The budding entrepreneur also married and fathered children during this period.

By and large, life here was peaceful, unlike on the mainland, where people squabbled with one another over trifles and fought bitterly over religion, caste and community. Despite harbouring a diverse population from Tamil Nadu, Andhra Pradesh, Maharashtra, Punjab and several other parts of the country, people in Campbell Bay lived in harmony and helped one another out in times of crisis. Kathiresan was soon so engrossed in life at Campbell Bay that the thought of visiting his parents on the mainland did not occur to him for more than a dozen years.

'But all that changed completely after the tsunami,' he recalled. 'Until then, Campbell Bay had been a beautiful place, whose population and business potential were on the rise. After the tsunami devoured our peaceful little island on 26 December 2004, life was never the same. We are yet to recover from its impact, even after so many years.'

Over the next few days, I was to discover that no conversation with an islander could take place without the word 'tsunami' cropping up at least once. Such had been the impact of the killer wave on this little paradise. In fact, while waiting for the shipping ticket counter to open so that I could purchase my return ticket to Port Blair, I had learnt from a software engineer from Bengaluru, who had come down to Campbell Bay to run maintenance routines on Indian Navy radar software, that the island administration had issued a tsunami warning on the very eve of my arrival, after an earthquake struck the Indonesian coast, a mere 80 nautical miles away.

'We were asked to keep our essential belongings ready, in case we had to evacuate,' the man said. 'Fortunately, nothing happened. But I am not about to linger here. I want to get out on the next available vessel.'

* * *

The next afternoon, I visited B-Quarry Beach, situated less than a kilometre from the APWD guest house. A short walk from the guest house past the Tribal Welfare Office led me to a four-way junction from where I took a left turn and passed a two-wheeler mechanic shop, a locked Andaman and Nicobar Islands Integrated Development Corporation (ANIIDCO) retail outlet (it was the exclusive licensee for selling liquor on the islands and liquor was banned on the island) and the island's only petrol and diesel station – little more than a shed with corrugated iron roofing, stocked with dozens of barrels of fuel. I made my way up this steadily ascending road until I had reached its summit. A wooden board planted on the other side of it welcomed visitors to the B-Quarry Beach, an initiative by the Andaman and Nicobar forest department. A stone stairway, embedded with dry, faded corals, led me all the way down to a stunning beach hugging a C-shaped coast.

The emerald sea and white sands were flanked by tall ferns and colossal screw pines. Hammocks, bamboo huts and rustic benches carved out of the trunks of giant trees were so aesthetically arranged here that the beach looked as if it had been plucked out of a Hawaiian resort and replanted in this remote part of the world. Despite the heat of the midday sun, the shade from the tall trees ensured that the beach was cool and the mild breeze was soothing. As the only visitor on that serene beach this afternoon, I found it hard to resist the urge to dive into the waves. This had been my fantasy: to live on a remote, unspoiled seaside, surrounded by lush green vegetation, with no other human around; a place where time stood still and the individual could surrender wholeheartedly to nature's overwhelming beauty; a place so distant from urban civilization that living or dying here left no impression, not even on statistical records. Like the tonnes of dead corals that washed ashore during high tide and were bleached in the blazing sun, humans too ended up as mere bones that would be fossilized and added to the earth's calcium deposits.

Having savoured the pristine beauty of this little Eden, I could well imagine how the various aboriginal tribes, who had been its original inhabitants, must have felt when the influx of supposedly more civilized humans drove them deeper into the impenetrable forest that lay behind the guest houses, residential quarters and Defence establishments. On that balmy afternoon, I figured it was my one chance to live like an aborigine and give in to my natural instincts.

So I took off my t-shirt and jeans, wrapped them in a bundle and placed them on a wooden bench. Then I ran towards the inviting sea and was wading past the gentle waves, when two men emerged from nowhere and asked me to come right back.

'This beach is not suitable for swimming,' said one. 'You are not allowed to venture into the sea from here.'

The man was clean-shaven and middle-aged. His leaner, taller and much younger companion seemed kinder and said that I could go into waist-deep water, but venturing beyond that would be very risky, unless I was an expert swimmer. When I retorted that I could manage, the older man, who was wearing a khaki half-sleeved shirt and matching knee-length shorts, came up and explained that there was a coral reef just a few metres from the shore, where the underwater sand bed fell away without warning to a depth of several feet, causing many people to drown.

'We would advise you not to swim here. But if you really insist on doing so and find yourself in trouble at any point, remember that there are no lifeguards and there is no way we can save you,' he warned. 'Besides, there are no reliable hospitals here either.'

His last statement killed my urge to enjoy a swim. Sensing my disappointment, the older of the two invited me to a bamboo hut nearby, handed me the visitor's register and made casual conversation, perhaps to divert me.

His name was Sephal Majumdar and he was from West Bengal's North 24 Parganas district. He had come to Campbell Bay in 1991 with a job in the forest department. After serving in different locations, Sephal and his associate were now guards at the B-Quarry Beach and spent the day maintaining the facilities built for visitors. There were, however, hardly any visitors to speak of. The guest register had no more than two dozen entries, most of them made by government staff who would arrive here on official assignments and take time off to visit the beach.

'You spend every day on this beautiful beach and actually get paid for it,' I told him enviously. 'This is the best job in the world; I wish I were in your place.'

Majumdar nodded in agreement and admitted that he was, indeed, very happy with his job and that the town where he lived, Campbell Bay, was also a pleasant place.

'Unlike the mainland, it is very peaceful here. Back in West Bengal, you must always be on your guard. If you're not careful, they will snatch away your money, your home and even your wife. Here, there are no such threats. So many different communities live here – Bengalis, Tamils, Punjabis, Telugus and people from all parts of the country. But we don't quarrel among ourselves here like they do on the mainland,' he said. 'We live like brothers.' Then he added, 'Not that there are no problems.'

He kept up a running account and I did not interrupt him. By now, I had become familiar with such monologues. People like him, who lived in remote locations and rarely got to meet anyone other than close family members and colleagues, seldom had an opportunity to unburden their minds and hearts.

'I have a 12-year-old son,' Sephal went on. 'Tushar is studying in class VII at the Jawahar Navodaya School in Carnic [short for Car Nicobar]. He is one of the very few children from Campbell Bay to have got admission in this prestigious school and that too after sitting for a written test. I was quite happy to go and get him registered as a residential scholar at the school, after which I returned to Campbell Bay.

'A few months back, I got a call from the school principal. He informed me that Tushar was ill and had had to be admitted to the local hospital. The principal asked me to rush to Car Nicobar, as the boy was missing his family. I was desperate to see my ailing son, but there were no ships going to Carnic that week. The helicopter service was too expensive and reserved only for VIPs.

I had no way of reaching my son. I spent several sleepless nights agonizing over his condition and state of mind.

'A ship arrived exactly a week later and I left for Carnic. My son was still in hospital and said that he missed us very much. Luckily, he recovered and went back to school. It might look like a trivial incident now, but only I know what my wife Triveni and I went through at the time. Such is life in Campbell Bay.'

I nodded in agreement, lit a cigarette and offered him one. Majumdar declined it and continued to speak.

'Until the tsunami happened, I had never thought of leaving Campbell Bay, but the events of that one day changed me. And I am not the only one who feels this way. So many of the people who once lived here have already returned to the mainland. Those who remain are here to make enough money so that they can build a home in their native place.'

Majumdar vividly remembered the events of 26 December 2004, despite the twelve years that had passed since. It was a Sunday morning and he was alone at their home in Shastri Nagar, 35 kilometres from Campbell Bay. Triveni and Tushar were away in Port Blair, spending the winter holidays with Sephal's in-laws.

Although he didn't have to report to work, Sephal got out of bed at 6 a.m., as he had to collect drinking water that was supplied at fixed hours of the day from a public tap. But before joining the queue at the tap, he decided to have a cup of tea at a tea shop not far from his house and very close to the seashore. Four other customers were already there, seated on a bench. Sephal ordered tea and joined them. The tea-shop owner made the first round of tea with fresh milk.

Just as he was about to take a sip of his tea, Sephal noticed that the ceramic cup in his hand was shaking and the hot tea had spilled over on to it. At first, he thought that his hands were trembling because of the previous night's drinking binge. Trying hard to steady them, Sephal looked around and noticed that all the other customers in the tea shop were facing the same problem. Within seconds, the bench on which they were sitting began to rock and, along with it, the tea pot and even the stove. Earthquakes were not unusual in this part of the country and occurred almost every other month. The locals were used to simply laughing them off. Sephal thought it was just another tremor like the ones they were accustomed to. So he moved to a corner and held on to one of the wooden pillars supporting the roof, waiting for the rocking to stop.

Unlike in the past, the earth did not stop rocking this time. Instead, the tremors became more violent. When this went on beyond a few seconds, Sephal panicked and looked around. The homes around him were shaking and the coconut trees were swaying so violently that their tops almost bent over to sweep the ground. Due to the movement of the earth, water was gushing out from a nearby drain. People were stunned and howling in fear. After a while, the rocking ceased.

Until that day, no settler or native of Campbell Bay had heard of the word 'tsunami'. They had not even known that such a phenomenon existed. So as soon as the rocking ended, the men resumed whatever they were doing and Sephal even joked with the tea-shop owner that he was not about to pay for the spilled tea, as he had not even had the chance to taste it.

About fifteen minutes after the quake had subsided, the customers at the tea shop were waiting for fresh tea to be brewed, when Sephal saw a young boy who had gone to complete his morning ablutions on the seashore sprinting towards them and screaming, '*Bhago, bhago*!' Majumdar did not know what to make of it and stopped the boy to question him.

'He replied that the sea was rushing in towards us and raced away like a madman. I ran out to check for myself. The sea was not coming towards us, I discovered, but had backed off up to a kilometre and we could see the buried rocks far into the distance. Just a few seconds later, even as I was gazing at the scene, a giant wave headed towards us. As soon as I saw it, I too screamed a warning to the others and we all ran for higher ground.'

The massive wave reached the shore about a minute later and Majumdar still remembered how filthy and muddy the water was. It rushed in and drowned Shastri Nagar, sweeping away everything that was in its path.

'Standing on a mound, I watched my home being washed way in a matter of seconds,' Sephal recalled. 'Curiously enough, that wave destroyed only two homes and one of them was mine. I was standing there, bemoaning my fate at being one of the unfortunate few on the island, when another giant wave, much bigger and more powerful, engulfed the entire village, devouring all the homes, the tea shop, the marketplace and everything along with it. Fortunately, except for two or three unlucky persons, everyone was already on the hillock and survived.'

A third, much smaller wave swept in and cleaned the remaining debris, leaving nothing behind. Even then, the islanders were not yet aware of the extent of the devastation. Slowly, news trickled in and they came to know that all the other villages along the coast had suffered the same fate.

Until that day, settlers and businessmen in Campbell Bay had never thought of returning to their hometowns on the mainland. This was their little heaven on earth and they would do anything to protect it. But that black Sunday changed its fate. People who had lost touch with their relatives on the mainland re-established ties and bought property there with whatever money they had saved.

'Even I have a bought a small house near Kolkata,' Majumdar confided. 'What do we live for, sir? Isn't it for our children? We want our children and grandchildren to be safe. How can anyone feel safe in this land which is rocked by tremors every so often? I no longer wish to remain here. Who knows, another tsunami might occur only a hundred years later, but I won't be around to warn my children and grandchildren about it, will I? All the fruits of our hard work, our investments and property could vanish again. I do not want my family to live in such a place.' His words were uttered with a sad smile.

After recounting the experience, Sephal probably felt that he had said too much. He quietly left after shaking hands with me. Before parting, I wanted to take his picture, but he turned down my request, stating that he was on duty, and walked off. I returned to the wooden bench facing the sea, where my clothes still lay in a bundle. The sea and the beach that had seemed so inviting just an hour ago now looked ominous.

* * *

Like most other coastal settlements, Campbell Bay begins at the Harbour Jetty and stretches along the coast up to 35 kilometres in the south. The main bazaar, located in the town centre, a little more than a kilometre from the jetty, has several retail outlets, eateries and saloons. Besides being a commercial hub, Zero Point also houses the APWD guest house, the Great Nicobar Assistant Commissioner's bungalow and other government offices within a radius of half a kilometre. The residential neighbourhoods, situated mostly to the south of Zero Point, are commonly referred to by names coined on the basis of the distance between the settlement and Zero Point. Joginder Nagar, for example, which is 8 kilometres from Zero Point, does not go by its given name, but is usually called the Eighth Kilometre Settlement. Similarly, Gandhi Nagar is the Thirtieth Kilometre Settlement, while Shastri Nagar is commonly known as the Thirty-fifth Kilometre Point. Beyond this last settlement lies Indira Point, the southeastern tip of India at Fifty-first Kilometre, but it is no longer accessible by road after the tsunami of 2004. The island administration provides daily bus services from the jetty to Shastri Nagar and back between 5 a.m. and 7.30 p.m. Private autorickshaws and taxis are also available for hire on a daily basis. Apart from the North–South Road that runs up to Shastri Nagar, the Campbell Bay area has one other major road running east to west, again starting at Zero Point and extending to about 11 kilometres west right up to the entrance of the Campbell Bay National Park.

The earliest settlers in Campbell Bay were families of ex-servicemen brought over from the mainland by the Union government in the late 1960s and early 1970s as part of the Accelerated Development Programme of the Ministry of Labour and Resettlement. The intention was to populate the largely uninhabited forest areas and secure the country's borders. Ex-servicemen were particularly chosen for these settlements, as their military skills could also come into use if there were signs of aggression from hostile neighbours. Most of the current residents of Campbell Bay are the children, grandchildren and relatives of those original settlers who cleared the forests and laid the foundations of a community here.

After spending the first few days roaming around Zero Point, meeting locals, walking into government offices and police stations and bumping into bureaucrats at random, I went off to meet the original settlers of Campbell Bay on a Sunday, taking the 11 a.m. bus from the jetty's bus depot. Despite it being a holiday, most of the seats in the old State Transport Service bus were already taken when I reached the depot fifteen minutes before the scheduled time of departure. The passengers, who seemed to know one another, spoke in Tamil, Malayalam, Punjabi and other Indian languages that I could not even identify. I had taken a window seat behind the seat reserved for senior citizens and was casually observing the other passengers, when a tall, well-built elderly man with shiny brown skin that dripped with sweat under the flat black cap covering his balding head approached and asked me with a friendly smile if I was visiting Campbell Bay. I replied that I was, indeed, and had put up at the APWD guest house for the duration of my stay. I added that I was headed to Shastri Nagar to meet some of the earliest settlers.

'Oh, really? I am one of those early settlers,' he replied and shook hands with me. 'I arrived in 1972 and have been living here since.'

The man introduced himself as R.C. Kurup or Rama Chandra Kurup from Trivandrum, Kerala, and invited me to his home in the Thirtieth Kilometre or Gandhi Nagar.

The bus left the depot at 11 a.m. sharp with a full load of seated passengers and headed south, taking in more passengers at every halt, along with rations and other goods packed in metal boxes and cartons that were all stuffed into a luggage cabin under the passengers' area. The scenic route passed through dense forests, where tall palms, ferns, *rudraksh* trees, wild almond, mango and other fruit trees, with giant creepers twined around them, occupied every square foot of land and every square inch of open space, blocking out the sun completely. As we drove through the forest, I learnt from Kurup that the road we were taking had been recently constructed; the old one that had run adjacent to the coast had been completely destroyed by the tsunami. Every time the bus turned towards the coast, I could see vast stretches of land where the severed, decaying trunks of coconut and areca-nut trees stood pale and desolate in the slushy soil. In most places, the land itself still lay wallowing in sea water, utterly spent, robbed of its nutrients and useless for cultivation. Every now and then appeared the dilapidated walls of abandoned homes, stripped of their doors, windows and other woodwork, standing starkly in the slush – a reminder of how the land once used to be – firm and solid enough to build on. Little canals had since been dug along the coast, with one-way shutters to ensure that all the water that washed ashore at high tide would return to the sea.

As we passed various settlements along the 35 kilometre journey that would take approximately an hour, more passengers alighted at their stops and the bus started emptying out. A time came when all the seats lay vacant but for those occupied by me and one five-member Punjabi family. And that is how we travelled until the bus reached its final destination. The vehicle halted on a dirt road facing a desolate beach and the conductor announced that we had reached Shastri Nagar. The Punjabi family got off with their picnic baskets, tiffin carriers and water bottles and headed towards the beach, padding through the soft white sand and looking back at me curiously, again and again, as if to see if I was headed their way.

I turned away from the beach and stood next to a blue signboard with 'Shastri Nagar' written on it. A gravel road ran beyond it and into a bush jungle that revealed no signs of human habitation. To my left was a petty shop selling cold drinks, cigarettes, biscuits and other provisions, where two young men, one clad in a red t-shirt and white shorts, the other in a blue checked shirt and white dhoti, were engrossed in a serious discussion. I approached the shop and asked them for a cold drink, as I felt completely drained and dehydrated because of the scorching heat.

'We have Sprite, Maaza and Mountain Dew – which one do you want?' asked the young man in the red t-shirt, who was slightly taller and more broadly built than his companion.

I asked for a 500 ml bottle of Sprite and glugged down its contents in a matter of seconds. Then I bought a pack of Flake cigarettes, the only brand available here, and asked for directions to the village pradhan's home.

'We don't have a pradhan here,' the man in the red t-shirt replied. 'There is a panchayat ward member for Shastri Nagar, though.'

It turned out that he himself was the Shastri Nagar panchayat ward member M. Shankar. I also learnt that he belonged to the BJP. His friend Anil Kumar, a carpenter who worked as a contractor with the Border Roads Organization (BRO), was engaged in rebuilding the roadway between Shastri Nagar and Indira Point. Born and raised in Shastri Nagar, the two childhood friends were third-generation descendants of the original settlers.

Shankar's grandfather Govindasamy, then a washerman in the Indian Army, had married a Brahmin woman from Thanjavur, creating a furore in their conservative native village. Consequently, after he had completed his full service in the army, neither Govindasamy nor his wife Rajammal were keen on returning to the village. They opted, instead, to be resettled here as part of the Accelerated Development Programme of the Ministry of Labour and Resettlement. Given 11 acres of land, in addition to livestock, equipment and other basic necessities that would help them start life afresh, the couple moved to this remote island with their two sons and two daughters and began a new life, along with fifty other families of ex-servicemen from different parts of the country, resettling in Shastri Nagar in 1974.

'Actually, their last child, a daughter, was born in Campbell Bay and our family has been living here since,' Shankar informed me.

Raised in a small community of ex-servicemen and completely cut off from all other human contact, Govindasamy's second daughter Durgambal would fall in love with the son of another first-generation settler, a Keralite who was employed at the time by the Andaman and Nicobar government.

Durgambal and Manmadhan Nair tied the knot in Campbell Bay and started a new life together in Shastri Nagar, where

Shankar and his siblings would be born. The children attended the Shastri Nagar Primary School and, on being promoted, continued their education at the government middle school at Gandhi Nagar, until it was time for them to go to the government high school in Vijay Nagar.

'Unfortunately, I could not clear my class X exams and dropped out of school, but my siblings continued their studies,' Shankar confided.

His friend Anil Kumar shared a similar past. Sometime in 1974, the young man's grandfather, an ex-serviceman from Kerala, had been resettled with 11 acres of land in Shastri Nagar. Anil's parents, Sarala Devi and Ravindran, had come down to Campbell Bay soon after their wedding in Kerala, when she was just eighteen and he in his early twenties, to assist his grandfather. After settling here, Ravindran would work as a road-construction contractor, while developing the 11 acres of land their family had been allotted. Since then, Anil's parents had been living in Shastri Nagar. Anil and his siblings were all born and raised in Campbell Bay and had never lived elsewhere.

Earlier that morning, residents of Shastri Nagar had gathered outside Shankar's shop and conducted a meeting to discuss the renovation of the Pandimani Temple on the seashore that the tsunami had washed away.

'If you had arrived a little earlier, you could have met all our residents at one go. They've just left,' Shankar said.

According to the two men, the Pandimani Temple, a south Indian shrine, had been the last Hindu place of worship on Great Nicobar. It had played a very important role in the lives of the locals, many of whom would visit it every day to offer their prayers, until the tsunami wiped it off the face of the earth.

As the temple had been extremely popular in Shastri Nagar, its residents had decided to rebuild it. The final decision regarding the costs involved in its construction and other related matters had been taken mere minutes before I had reached the locality.

'We are slowly trying to put our lives back together,' Anil declared. 'After the tsunami destroyed nearly all the homes in the coastal settlements, the families that had survived were evacuated to temporary shelters in Campbell Bay and provided free rations, clothes and other supplies. But we were kept languishing there for too long. Most families like ours had been living in makeshift shelters for nearly ten years and it was only a couple of years ago that we were allowed to move back to our lands and homes. Those ten years of our lives were completely wasted.'

As the original settlers and even their offspring were now in their sunset years, youngsters like Shankar and Anil were taking up the initiative of rebuilding their colony.

'While sea erosion has destroyed most of the plantations, the farmlands are still suitable for agriculture,' Shankar said. 'But having been idle for ten long years, people seem to have lost the will to work as hard as their ancestors did when they first settled here. Unless we strive to rebuild our lives and our economy, Campbell Bay will stagnate.'

Both Shankar and Anil loved their neighbourhood and claimed that their childhood had been simply wonderful, with a beautiful beach on one side and a dense jungle on the other. Not for them the attractions that kept most urban children absorbed, like motorcycles, satellite TVs and movie theatres. They claimed, in fact, to never have missed or pined for these sources of entertainment.

'We just wandered these forests day and night,' Shankar recalled. 'Occasionally, we went on little hunting trips, caught fish from the streams and reservoirs, plucked wild fruits and ate them without a care. While growing up on this island, we never knew the meaning of fear.'

Over the years, the island's roads were modernized and the bus service became more regular. The convenience of paid cable TV was still a distant dream, but most homes were equipped with giant dish antennas, each 8 to 12 feet high. People could watch free TV-channel programmes transmitted from different countries, including India.

'But I hate cities,' Shankar declared emphatically. 'I went to the mainland for a few months and found it suffocating. Its people, politics, traffic and pollution just do not suit us islanders. Here, we lead simple lives. If anyone is in trouble, we come together to help. My father is a Malayali, my mother a Tamil. My sister is married to a man from Ranchi, while a cousin recently married a Punjabi girl from another village. There is neither communal tension nor any hint of casteism here; we are all one. Where else would I want to raise my children but in this place?'

Both Shankar and Anil were pinning their hopes on the tourism industry that had, of late, received an encouraging boost from the island administration. The men informed me that the government was taking serious measures to promote eco-tourism in Campbell Bay, using its natural beach and rain-forest environment as attractions.

'It is our only possible path to progress,' Shankar declared. 'If tourism develops in a big way in Campbell Bay, all other amenities will soon follow and greatly help in reviving our economy. Until then, we will have to subsist on coconuts and areca nuts.'

* * *

Later that afternoon, Anil took me to his home at the far end of Shastri Nagar. The modest wood cabin was the last recognized residential address on India's southeastern coast. Beyond it lay dense jungles, stretching all the way to Indira Point and further as the coast turns towards the east. Yet, somewhere deep within them, groups of Shompen tribals and probably a few isolated Nicobarese could be living surrounded by, and in harmony with, nature.

When I visited their home, Anil's parents Ravindran and Sarala Devi were watching a Malayalam movie telecast on Asianet's Middle East channel. I had noticed the huge dish antenna planted outside their house. Apart from Anil, the couple had three older sons, who no longer lived with them. While the eldest was living in Port Blair, the other two sons had made their homes in the Vijay Nagar settlement about 8 kilometres away. Although the family had its roots in Trivandrum, none of the sons had ever visited their ancestral house and did not consider any place other than Campbell Bay their home.

I asked Ravindran if he ever missed his village in Kerala and wanted to return there some day.

'What is left there for us to return to?' Ravindran said. 'We sold whatever little we had to migrate to this part of the country. The Indira Gandhi-led government that had come up with this resettlement policy gave us everything we needed at the time. They gave us land, money to build homes, vessels, furniture, livestock and even free rations for the first four years to help us resettle in this new land. We were all quite happy with the arrangement and had settled down here comfortably. Unfortunately, after the change in government, successive administrations seem to have forgotten about us completely. This region has seen no development since those early days.'

Back in the early 1970s, the construction of the road connecting Campbell Bay and Indira Point was under way and a network of schools, primary health-care centres and public-distribution outlets for supplying rations and other basic commodities had come up.

'If you go and check this out now, you will not find any

additions to the facilities that were in place forty years ago,' Ravindran went on. 'We have been living in a kind of limbo for these last four decades. Even now, if someone has a health crisis here, the only way to get him treatment and save his life is to rush him to Port Blair or to the mainland. And unless it is an extreme emergency, the helicopter service is out of bounds.'

Despite all these setbacks, the 300-odd families from across India who had arrived in two batches between 1969 and 1974 would work hard on the land allotted to them in their new homeland and make a decent living from their farms, which had, by then, started yielding the hoped-for returns.

'But with the devastation wrought by the tsunami, all the hard work came to naught and our settlements were set back by forty years,' Ravindran lamented. 'We lost our plantations to the sea. Moreover, since we were away from our homes for several years, weeds grew on the road leading to our paddy fields, cutting off access. Now even if some of the residents wish to restore their paddy fields to their original condition, there is neither money nor adequate manpower to start afresh.'

He believed that unless the government came up with a detailed scheme to revive these areas, the settlements could well vanish altogether in the not-too-distant future.

'Tourism has to be developed in a big way,' Ravindran said with conviction. 'It is the only available option, as the land here is too fragile for anything else. As recently as last month, there was a quake. Our homes were shaking. It is such a common occurrence here. Every now and then, the earth under our feet begins to move. *Ithar toh hamesa hilta rahta hai.*'

Ravindran and Sarala vividly remembered the year 1982, when a series of earthquakes rocked their lives continuously for over a month.

'It was the worst period of our four-decade stay. The earth

would shake four or five times a day and continued to do so for an entire month. We had to put up tents outside our homes and would rush out whenever there was a tremor,' Ravindran recalled, laughing out loud at the memory. '*Ithar toh pehle se hilta rahta hai.*'

* * *

The last bus to Zero Point left Shastri Nagar at 6.30 p.m. and reached the jetty an hour later. I decided to catch the one scheduled to leave an hour earlier so that I could get off at Gandhi Nagar or the Thirtieth Kilometre and meet R.C. Kurup at his residence, as I had promised that morning. Since I had a little time in hand before the bus arrived, I requested Anil to accompany me on a short trek in the jungles behind his home so that I could get a feel of the evergreen forests. He was only too happy to oblige.

My young companion led me down a dirt track that cut right through the thick vegetation behind their home. Hardly a hundred metres or so along the trail, I started feeling utterly lost, surrounded as I was by the gigantic wild mango, jackfruit and other fruit-bearing trees whose dense foliage seemed to completely shut out the sun, leaving the soil underfoot moist and leafy. Growing in the shade of the taller trees were shorter varieties of pine and wild palm. Wrapped around them were lush green creepers of different shapes and sizes. The ground below lay strewn with ripe mangoes half-eaten by bats and monkeys and tossed away for ants and other insects to scavenge on.

Anil picked up a large mango from a ditch and asked me to taste it. It was so sour that my body shivered involuntarily in reaction as the tartness of the juice hit my tongue and palate.

'These fruits grow wild here,' he explained. 'We grew up eating them straight off the trees in the jungle.'

We continued on our way and reached a locked forest outpost with an abandoned water tank near it. Anil helped me climb to the top of the tank, where we sat for a while, admiring the rain forest. Unlike in the jungles to be found in other parts of India, there were no ferocious beasts or poisonous reptiles here to worry about. In fact, I was reassured that no venomous snakes or insects lived in these jungles. The only animals found here were monkeys and wild boars.

'Reticulated pythons are present, but they do not attack humans,' Anil informed me. 'They prey on hens and other small creatures and rarely come out in the open.'

The only other predators in these jungles were salt-water crocodiles, which were quite common along the estuaries and canals that flowed into the sea. Anil reported that there had been a few incidences of crocodiles attacking people who had ventured unknowingly into the water.

'Otherwise, it is quite safe to walk in these forests,' Anil declared. 'As children, we had trekked deep into their interiors and even stayed there for a few nights without returning home. It was our favourite timepass.'

Sitting on the tank's parapet, I wondered what life must have been like for Anil, Shankar and others to grow up close to a dense jungle. They were so far away from civilization, with no TVs, cinema halls, restaurants or any of the other modern amenities that urban youth growing up in the 1980s and 1990s were used to. They must also have been unaware of the terrorism that had devastated Punjab and Kashmir and remained oblivious to the assassination of prime ministers and other major events that had shaken the country. Until recently, the only source of information here had been the radio and people like Anil and Shankar hardly listened to news broadcasts over the radio. Before the tsunami came and wreaked havoc in their lives, the settlers and their children had lived in a little paradise, with precious little to worry about. All they needed to buy was rice, dal and cooking oil. Everything else was either available on their farms or in the forest.

* * *

When we returned to the Shastri Nagar bus depot, the 5.30 p.m. bus was ready to leave. Other than myself, there was just one passenger. I purchased a ticket to the Thirtieth Kilometre stop and reached Gandhi Nagar Primary Health Centre in less than ten minutes.

Kurup and his wife lived in one of the row houses built for the rehabilitation of tsunami victims in Gandhi Nagar after their traditional homes had been washed away. I arrived at the home of this elderly couple while they were busy supervising construction work in their portico area where a new wall was being built to replace the corrugated iron sheet that had served as a partition between the living room and the portico. As in any Malayali home on the mainland, in the living room of Kurup's modest home was a Mathrubhoomi calendar (brought out by a leading Malayalam daily in Kerala) hanging from an iron nail on the wall facing the main door. Portraits of Guruvayoor Appan (the most popular deity worshipped by Malayali Hindus) adorned the rest of the wall.

Kurup introduced me to his wife as a writer from Chennai and hastened to the kitchen to prepare some tea. From there, he yelled out the explanation that his spouse was not well enough to handle kitchen duties. Within a few minutes, he had returned with a cup of milky tea, Good Day biscuits and some deep-fried snacks, which he placed before me.

On his retirement from the Indian Army following eighteen years of service, this veteran soldier had arrived in Campbell Bay with his family in 1977. Kurup had clear memories of his early days on the island, when its forests were being cut down, day and night, to make way for arable land that could be cultivated by the settlers. He also recalled that the first batch of settlers in Shastri Nagar had begun with the cultivation of paddy.

'When we first arrived here,' Kurup said, 'their paddy fields were ready to be harvested. The crop was bountiful, but there was no labour to reap it. The paddy was getting wasted in the fields. So we were asked to help out and take half the produce to meet our needs, which we gladly did.'

After the settlers in Gandhi Nagar were provided with paddy fields and plantation land, Kurup toiled hard on his farm and earned enough to take care of his son and three daughters, who were attending school in Campbell Bay. He made a decent living harvesting coconuts and areca nuts from their five-acre plantation and rice and vegetables from their paddy fields.

'There was a time,' Kurup reminisced, 'when I could make a few lakh rupees every month by selling coconuts and areca nuts alone. Those were the best days of our lives. We had cows, goats, hens and ducks that roamed freely on our farm. I would go all the way to Port Blair to buy strong, healthy bulls that could be put to use ploughing my land. We worked tirelessly and made a good life for ourselves.'

With the assassination of Indira Gandhi, the central government's policy towards settlers changed and, according to Kurup, the ex-servicemen resettled in faraway Nicobar were completely forgotten. All development activity was stalled here and the promise of a decent township on par with any developed town on the mainland remained an unfulfilled dream.

When Kurup's children grew up, they found jobs in Port Blair and elsewhere in the country, where they chose to settle. Over the years, these young people had become preoccupied with their own lives and their visits had tapered off. With the birth of their own children, Kurup's offspring rarely had the opportunity to visit the elderly couple, particularly as a round trip to Campbell

Bay was fraught with many uncertainties. However, Kurup and his wife had chosen to remain in Campbell Bay, taking care of their farm and going about their daily lives.

'Who would want to live in such a backward area?' the old man now remarked. 'The public-transport service is as unreliable as ever. If my wife or I, both heart patients, were to fall ill, where would we go for medical attention? Getting a helicopter ticket is next to impossible and the ships are available only once a week, sometimes once a fortnight. If a local were to develop sudden health complications, he or she would have no choice but to die alone here. Who would willingly come and live in such a place?'

The former soldier's biggest concern right now was whether his children would be able to make it to Campbell Bay in time to light his funeral pyre after he passed away.

'I am 78 and my wife is just a few years younger. How long can we go on?' he asked.

Even as we were talking, Kurup's next-door neighbour, an elderly Malayali woman, entered and introduced herself as Ammu. Her husband E.C. Damodaran was an ex-serviceman settler as well.

'I just want to say one thing,' Ammu began purposefully. 'We were brought here to defend the country's borders and given land, money and all assistance. We are grateful for that. But now our children are grown up and have moved elsewhere. They do not want to live in these remote backwaters. We are too old to continue working on our farmlands. In fact, all the settlers are either in their late seventies or late eighties. We no longer need this land. But we are unable to sell it, as there have been no buyers after the tsunami. My plea to the government is that it should take back the lands given to us and arrange for our relocation to the mainland. We are trapped here, with no way out.'

Even before Ammu could finish venting her woes, I heard

the roaring engines of the last bus to Campbell Bay passing by. Kurup and I ran out of his home to flag it down. If I missed that bus, I would not be able to return to my room at the guest house until the next morning. Even as Kurup held up the bus for me, I clasped Ammu's hand in my own and assured her that I would do my best to convey her message to the concerned authorities. Then I ran to board the waiting vehicle. As this was the last trip of the day, the bus was nearly full and I had to travel standing, leaning against a pole for the journey. As the bus sped along the winding road to Zero Point, I could hear Hindi film songs playing on a mobile phone that belonged to someone occupying one of the back seats.

* * *

For all practical purposes, Shastri Nagar is the last civilian settlement at the edge of this slice of Indian territory. Beyond it lies a vast coastline inundated by the sea up to Indira Point, 51 kilometres from Campbell Bay. Beyond Indira Point, approximately 30-odd kilometres away, as the coast curves southwest, lies Pilovavi, home to a modest settlement of Great Nicobarese families. They are the original inhabitants of this borderland and bear less physical resemblance to Indian settlers from the mainland than to Indonesians, Malays and other South East Asians. The Anthropological Museum in Port Blair classifies these tribes as Deutero Malays, while the Car Nicobarese belong to the Proto Malay tribes. Distinguished by their short, lean, athletic physiques and yellowish brown complexions, these people speak a dialect of Nicobarese. In their language, Great Nicobar is referred to as 'To Kirong Long'. Thanks to the missionaries who arrived on this island before others, the entire native population in Pilovavi has been converted to Christianity.

Until 26 December 2004, more than 350 Great Nicobarese

had lived scattered in and around Pilovavi. But when the tsunami came, its monstrous waves would leave their most brutal impact on these tribal villages, swallowing close to 300 people in a matter of minutes. The few dozen survivors, who were evacuated to Campbell Bay, have continued to live in temporary tsunami shelters built in Rajiv Nagar, also known as the Nicobarese Basti, for the past twelve years.

I visited the Nicobarese Basti on a hot, sunny afternoon to meet a young man named Hopeful. He was referred to me by an ornithologist in Coimbatore who had once taken him along on a 15-day voyage down the Great Nicobar coast in search of the Megapode, an elusive bird endemic to Andaman and Nicobar, the Australasian region and other Pacific islands. After completing his research, the ornithologist had returned to Coimbatore, but remained in touch with Hopeful. Using the ornithologist's name as reference, I had called the local with the interesting name a day before my proposed visit to the Nicobarese Basti.

Hopeful was delighted. 'He's a good friend of mine, sir,' he said enthusiastically. 'Come to our *basti* any time you wish. I'll help you out in every way I can.'

Rajiv Nagar was located barely a kilometre from Zero Point and, like most settlements in this group of islands, consisted of Tamil, Telugu and other families of mainland origin who lived alongside the Nicobarese. While the settlers lived at the entrance to the *basti*, the Nicobarese had been provided wooden cabins built several feet above ground level at the top of a mound. In the space beneath each home were pig pens and cages for hens and other livestock. As I approached the Nicobarese Basti, several white and grey piglets ran around the neighbourhood, mother hens and their chicks pecked at tiny insects and spilt grain by the roadside and little children clad in nothing but boxer shorts played football with enthusiasm.

At the entrance to the *basti* stood a huge community centre, the only concrete structure in the locality. To its right was a health centre, a little room that was now locked. Outside it sat three young men in boxer shorts, their bodies lean and toned. When I reached the community centre, one of the men waved out and beckoned me to join him. It turned out to be Hopeful. He shook hands with me and introduced his friends Morris and Matthias. While Hopeful and Matthias each sported a thin moustache, the other man was clean-shaven. In their early thirties, all three were unemployed and looked as blank as a classroom blackboard on a Monday morning.

For a while, none of us said a word. To end the awkward silence, I told Hopeful of my wish to talk to some of the older men in the *basti*.

'Nobody will talk to you,' he said. 'Actually, there is only one *budda* [old man] who might have, but he is very ill.'

Morris, who had ignored me until that moment, turned to me and declared that there was nothing in their lives worth sharing.

'We have no jobs, no homes, no money. What is there to talk about?'

Before the tsunami, these Great Nicobarese, who were not, until recently, conversant with the concept of money, had led simple lives with their extended families at Pilovavi. They had lived off the land, for the wild fruits and vegetables that grew in the jungles surrounding their villages and the pigs they reared had provided them with adequate food all through the year. They had made a living from the coconut and areca-nut plantations they owned by selling coconut and areca nuts to dealers from Port Blair. With the income they earned, they would shop for clothes and other basic commodities. Every once in a while, the government sent them free supplies of kerosene, rice, sugar and cooking oil by boat. Their village had a police outpost, a primary school and a health centre of sorts. The Assistant Commissioner of Campbell Bay visited them routinely once every few years to renew ties with them and enquire about their needs and welfare.

'But now, we have nothing,' said Morris. 'We have been brought here and given homes, but no jobs. Our plantations are all gone, taken away by the sea, and we have no source of income.'

Like most other men in this *basti,* he had attended school only up to class V or VI. He was not quite sure which.

'But what is the point? The teacher never came to school, anyway, and we were taught nothing.'

All the men here were, by and large, jobless and took up temporary work, such as clearing forests, paving roads and so on for a few months in a year. Every month, a group of men from the *basti* would take a dinghy and go all the way to Pilovavi to check on the condition of their former homes and neighbourhood.

When I asked what drove them to do so, Matthias, the oldest of the three, reminisced about their old way of life, when they had lived among their own people and would roam about in the jungles, carefree. Their interactions with the settlers from the mainland had been minimal. They were more frequently in touch with sailors from Myanmar, Thailand and even Malaysia, who halted at their village, every now and then, and brought in groups of smugglers from various South East Asian countries. The latter always carried enough food, clothes and other rations for a long stay on the island. They felled trees, hunted game and fished in the lagoons until they had enough to take back home. The visitors, whose physical features resembled those of the Great Nicobarese, got along well with the locals, stayed in their homes and roamed around Great Nicobar freely. When they went back home, the smugglers left behind their surplus rations and clothes for the Nicobarese, which made them hugely popular.

'They were so much fun when they arrived,' said Matthias.

'Sometimes, they would even sneak into Campbell Bay at night to do some shopping and then return to our settlements. All that ended after we were relocated to Campbell Bay. All we want is to return to our old village and revive our plantations. Please write that in your book.'

A little later, Hopeful took me along to the home of Justin, the 'captain' of the *basti*. In these predominantly Christian villages, the pradhan or head of the village was called a captain. Earlier, when these families had lived in Pilovavi, Justin's father had been the captain. Following his demise in the tsunami, his son had been given the post of the new captain.

Although well-built, Justin was less than five feet tall and noticeably shorter than the other men. When we visited him at home, he was neatly dressed in a pair of black jeans and a white round-necked t-shirt, with dark sunglasses tucked into it. He was also among the few in the *basti* who spoke English. The 39-year-old was married to Maryann and the couple had two children: R. Dhoni (named after Indian cricket captain M.S. Dhoni), who was nine, and Adanashish, who was two years younger. Justin's living room was a neat, spacious enclosure, bare of furniture. The walls were adorned with two large posters of Jesus Christ and smaller posters of quotes from the Bible. I did not see any signs of Maryann or their two children at home. From the way he eyed me, I sensed that the man was wary of me and was weighing every word he uttered.

Justin belonged to the first generation of Great Nicobarese who had been to school and could speak fluent Hindi. He had lost as many as twelve members of his family to the tsunami, including his Appa and Amma, and revealed that the only reason he was still alive was because he had taken a canoe out to sea that morning, unaware that in his absence, the tsunami was devastating his village. With almost the entire place swept away and, along with it, most of its residents, the twenty-odd survivors would marry soon after the tragedy, their sole aim being to procreate and make up for those lost lives.

'Children born here after the tsunami are around the same age as my own sons,' Justin said. 'When they grow up and have their own families, we would like to return to Pilovavi and settle where our ancestors had once lived. Right now, we are too few in number to make living in such a remote place feasible.'

In the interim, Justin and the others had been provided a plot of land each at Coledegree, where they had been cultivating coconut, areca nut and other trees for the last few years.

'The banana trees have borne fruit this year, but it will take a long time for the other trees to do so,' Justin said. 'Life is a struggle, but do we have a choice?'

I asked him if any of the country's national leaders or politicians had ever visited them or even knew of their existence.

'After the tsunami, Manmohan Singh and Abdul Kalam did visit our *basti*, but we did not get a chance to meet them and share our problems with them,' he replied. 'It was the settlers who stage-managed the entire affair and ensured that they were the only ones to interact with the visitors and air their grievances. We were completely sidelined.'

* * *

On my last afternoon in Campbell Bay, I visited the Tribal Welfare Office near the APWD guest house to meet a few Shompens, an indigenous tribe of Great Nicobar, who had turned up at the office to collect monthly rations for the rest of their community. The Shompens lived deep in the jungles and continued to carry on the traditions of their hunter-gatherer ancestors. Though not considered as hostile as some of the other tribes in the Andaman and Nicobar islands, the Shompens rarely interacted with outsiders.

When I arrived at the office, the only staff member present was a driver; the Tribal Welfare Officer had gone to Port Blair. I told the driver that I wanted to meet the tribals and was led into the next room, where they had been locked in. When the driver opened the door, I found two perplexed young men with straight, silky hair, pale yellow skin and strong limbs staring at me with open curiosity. Barring a soiled loincloth wrapped tightly around their groin and buttocks, they were naked. Then an older, taller man with similar features, whose teeth were stained red and full of cavities, approached with a broad smile. I extended my hand. He did not understand my gesture and said something in his native language.

'He says, "*Saab aye hain,*"' the driver translated.

I smiled back at the man and asked, 'How are you?' and extended my hand again.

The man came closer and hugged me tight. I was a little alarmed at the proximity of his naked body and his strong odour – a scent I can only describe as a blend of the salty seaside air and the moist, rotten bark of decaying forest trees rubbed on an unwashed human body. But after the initial few seconds of revulsion, I could feel his warmth, his smooth skin and the innocence of his embrace. I hugged him right back. Then he said something again and loosened his grip.

'He says, "*Bade Saab aaye hain,*"' the driver translated for me.

Soon, three more staff members arrived and requested me to leave. A visitor was not allowed to interact with the tribals without the permission of their superiors, they informed me.

'Besides, they are cooking their lunch now and will become agitated if we linger here for too long,' one of them explained.

The building's caretaker shut the door and locked the room again, with the Shompens inside. I went back to the Tribal Welfare Office. Matthias, whom I had met at the Nicobarese Basti, was sitting there. I asked him what he was doing there, to which he replied that he had been working as an interpreter, as he knew a little bit of the Shompen language. I asked him if he would act as an interpreter between the tribals and me, putting my questions to them in their language and translating their responses for me. But he turned down my request with the same blank, indifferent look that he had sported the previous day.

The tribal welfare staff who had insisted on my leaving their office informed me that the Shompens would cook rice and dal for their lunch and eat it before returning to the forest with their rations later in the evening. If I was keen to interact with them, I would have to come back when the officer was present.

As I left their office, I heard the tribals making strange sounds and stomping their feet heavily on the floor. Unable to contain my curiosity, I peeped through the window into the locked room. The three Shompens I had seen earlier were facing each other, as though to form a triangle, and leaping as high into the air as they could go. They seemed really happy and I was left wondering what had caused their elation.

#### Acknowledgements

During the eighteen months that I took to travel to remote parts of the country and write this book, countless people have gone out of their way to help me. Strangers have welcomed me into their homes and treated me like family; I thank each and every one of them.

Besides, I owe special thanks to my good friend and senior journalist Arup Chanda who took on the role of a big brother and guided me through most of my travels. Thank you, Dada!

I thank the members of the All Manipur Working Journalists Union for facilitating my stay and travel in the state and senior journalist Loganathan from Rameswaram for ensuring my stay in Dhanuskodi.

I extend special thanks to my friend Jayaparakash Radhakrishnan for constantly encouraging me whenever I was down and doubtful.

Most of all, I thank Prabha, Varsha and Vidhur for practicing 'frugal living' during the course of writing this book and ensuring that I had a warm home to return to, and to my parents and brother for always being there.